Cities and Urbanization

VIEWPOINTS IN SOCIOLOGY

NORMS AND HUMAN BEHAVIOR
Arnold Birenbaum and Edward Sagarin

A SENSE OF SOCIOLOGY
Lee Braude

WORK AND WORKERS: A SOCIOLOGICAL ANALYSIS
Lee Braude

MARRIAGE AND OTHER ALTERNATIVES, SECOND EDITION
Lucile Duberman

CITIES AND URBANIZATION
Richard T. Geruson and Dennis McGrath

CRIME AND CRIMINALIZATION
Clayton A. Hartjen

ANALYZING SOCIAL PROBLEMS
Jerome G. Manis

JUVENILE DELINQUENCY
William B. Sanders

METHODOLOGY AND MEANINGS: VARIETIES OF
SOCIOLOGICAL INQUIRY
George V. Zito

Cities and Urbanization

Richard T. Geruson
La Salle College

Dennis McGrath
Community College of Philadelphia

Praeger Publishers
New York

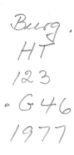

Published in the United States of America in 1977
by Praeger Publishers,
200 Fifth Avenue, New York, N.Y. 10017

Library of Congress Cataloging in Publication Data

Geruson, Richard T
    Cities and urbanization.

    Bibliography: p. 207
    Includes index.
    1. Cities and towns—United States. 2. Urbanization
—United States. I. McGrath, Dennis, 1946–
joint author. II. Title.
HT123.G46   301.36'3'0973   76–17251

ISBN 0–275–64660–2 pbk.
ISBN 0–275–23440–1

Printed in the United States of America

789 090 987654321

Foreword

Arthur J. Vidich

Each volume in the Viewpoints in Sociology series seeks to transmit to the beginning student a sense of the sociological attitude and an analysis of a significant sociological problem. In *Cities and Urbanization,* Professor Geruson, an economist, and Professor McGrath, a sociologist, have combined disciplinary viewpoints to improve the understanding of the nature of the city and the processes of urbanization, two of the central features of industrial civilization. Their work, which is informed by a deep historical awareness of the place of the city in the history of civilization, rewards us with a clear, comprehensive, and succinct introduction to one of the most intriguing subjects of modern sociology.

The great increase in the growth rate of cities and the acceleration in the processes of urbanization are associated with the beginnings of the industrial revolution in England in the mideighteenth century. Those beginnings were followed by parallel changes that took place in America, where the small settlements of the seventeenth century first evolved into urban towns and later in the nineteenth century into industrial cities. But, up to 1900 only one country, Great Britain, could be regarded as a mainly urban society. Yet only three-quarters of a century later, all industrial societies are highly urbanized and the dynamic of urbanization has reached all but a few areas of the world. Moreover, as the authors of this book tell us, cities of more than a million inhabitants grow faster than cities with less than a million; and multimillion cities, with over 2.5 million people, fastest of all. "The result is that, by the year 2000, New York and Tokyo will be joined, on present trends, by at least twenty-five other contenders in the super-city class. Of these, no fewer than eighteen will be in the under-developed countries." Within no less than a few hundred years, the world's populations, which for millenia were primarily rural in life style and community structure, have been transformed into urban inhabitants freed from the restraints of rural ways of life and culture.

The phenomenon of world-wide urbanization is as dramatic in its revolutionary implications for the history of civilization as were the earlier agricultural and industrial revolutions. It has reordered social relations and has brought forth new patterns of political, familial, and religious institutions. Older ethnic, racial, and cultural traditions previously linked to rural society have been adapted to urban settings. Vast numbers of people—perhaps as many as a half-billion—in our own generation have been migrants to the city. Clearly, an understanding of urbanization poses large problems for the sociologist.

In the view of Professors Geruson and McGrath, the city and urbanization are best understood by focusing on three critical functions:

1. The city's "functioning as exchanger and transmitter of values, culture, and wealth" and the impact of these on the multiplicity of life styles found in the city.
2. The city as the "producer, creator and developer" of new styles, social forms, and *technics* that ultimately transform civilization.
3. The city as a "magnet and liberating force" for the poor, the disenfranchised, and the less fortunate people of the world who, in turn, add to the richness and diversity of culture and supply the energy that keeps the motors of the city running.

The authors use these functions, which they call the *interactive,* the *generative,* and the *upgrading,* to analyze within concrete historical contexts those features that differentiate ancient, medieval, and modern industrial, commercial, and administrative cities. Their brief, but imaginative and informed, discussion of the nature and origins of ancient and premodern cities serves as a solid foundation to the core of the book, Chapters Two through Eight, which focuses on the emergence of modern cities and the forces shaping the modern metropolis. It is appropriate in a book designed for American students that a major portion of these chapters should treat the American city. In their concluding chapter, however, the authors embrace a worldwide perspective and suggest hypotheses about the long-term prospects for modern cities.

It is an irony of our times that disillusionment with industrialization and urban life has penetrated most deeply in those countries where the institutions of industrialization have reached their highest level. Paralleling this disillusionment has been a revival of anti-urban ideologies such as pastoralism, communalism, primitivism, ruralism, and nativism. Yet, even as such ideologies are revived and acted upon, they continue to be vitiated by the deeper and more extensive urbanization and more intensive capitalization of industrial civilization.

Countries in the underdeveloped world are only now beginning to achieve some of the benefits of modern urbanization and industrialization. They have been willing to abandon their traditional ways of life because they hope for a share in the material benefits to be derived from industrialization and urbanization. It is expected that success in these endeavors will enable them to eventually emulate the life and consumption styles of countries whose industrialization is already advanced. Their hope for the future is based on their image of life in distant places. However, their image excludes the negative features of industrial civilization that are becoming apparent to those groups and classes within the metropolitan countries who are the beneficiaries of the successes of industrialization.

It is too early to say how deeply the reaction against urban industrial life will penetrate the metropolitan countries, but even at its present rate such a reaction is sustained by a utopian image of preindustrial and rural life.

The irony then is that the underdeveloped world sustains itself partially by its own myth of a utopian urban future while the metropolis sustains itself partially by the myth of a return to a preindustrial past. It would appear that while large numbers of the world's populations have been embraced by urban and industrial life, urban men and women have not yet come to accept this new world-wide urban reality directly and on its own terms.

Preface

Cities and Urbanization attempts to develop a general perspective on cities and urbanization and to examine in detail the American urban experience—tasks made all the more difficult because of the amount of material that must be covered, as well as the complex nature of the subject matter.

The study of the development and functioning of cities requires an understanding of the interrelationships among social, economic, and political activities. It also requires an investigation of how these aspects of life are influenced by spatial patterns of human settlement. One student of the city, Maurice Stein, has suggested that three metaphors are most useful in studying urban life: history, system, and drama.

A focus on history emphasizes that urban life is open-ended. Urban areas have developed over time, and an understanding of them requires a close analysis of their particular historical records. A focus on system emphasizes that urban life is composed of many patterns and interrelationships. Technological innovations, such as a new transportation system, quickly influence living patterns and the location of industry. These in turn have other social and political consequences. Thus, beneath the mass of historical fact lie basic relationships that must be identified. A focus on drama emphasizes the human dimension of urban life, its impact on people's lives and experiences.

This book strives for a balance between history and system, a balance we have attempted to maintain in several ways. One is by using a multidisciplinary approach. We believe that sociology provides important and necessary insights into the urban process, but the sociological perspective must be complemented by ideas and theories from other social sciences. Since one of us is a sociologist and the other an economist, we draw primarily upon these disciplines, but we include much work from history and some from geography and political science. Since urbanization is a complex phenomenon, it both requires and lends itself to such a perspective.

The sociological dimension can be integrated into a multidisciplinary view by focusing on how changes in economic, technological, transportation, and other systems affect and interact with the institutions people act within, the statuses they occupy, the roles they play, and the communities in which they live.

This can be illustrated with reference to the status people occupy and the role they play as neighbors. Using technical sociological language, we can identify the neighbor as a status because it is a position in a group or community; it is a "type of person." People have conceptions of what neighbors are and expectations of what neighbors should do. In some communities neighbors are expected to join in local events and to help out in emergencies: they offer assistance if another neighbor is sick or needs a baby-sitter at the last minute. In other communities neighbors are expected to be polite but distant, to respect other's privacy and mind their own business.

In both cases it does not matter who the individuals are; there are shared conceptions of what neighbors are and what role they should play. There are shared sets of beliefs and standards of behavior (norms) to which all neighbors are expected to conform.

If we maintain a sociological perspective on neighbors, we can also study the patterns of relationship they develop—that is, the patterns or styles of neighboring. We can also study the type and nature of the communities they develop, which we term *neighborhoods*. Going deeper, we can study how changes in the economic, technological, transportation, political, or communication aspects of urban society make an impact on the role of the neighbor, the pattern of neighboring, and the nature of neighborhoods. To complete the cycle, we can observe the ways in which city dwellers experience, interpret, and adapt to such changes.

A second means of integrating the sociological perspective with other disciplines is by focusing on work and occupation. While the role of neighbor is an important one, occupational status—whether people are managers or workers, laborers, or machinists—has great impact on their behavior and the nature of their communities. Thus, in studying urban communities we can ask how people earn a living. This permits a sociological interpretation of the effect of societal changes on work and occupation, which in turn have impact on community and urban patterns.

Thus, a sociological perspective studies how societal changes affect the institutions people act within, the statuses they occupy, the roles they play, and the communities in which they live. The roles of neighbor and worker will be accorded particular attention here. This focus will help us to better understand the linkages between community and work-place, between urbanization and industrialization.

The economic dimension can also be included in an integrated view of cities and urbanization. This is best done by using the economic viewpoint to focus on changes in social, technological, political, and other systems. The economic viewpoint looks at various aspects of the question of choice. These include the alternative costs of using resources to satisfy human wants; the incomes generated, spent, and invested by the decisions of workers, consumers, and business people; and the markets for land, housing, and labor within which they make these decisions.

The integration of the economic perspective can be illustrated by concepts such as industry, income, institutional change, industrialization, and productivity. An industry is a group of business firms generating money income for a group of workers and goods or services for a market. The workers fill occupational roles by exchanging their skills for the products of industry, and the amount of income they earn is a main measure of prestige.

We can then analyze a household's patterns of consumption, wealth-holding, aspirations, education, and other such characteristics in terms of changing income levels. Income patterns change with industrial change, and industries appear, grow, and decay as a result of changes in technology and social and political institutions. Their growth or decay is based on the resources and wants of the population. It is these patterns we label industrialization, and they interact so closely with urban change that in exploring one set of patterns we throw light on the other.

Another major point of interaction is the process of institutional change. This is the stage upon which the economic roles are acted out, where the interactions among family, neighborhood, or school and the economic order become realized. These interactions reflect back on the industrial order—shaping its goals, values, and motivations. The industrial order organizes itself spatially in and around cities, thus taking advantage of the external benefits of producing where transport costs are lowest and markets closest. It also seeks out labor supplies, the economies of large-scale consumption, and adequate public services. The end product is the pattern of industrial and residential location within the metropolis.

So organized, the urban industrial region can increase productivity of the firms and households within it. The productivity of the city has provided avenues for upward social mobility to millions of workers over the past 200 years. It has been the generative and innovative center for the expansion of trade in a dual manner: each such market area produces for local use and for export to other regions. It is also an importer from any complex with a differing resource base. This pattern of production and exchange determines the distribution of cities by size in a network across the country. Within the network, each urban area can further specialize in efforts to produce a best mix of goods and services for its residents. In this process the system creates populations with a great diversity of life styles and values.

The strength of economics lies in the fact that it can microscopically examine certain behavior patterns (the rational, self-seeking satisfaction of material wants) for certain actors (households and business firms). It also can take a macroscopic picture of the ways in which nation-states and governments perform certain jobs (stabilizing the total level of output, employment, and prices).

In summary, sociology provides an overview of the terrain of the society and social change. It suggests a camera sweeping over the landscape, revealing patterns and details. Economics digs into the terrain. It looks at the composition of the social layers that were laid down over time and the shaping forces that were at work. Together perhaps sociology and economics can tell us how the "mountains and valleys" of modern urban life were formed—and how we can survive in them.

In attempting to show both the historical development and complex nature of urban life, we emphasize the interrelationships among social, economic, political, and technological factors. The general framework employed views urbanization as resulting from two related processes, economic growth and city growth. Our aim is integrative, to do justice to the complexity of urban life and to show the utility of work done in several disciplines. To further such an aim, we analyze the functions performed by cities over time. Since these are discussed at length throughout the book, we will only briefly mention them here.

Throughout history cities have performed several important functions for the larger society. One is the interactive function. As areas of population concentration, cities provide the opportunity for increased interaction among people, which promotes the development of new ideas and innovations, as well as deeply affecting social and cultural life. Within sociology the work of the Chicago School has focused particularly on this function. Both Robert Park's view of the city as a "mosaic of social worlds" and Louis Wirth's essay, "Urbanism as a Way of Life," analyze the consequences of the interactive function.

Second is the generative function. Population concentration and increased interaction encourage the development or generation of new goods, technologies, services, and ideas that in time diffuse throughout the society. Cities are innovative centers and, as such, are vitally involved in the process of socioeconomic growth. Many economists and students of development have focused on this function.

Third is the upgrading function. Cities have historically provided more opportunities for an improved quality of life than was available in nonurban areas. The successful performance of the interactive and generative functions produces a greater range of employment and educational opportunities, as well as improved public services. This draws more migrants to the cities, which has an impact on the interactive and generative functions. Many sociologists, economists, and historians concerned with mobility and stratification have focused on this urban function.

Throughout the book the functions of cities are analyzed at different historical periods and during different stages of the urbanization process. This is yet another way of doing justice to both history and system and integrating the work of the various social sciences.

We thank our friends and colleagues—Andreas Athinaios and Dino Fiabane of Community College of Philadelphia, Ed Schwartz of the Institute for the Study of Civic Values, and Finn Hornum of La Salle College—for commenting on an earlier draft of this book. We also wish to thank Maryann Baranek for her typing and Joan Geruson for her assistance in editing and completing the manuscript. Finally, we thank Jim Bergin of Praeger and Arthur Vidich of the New School for Social Research for their advice and assistance.

R.T.G.
D.M.

Contents

Chapter Nine   Conclusions and New Perspectives   194

CHAPTER ONE

The Nature and Origins of Cities: Ancient and Premodern

DEFINING THE CITY

Since urban areas are complex systems, economists, sociologists, and others continually discuss the most appropriate definitions for the various units being studied. Also under discussion are ways of analyzing the functions performed by such units. An example of the issues involvèd is to consider the meaning of two terms often used by social scientists—rural and urban.

The terms *rural* and *urban* are usually thought of as opposites. Considering them in sharp contrast makes sense in any study of ancient and medieval societies, for then the city was a fortified town with a wall separating it from the surrounding countryside.

Today, however, the walls have long been torn down, and the distinctions are less rigid. The basis of a useful characterization of an area as rural or urban is by size and density of population, that is, the total number of people living in a given area and their degree of concentration. This is the basis of the U.S. Bureau of the Census distinction.

Since an urban area is defined as one that is densely settled, we must identify the distinguishing characteristics of cities. The popular concept of a city is based chiefly on size. People coming from a rural area will immediately notice the greater concentration of people, the density of housing, the number of large buildings. Were they to think also of functions, they would notice that the city has whole sections given over to factories, along with a wide variety of businesses and services.

The city also has a legal meaning. If an urban area has a population of 20,000 or more, it is probably incorporated as a city according to the laws of the state in which it is located. The central and dominant unit of any substantial urban area is the incorporated city, which has boundaries fixed by law and is governed as a unit.

When driving through a city, one may not realize that he has crossed the city limits because the area outside the city line may be identical to the area within. The metropolitan area refers to the city as the center or nucleus along with the adjacent areas that share a community of interests with the nucleus. The concept recognizes that the definition of the legal city is important because it designates political boundaries and legal responsibilities. However, the concept of metropolitan area stresses that political boundaries are arbitrary, with many people and businesses located outside the city limits linked to it economically and socially.

Most people who study American urban areas use the terms and definitions developed by the U.S. Bureau of the Census, so they can utilize the extensive data the bureau collects. The Census Bureau argues "that for many types of social and economic analysis, it is necessary to consider as a unit the entire population in and around the city whose activities form an integrated social and economic system." The major terms used in Bureau of the Census studies include: urbanized area, urban population, *standard metropolitan statistical area (SMSA), central city, central business district,* and *suburban ring.* Below is a brief summary of these terms.

1. *Urbanized Area:*   An area containing a central city of 50,000 or more population, and the surrounding closely settled territory.

2. *Urban Population:*   All of the inhabitants of urbanized areas, plus the inhabitants of incorporated or unincorporated urban places of over 2,500 population in the rest of the United States. The purpose of this concept is to separate urban or city dwellers from the rural population.

3. *Standard Metropolitan Statistical Area:*   Combines the definition by political boundary with the concept of urbanization. SMSAs are defined as counties containing at least one city of 50,000 inhabitants, plus adjacent counties integrated with the central city. Within the SMSA it is common to identify the central city, central business district, and suburban ring. The central city is the large city within the SMSA, from which the SMSA takes its name. The area outside

the central city is called the suburban ring. The central business district consists of the few square miles of downtown area characterized as the center of the city's business activity.

SMSAs include most urbanized areas in the United States. The term describes the population and businesses located in and around cities, and recognizes that people may live in one place (for example, suburban ring) and work in another (that is, central city). An SMSA can be described as the smallest area that is large enough to contain the work places of most people who reside in it, as well as the residences of most people who work in it. The largest urbanized regions encompass more than one SMSA. These are called *SCSAs (Standard Consolidated Statistical Areas)*.

In studying urban areas, it is necessary to identify units and understand their interrelationships and dynamics of growth.

Urbanization refers to the concentration of population through movement and redistribution. In the strict sense, the term refers to the *demographic* aspect of society, the pattern and size of human settlements. However, changes in the distribution and size of populations have many consequences, affecting people's economic and political activity, their way of life, culture, and social organization. The most basic problem in studying urbanization is to understand both the causes and consequences of changes in human settlement. In other words, an integrated view involves understanding how urban change interacts with the growth and concentration of industry and the development of new technologies. It also includes changes in family structure, relationships between neighbors, political activity, as well as all the other aspects comprising a way of life.

An urban area is a dense settlement that results from the process of urbanization. The metropolitan area or *region* defines the system; it is the whole area that is linked economically and socially and includes both city and suburb, areas where people live and where they work, transportation routes and various types of land use.

A city is an element of the metropolitan area. It is a dense settlement that performs certain functions, and is defined by political boundaries.

A neighborhood is a component of a city. It is a small-scale area with informal but well-recognized boundaries, in which much of the resident's social life takes place.

Taken together, these are the most basic terms needed to define urban areas and to capture the social, economic, political, and cultural aspects of urban life.

The metropolitan area or region is a geographic area that is functionally and economically integrated, the system containing jobs and residences, the production and distribution of goods and services. A city is a more arbitrary entity, since its boundaries are legally rather than socially or economically defined. However, the city performs functions essential for the whole metropolitan area. The neighborhood is the basic component of the social and cultural unit where people live and interact in terms of the common concerns and interests they share as consumers, citizens, and householders.

CITIES IN THE ANCIENT WORLD

Let us apply the terms and ideas introduced above to a brief discussion of the initial origin of cities in the ancient world. The issue of urban origins is important because it raises questions that are relevant when studying any city in any historical period; these include: the nature of cities, their dynamics of growth, and the functions they perform.

Until about 1000 B.C., it is believed that no more than 1 to 2 percent of the world's population lived in cities and that these prehistoric settlements did not exceed 100,000 people. Most were much smaller. These first cities were different in two ways from all previously existing human settlements. First they were larger in total population. They were dense settlements and contained more people than had previously lived together. Second they contained a larger number of workers who were not directly involved in producing food.

Many archaeologists trace the origin of cities in part to what is called the Neolithic or New Stone Age (about 8000 B.C.), a period that saw a gradual transition from the nomadic existence when people were dependent on the fluctuations of natural food supplies. Groups slowly learned to domesticate animals and to grow a variety of crops, changing from food gathering to food producing.

As a result, divisions arose between pasturers and cultivators. Herdsmen continued to move with their flocks, constantly searching

for new grazing areas. Farmers, on the other hand, located in permanent settlements where water was readily available and where manur-
ing and crop rotation were found to be satisfactory means of renewing
the soil.

These developments took place during what is called collectively
the *Neolithic Revolution*. Increasing food surpluses, the growth of
permanent settlements, improved tools and techniques, and the beginnings of specialization of occupation all laid the foundation for the
emergence of the city in the ancient world.

The most direct ancestors of contemporary urban communities
were the cities that grew up in Mesopotamia between 4000 and 3000
B.C. The people living in this area, building on the inventions of the
Neolithic Revolution, increased their agricultural productivity. Dis-
covering that some animals, such as oxen, could be used for power as
well as food, farmers began to work with heavier and more efficient
plows and turned over more land during a workday. When irrigation
was systemically introduced, more land was available for cultivation
and the effect of drought more easily controlled.

Since cities required a constant interchange both with their surrounding rural areas and with other cities, transportation systems
were improved to foster increased trade. The widespread use of two-
and four-wheeled carts, advances in boat building, and the introduction of sails permitted more rapid transportation over wider areas.

These early Sumerian cities developed along the waterways of the
Southern Mesopotamian plain. The waterways served both as sources
of crop irrigation and as natural routes for trade that helped the cities
to extend their influence to surrounding villages and rural areas. They
used their locational advantages and military power to increase their
wealth, and evolved complex social structures with a number of specialized occupations. City dwellers developed systems of writing, and
a rich tradition of literature grew over time. Their monuments and
temples show evidence of a high degree of engineering and architectural ability. Complex religious beliefs evolved, with the priesthood
wielding great power in economic and political life.

Each city was surrounded by a countryside of farms, villages, and even
towns. Despite tensions between the urban and rustic populations, contact and interaction was common. ... Cities usually had three main

parts. An inner city housed within its walls the temples of the city's gods, the palace of the ruler, and private houses. . . . The suburbs contained houses and gardens and cattle pens, for the immediate support of the population. Finally, there was a commercial section. . . . In short, the cities provided their inhabitants with material security, prosperity, and efficient government and with an assurance of divine protection and favor. (Hammond 1972:38)

The existence of these cities demonstrated the emergence of *specialization*. One could argue that specialization and *innovation* were the unique contributions of early cities. Rural and village life limited the exchange of goods, ideas, and people, as well as the complexity of technology and the division of labor. As cities grew in size, more of their people specialized in providing goods and services unavailable in rural areas or in other cities. Thus, trade became the lifeblood of early cities. Trade, in turn, was spurred on by the attraction of new goods and services produced by urban artisans and craftsmen. In sum, early cities were linked to the surrounding rural areas and to other cities by a complex system of production and distribution, as well as religious, military, and economic institutions.

THEORIES OF CITY ORIGIN

Many authorities discuss preconditions for the emergence of cities in terms of the development of an agricultural surplus. This theory has implications that must be questioned. There are at least two general and conflicting theories of the origin of cities to be considered. We do not have the archaeological evidence to fully resolve the differences between the two theories, but it is important to examine both since they involve quite different ways of viewing urban growth and the functioning of cities.

Surplus Value—Parasitical View

One can argue that before cities could develop, food surpluses had to be produced to feed the city dwellers who no longer grew their own food. This suggests a particular image of urbanization, that of development resting on the efforts and ingenuity of rural farmers to increase the yield of their crops. This view, the assumption of agricultural primacy, states—agriculture first, cities later; that is, no cities without industrious and crafty farmers giving up the bounty of their harvests. Pushing this image, one could say it implies a parasitical view of cities: cities and city dwellers are parasites, feeding off and growing fat from the labor and efficiency of agricultural workers.

This view is probably the dominant one in the social science literature. There are many variations, but at their heart lies the assumption of agricultural primacy. As one noted anthropologist writes:

> ... the urban revolution ... rested ultimately on food surpluses obtained by agricultural producers above their own requirements, and somehow made available to city dwellers engaged in other activities. (Adams 1960:3–4)

If one holds to this theory, then to understand the origin of cities two questions must be answered. The first concerns the cause of food surpluses and involves an examination of the development of agriculture leading to the generation of higher yields. The second question is why farmers parted with this surplus; what caused them to give up part of their harvest to the parasitical city dwellers? This typically involves an examination of religious, political, and military factors, and the assumption that force or coercion was involved.

Nexus of Exchange—Mutual Cooperation View

However, it is possible to develop a totally different view of the course of city growth. This approach stresses the benefits that cities confer on the countryside, the terms of trade between city and country, and the city as the source of needed innovation and development.

This counter-view has been most forcefully argued by the urbanist Jane Jacobs. She attacks the view of agricultural primacy by noting:

> ... it can readily be seen in the world today that agriculture is not even tolerably productive unless it incorporates many goods and services produced in cities or transplanted from cities. The most thoroughly

rural countries exhibit the most unproductive agriculture. The most thoroughly urbanized countries, on the other hand, are precisely those that produce food most abundantly. (Jacobs 1969:7)

Thus, Jacobs tries to undermine and reverse the assumption of agricultural primacy by stressing the improvements in farming that result from the application of new techniques, goods, and services originating in cities. Rather than being parasitical, cities are centers of innovation, generating new ideas and technologies, as well as providing goods and services needed in the countryside. The types of exchange and trade conducted between city dwellers and rural populations are seen as much more equitable and cooperative than the first theory would suggest.

If one holds to this theory, then an understanding of the origin of cities requires answering two quite different questions based on the view of cities as centers of innovation and trade. The first concerns the process of innovation, that is, how new work develops in cities and how new goods and services are produced and distributed. The second question concerns how innovations generated in cities radiate out to the countryside, that is, how cities act as growth centers for the surrounding region.

The present analysis of cities and urbanization is rooted in this second view based on the belief that the processes of innovation and specialization are at the heart of city life and growth. In later chapters an attempt is made to trace how these processes link with the functions that cities have performed in different historical periods.

THE FUNCTIONS OF CITIES

Besides speculating on the origin of cities and considering alternative theories, one can also study the functions of cities. The authors' belief that cities served several historical purposes in both the ancient and modern world provides another way of understanding why cities have emerged in human society, as well as suggesting the major reasons for their continued existence. A careful examination of how well or poorly particular cities perform such functions also tells a great deal about their structures, processes, and probable futures. The following are three principal functions.

Interaction focuses on the concepts of interchange and exchange, and refers to the transfer of ideas, resources, and output in both the physical and psychic sense. It also includes the private market for goods and services as well as the production of collective goods for public consumption. Interaction encompasses the exchange of information and social contacts and illustrates the benefits available to city dwellers from both large-scale and minute specialization. This is the city functioning as exchanger and transmitter of values, culture, and wealth.

Generation focuses on the concepts of creation and innovation. The presence of new ideas changes the form of the city as each novelty leads to new wants and goals. New styles, forms, *technics,* ways of doing and dreaming all originate in the centers of civilization. Increasing productivity and technical invention take social form. This is the city functioning as the producer, creator, and developer of change agents for society, which is measured in rising standards of living and the creation of new industries and jobs.

Upgrading focuses on the concepts of *assimilation* and *opportunity.* The city, in the processing of in-migrants, is permanently shaped and reshaped by contact with their pluralistic backgrounds. The city provides education, skills, safety, and economic opportunity to its inhabitants, offering new hope and opportunity. This is measured in terms of new occupations, income, and access to services. In return, the city is immensely enriched by the heightened human activity. This is the city functioning as magnet and liberating force for the poor and less fortunate of the world.

The bulk of this book deals with modern American urbanization, its dynamics, growth, and functioning. However, we will briefly examine cities that existed prior to the Industrial Revolution so as to provide a basis for evaluating the changes that took place in the eighteenth and nineteenth centuries—changes that ushered in the current era.

PREMODERN CITIES—ROMAN EMPIRE
TO MIDDLE AGES

Several thousand years of urban development spanned the period from the ancient cities to the cities that flourished within the Roman Empire. However, the empire's fall in the fifth century A.D. marked the effective end of urbanization in Western Europe for over 600 years. Thereafter, the gradual revival of urban life heralded another historical period—one we can use as a social science laboratory for studying the dynamics of urbanization.

Logically, the first question to raise is why urbanization was halted for so long, why cities stagnated. The major reason was that the collapse of the empire meant that each locality was isolated from every other, and had to become self-sufficient in order to survive. From their very beginnings, cities had survived and grown because they were tied to their rural *hinterlands* and to other cities by a system of production, distribution, and exchange. The disruption of the Roman transportation system, the advance of Islam in the seventh century, and the pillaging raids of the Norsemen in the ninth century almost completely eliminated trade and commerce. These events, plus the periodic great migrations of barbarians across the countryside, resulted in an almost complete disruption of urban and rural interaction.

Barbarians had been migrating into the Roman Empire for centuries before its fall. They came as traders and buyers of goods, as settlers in search of land, and as recruits for Roman legions. The peak was reached with the unseating of the emperor Romulus Augustulus in 476. A period of fighting and mass destruction followed. The Visigoths captured and sacked Rome and then moved into Gaul. The Ostrogoths moved through the Balkans and into Italy. A number of other tribes migrated shorter distances, contributing to the final convulsive death shudders of the empire. Towns were ravaged, villages burned, and crops destroyed.

This historical period provides a classic case of almost complete disruption of urban interrelationships. Both the rural and urban populations declined. Many took refuge behind the ruins of the walls of the Roman cities. The peasantry occasionally moved back into areas where they were strong enough to establish settlements and reclaim their previously cultivated fields. With the loss of trade, regions became isolated, with the result that there was little communication or diffusion of ideas, agricultural productivity was low, and people were preoccupied with defense and survival.

Compounding this pattern was the breakdown in administration. Services, especially roads and communications, could not be maintained—and urban life turned inward. The lack of innovation and technical change reinforced the stagnation pattern. Small wonder that this period is sometimes called the "Dark Ages."

Revival began very slowly. At first most urban areas were of two types. One type was represented by numerous fortified settlements built for physical protection from the pillaging bands that wandered throughout the countryside. The castles of the nobility represented new security and became centers of population. Many historical documents record how impressed the barbarian tribes were with such defenses built upon the ancient Roman towns. They were almost indestructible and gave residents a sense of safety against bands of marauders.

The second type of urban area was the ecclesiastical center, where bishops established their residences. With the collapse of the empire, the only large organization capable of any overall administration was the Roman Catholic Church. It was the church, more than any other institution, that gave continuity to the life of the town. As social scientists such as Max Weber have noted, Christianity was, in origin, an urban institution. During the latter part of the empire, its basilicas were built alongside the castles of the emperors. Bishops lived in towns and administered dioceses that closely paralleled the political boundaries of Roman administration. This was important because the church was quite significant in people's lives, and religious beliefs and institutions influenced urban revival in numerous ways.

> The closest link between the classic city and the medieval city was that formed, not by the surviving buildings and customs, but by the monastery. It was in the monastery that the books of classic literatures were transferred from crumbling papyrus to tough parchment; it was here, in the Benedictine Abbeys at least, that the advanced practices of Roman agriculture and Greek medicine were maintained, with a corresponding rise in productivity and health. (Mumford 1961:247)

THE MEDIEVAL CITY

As these settlements slowly gained in size, their representative symbols became walls and churches, the walls representing the secular power of the feudal lords, the churches the religious power of the bishops. As trade expanded and as traveling merchants grew in social importance, the market became a new center for generating urban institutional change. However, it took several hundred years for long-distance or international trade to fully develop since it was conducted only by a small number of people and was quite dangerous. The merchants had to travel in convoys guarded by heavily armed soldiers and, as the Old Roman roads were in bad condition, travel was slow and uncertain.

As a result the early medieval city was a closed and relatively self-contained social world. Exchange was largely conducted with inhabitants of the immediate surrounding region, with most urban residents spending their lives within the walls of their city. During this period urban communities had very close-knit social structures.

Power was shared between feudal lords and religious leaders. The economy was organized according to *guilds,* with each craftsman, artisan, and merchant belonging to a particular guild. It was a world in which each person had a clearly defined place. One's position in guild, family, church, and feudal administration determined one's status and responsibilities. There was a high degree of solidarity and loyalty among city residents as their lives were closely interrelated. They were always prepared to rush to the walls in the collective defense of their city.

The early revival of towns does not center on any one variable; rather a positive interrelation developed among many factors. These included the slow diffusion of agricultural innovations (pioneered in the monasteries); increases in local trade; new population growth and settlements; the strengthening of a formal institutional structure and administration around guild, church, and manor. These were organized into a new, self-reinforcing pattern of social and public order built around a shared culture. The slowness of urban revival can be seen in that this occurred 600 years after the fall of Rome. These interacting factors moved cities out of the pattern of stagnation, however, the system operated at a low level of *equilibrium,* and growth in population and production was quite slight.

The next phase in the story of urbanization and cities brings us to 1750, covering the next 600 years to the eve of industrialization. Examining the forces that disrupted this stability, destroyed medieval urban life, and created the modern unwalled city, this section relies on the splendid descriptions of the period by Lewis Mumford in *The City in History* and Max Weber in *The City.*

THE RISE OF MODERN URBAN LIFE— POLITICAL, CULTURAL, ECONOMIC

One trend was the increasing impact of cities on the rest of society. This was aided by the clashes that developed between feudal lords and church officials, and later between emperors and popes. These conflicts between the major political powers of the time gave greater scope to self-government by city residents. The discussions and struggles of urban residents to secure the rights to self-government provided the roots of the ideas of Western democracy.

> The Middle Ages revived the Roman definition of a town—the town is a community of men joined together by social bonds. And even more: a genuine civitas demands political independence and internal liberty. (Gutkind 1964:72)

One of the major factors that distinguished the medieval city from the village and rural area was the special status enjoyed by its citizens. Individual residents had more rights than most other members of society. Collectively, the city as communal organization was freer than rural communities to organize its own affairs.

Citizens' rights and degrees of freedom were spelled out in charters by which the cities were incorporated and granted their privileges by feudal lords. The lords originally granted the merchants and craftsmen, called *burghers,* restricted opportunities to practice trades and crafts. However, the lords maintained the authority to collect rents and taxes and to levy fees, all of which brought them a great deal of money and economic power.

As cities grew in size and wealth, the burghers demanded that the feudal lords grant them increased control over their own affairs. This rebellious tendency first appeared in Italy, which had the oldest tradition of urban life. From there, the idea of the city as an autonomous *community* of merchants, traders, and craftsmen spread into northwestern Europe.

For Max Weber one of the key features of the medieval city was that it became a self-determining institutional association. It was a special kind of community, based on an oath-bound fraternity of burghers and secured from the rural-based feudal lords. This movement created a new urban law that conferred a special status on urban residents and promoted trade and commerce. Weber shows in his study, *The City,* that the modern conception of deomocracy developed both in these battles for urban autonomy and in the internal urban clashes that later developed. When the burghers won economic control from the manorial lords, they extended their authority to the urban political system. This centralized power triggered a long period of internal problems over the extension of rights and political power from the merchants to other groups.

Many of the forces that ultimately changed the medieval city were spawned by the city itself. Medieval cities were tremendous sources of innovation, affecting both themselves and the larger society. From the tenth to the fifteenth century, cities and towns multiplied and grew. But there were limits to the growth of any particular urban area. All were encircled by walls for protection and usually none extended for more than a half mile from the center. Besides the physical limits to growth imposed by walled fortifications, other limits were imposed by meager water supplies, local food production, and guild restrictions that controlled the entry of outsiders.

Medieval cities functioned at a relatively low level of equilibrium. However, there was a slowly increasing tempo of growth. As individual cities and towns reached their growth potential, they gave birth to new settlements. The surplus populations built new communities nearby, which in time became self-sufficient and independent units.

Another aspect of innovation was cultural. The medieval cities, rising out of the Roman collapse and barbarian invasions, created an urban culture. This urban culture, and the ideals of city life, transformed the countryside. Later it was carried to the new world of America by Dutch, English, and other European settlers.

These urban communities were "works of art," symbolizing in their very layouts, their physical designs, the ideals of civilized life. At first the cities primarily offered the security of physical protection. Over the years, however, a way of life and a culture developed within the walls that promised much more—an opportunity for the citizenry to live a full life, both materially and spiritually.

During this period urban culture was closely intertwined with Christian culture, since the Christian church was the dominant and most universal institution in Europe for many centuries. The ideal form of a city was circular like the celestial city, and the usual twelve towers or gates symbolized the Twelve Apostles. The first and most important church was built at the symbolic and actual center of the city, and the location and interrelation of other churches were central to medieval "urban planning."

Since the cities were a visible representation of the shared religious culture, they exercised great influence over the countryside. Pilgrims continuously came to worship at the urban shrines, churches, cathedrals. This permitted many rural peasants to experience urban life and to report back their findings to the countryside.

A third aspect of urban innovation was economic. Cities aided the economic revitalization of first regions and then whole countries. There are differing interpretations of the origins of capitalism in the West; however, they converge in emphasizing the role of the cities that developed at the end of the feudal period. These early cities helped create modern industrial society both through their struggles for independence from existing feudal authorities and through their serving as the focal point for the production and distribution of new goods and services. The French historian Braudel writes that "capitalism and towns were basically the same thing in the West."

Medieval cities had a dual economic focus. A small part of their economy was based on national and international trade in luxury items. The much larger economic function was to provide a market for the surrounding rural region, a place of exchange for local agricultural and handicraft products. From the institution of the local market, which linked city to countryside, flowed the new ideas, goods, and technical inventions that revitalized rural areas. In conjunction with the spread of urban culture, these innovations helped promote the growth and urbanization of the countryside. Put simply—medieval cities fostered the growth of thousands of villages and small settlements in rural areas. Technical innovations and ideas developed in cities were applied in the countryside; they helped drain swamps, reclaim land, and increase agricultural productivity. And, to escape guild restrictions, craftsmen slowly moved out of the cities and settled in the villages. They took advantage of water power sites and thus created new economic centers that, in turn, attracted more crafts and trades. Thus, the achievements and innovations of the medieval city helped spell its end and laid the foundation for new forms of urban settlement.

The long-distance trade in luxury items, though at first economically insignificant also helped to transform the medieval city. As national and international *markets* were slowly established, a city's location in relation to trade routes became more important. By the eve of the Industrial Revolution, we find a well-established network of long-distance trade and the growth or decline of many cities dependent on their participation in it.

The expansion of an export base has been most crucial in the historical development of the largest international cities. Typically while a city grows in size, it develops certain comparative advantages in producing specialized manufactured goods. In growing from a village (less than 2,500 population) to a metropolitan center of 50,000 or more, the generation of new jobs is usually focused in a few key industries. During these times examples were silks and woolens, ceramics and pottery, brewing and spices.

DEVELOPMENTS IN CITY FUNCTIONS

During the ancient and premodern periods, cities evolved and developed slowly. Ancient cities, in fulfilling protective and priestly roles, provided a healthy environment for the interactive function. Gradually urban areas became centers for more widespread exchange and interchange as communications and transportation improved. But the growth pattern was interrupted by the fall of the Roman Empire, and societal disorganization led to urban stagnation. Cities turned inward.

The church provided continuity through the Dark Ages and was a leading force in shaping the revival of urban life in the Middle Ages. Rebuilt carefully with a strong physical and social structure, the medieval city stressed interaction of all phases of life and united itself with the neighboring manors in common defense.

Slowly specialization and trade again expanded as new ideas came from the Far Eastern trade. Then internal administration became more complicated as the city dweller attempted to develop political rights separate from feudal and church authorities. Merchants and craftsmen in guilds saw the innovative possibilities of free cities where a person could reach his full potential within a community setting. Trade and commerce expanded the generative function of the city and began to link up with the expanding power of the state. By the end of the premodern era, these forces had crystallized into a controlled system called *mercantilism*. Cities were its growth centers, specialization and trade its heart, and innovations its lifeblood. The new forces were not to wither away but rather they were to sweep away the last vestiges of feudal life and create a new central function for the city —generative. The name given to the new mix of forces, ideas, institutions, and technics was *capitalism*. It was capitalism that was to usher in the Industrial Revolution that led to the emergence of the industrial city.

CHAPTER TWO

The Emergence of the Industrial City

THE MODERNIZATION OF SOCIETY

At the heart of *modernization* is the shift from an agricultural to an industrial based society. Production multiplies and diversifies as new products appear, and population increases rapidly. Workers leave the countryside and flock, in great numbers, to towns and factories. Their occupations become specialized and change toward services, skilled trades, and machine operations. Fundamental social and political effects are brought about with the growth of manufacturing and services and the decline in farming.

Family size shrinks while the average age of the population rises. Political loyalties change focus from village toward new nation states. Under the impact of all the resultant mobility—of people, ideas, and trade—the older social class barriers dissolve. And a new middle class, led by *business entrepreneurs,* assumes wealth and power.

To understand fully the American experience, one must turn to its European origins. England was the first country to experience these changes, roughly speaking, between 1760 and 1840. Not only did Great Britain lead the way, but she also became the center for the diffusion of this process. It progressed across the Atlantic to North America and across the channel to northern and western Europe in the middle decades of the nineteenth century. We look for general explanations by examining the relations among changes in technology, population, institutions, and ideas in Europe between 1500 and 1750.

Let us begin with changes in ideas. The scientific concepts of Newton and Huygens were already well developed by 1700, but they had not been applied widely outside of astronomy. The voyages of exploration of the sixteenth and seventeenth centuries had taken place without an accurate means of measuring longitude. Navigators would sail along a coast until the desired latitude was reached and then sail east or west until they again reached land. This was a slow and dangerous method and in the northern areas of England and France trips were made much longer than was necessary.

It was the clockmakers, who used Newton's principles to design pendulums and balance wheels, and the instrument makers, with their telescopes and sextants, who together made the breakthroughs in the second third of the eighteenth century. Using the newfound abilities of the early machine toolmakers to create precise circles and straight lines, they began to measure longitude and time accurately enough to make possible quicker and safer crossings of the Atlantic by the shorter great circle routes in the northern latitudes.

Navigation voyages were supplemented by improved ship design. Ocean voyages became safer and swifter; trade increased and international rivalries turned toward commerce. Spurred by the discovery of riches, the rival European powers copied each other's administrative setups. Double entry bookkeeping, the joint stock company, and the roots of modern banking and finance were established.

This commercial revolution, as it is sometimes called, was completed by the shift from a barter economy based on direct exchange to a full monetary system based on money payments for wages, rents, and interest. Human and property rights now were defined by written laws and not by the traditions of personal and social responsibility built into the social order.

THE INDUSTRIAL REVOLUTION

Changes in institutions reflected changes in the technology, and these were linked by increased productivity and division of labor, setting labor free for the production of manufactured goods and services. The village economies of water and wind and wood were transformed into the urban factories of steam and coal and iron. The application of scientific methods to the production and distribution processes and the accompanying changes in societal organization are usually referred to as the "*Industrial Revolution.*" While the advent of experimental science and technological advances enabled man to understand and harness his environment, they also spurred population growth, thus providing more workers and markets for the advances in output.

Rurals areas grew more slowly and were disturbed by the changes in marketing, technology, and institutions. Urban areas, especially port cities and factory towns, grew very rapidly and their social and political unrest resulted from the swiftly changing nature of work and the community. It was in England that enough savings were first accumulated to construct large factories and machines in great numbers, and it was also in England that the idea of progress first reached into the life of the common man. However, in the words of the historian T. S. Ashton, change was not easy:

> . . . in each of the major industries there was some obstacle . . . before expansion could go far. In agriculture it was the common rights and the lack of winter fodder; in mining the want of an efficient device to deal with flood water; in iron-making the shortage of suitable fuel; and in textiles and inadequate supply of yarn. (Ashton 1964:40)

The best way to consider the Industrial Revolution is to closely examine the specific industries that led the way—the *leading industries* as they are sometimes called. By concentrating on the innovations in only a half dozen industries, we can see some of the more important historical interactions that underlay this event. The six industrial groups were farming, textiles, iron manufacturing, power conversion, commercial services, and transportation.

Farming

The introduction of new crops such as alfalfa and clover helped bring back nutrients to the soil and simultaneously increased food supplies for animals. This made it feasible to keep more animals through the lean winter months (formerly most had been slaughtered) and to increase the size of herds.

Other new crops such as potatoes and parsnips added new caloric sources to the human food supply. These could be grown in places where, and at times when, traditional crops such as rye, oats, and wheat could not. They also provided a good yield, with little tending, and they did not have to be harvested all at once—thus saving on labor costs compared to grains.

Using new methods of crop rotation and improved devices for plowing, cultivating, and harvesting, the British farmer by 1800 had markedly raised the nutrition level of the populace. The improvement in health that resulted enabled people to fight disease better, live longer, and work more efficiently and productively.

A final set of changes in agriculture which was of importance is called the *enclosure movement*. This meant that much of the common lands were claimed by individual landholders. The enclosure movement was strongest in sheep-raising regions because of the high rates of profit in the wool industry. As a result, animals were penned behind fences, their breeding was controlled, and their manure collected for fertilizer. This further reinforced the supply of protein foodstuffs as average animal size increased and dairy yields grew rapidly. Better health standards led to lower death rates and the resulting larger populations increased demands for textiles. Production of the traditional woolens and of the preferred softer, cleaner, cooler cottons expanded quickly.

Textiles

By 1800 textiles was the largest single manufacturing industry. A series of new mechanical gadgets—spinning "jennies," water frames, and "mules" enabled good quality thread to be made at very low cost. In finishing, new weaving looms and their powered adapters provided the next step in the cycle of increased output at lower costs. By the mid-nineteenth century the sewing machine brought the clothing revolution to the household.

The final stage of clothing preparation was thus specialized and mechanized. This in turn led to the rapid growth of an apparel industry in ready-made (factory) clothing in the latter half of the nineteenth century. By 1900 the circle was complete—all processes from raw material to finished product were incorporated into the industrial sphere of the market.

The advances in farming and textiles required the development of new kinds of implements (tools, machines) using stronger durable materials. The machines had to meet greater tolerance and run at higher speeds. The answer was found in the iron industry.

Iron Manufacturing

Changes in the iron industry made possible the widespread use of a superior, uniform quality iron in new and varied ways: plowing and cultivating edges in farming machines, cylinders and pistons in steam engines, rails and boilers for transport followed from significant improvements in the methods of producing iron. Another spur to the increasing use of iron was the shortage of wood. Two causes, visible as early as 1700, were rising wood prices and the shift of woodlands to farmlands to expand agricultural output. This last was in response to the food needs of an expanded population. Again, the interrelationships grew more complex. By 1750 iron was one of the few major industries in England that had not converted to coal. The problems were technical. How did one obtain a uniform fuel mix (as good as charcoal) and how did one redesign furnaces to accept this new fuel? During the next century these major problems of smelting and refining were conquered. Coking coal had become the fuel source and furnaces had grown in size and speed of operation. Puddling and smelting were carried through more scientifically. Rolling and finishing were standardized. The cycle was completed by Bessemer's creation of a furnace for mass producing steel, a new form of iron, with a controlled carbon content. Essential to the scale and speed of operation of machines using coal and iron was a more concentrated, dependable, year-round form of power converter. The answer was the steam engine—the new workhorse of the Industrial Revolution.

Power Conversion

Humankind knew of the power of confined steam from ancient times (the Egyptians and Greeks used steam toys). But it was not until the early eighteenth century in England that serious systematic thought was given to the problem of harnessing this power. Four elements were necessary: economic incentive, scientific insight, technical knowledge, and a common place where all would intersect. Economic incentive was provided by rapidly rising wood prices, flooding in deep coal mines, and the need to make England independent of Swedish iron. The meeting in Scotland of James Watt, a scientist, and engineer Matthew Boulton (a Birmingham manufacturer of extraordinary capabilities) provided the other ingredients. Watt developed the steam condenser needed to boost horsepower output and save on fuel by 75 percent. Boulton fabricated the giant piston and cylinder and seal necessary for the engine. He also helped obtain an extension on Watt's patents (originally dated in the 1760s) for producing and improving these engines. Where did British businessmen use this new power source?

Savery and Newcomen, two earlier innovators, had installed primitive, up-and-down beam, single-action steam pumps in the coal mining regions in the early eighteenth century. By 1800 they had evolved into flexible, double-action steam engines. These were adapted to rotary motion in all phases of manufacturing and transportation. Truly the steam engine can be viewed as a pivotal invention. By 1825 this new power source provided workers with the potential to control larger and faster machines. They could vary their speed and size in accordance with the job that needed to be done. Jobs were specialized by this interaction of man and machine. Innovations developed rapidly as men saw new ways of producing old goods and of creating new products for consumer and producer. The main limit to specialization was, as Adam Smith noted, the extent of the market—the market that was growing as a result of rising population and real wages.

Commercial Services

Facilitating the expansion of the market and all industry and trade were improvements in the organization and management of commerce. Among the most important of these were the diffusion of double entry bookkeeping and other accounting techniques and the expansion of credit and banking facilities. Other improvements were the formation of chartered companies (forerunners of the modern corporation) and the widespread use of fairs and markets to exchange ideas and to encourage production techniques through competitive contests. Finally, this period saw the beginnings of the great invest-

ment banking and international trading houses, the great Atlantic
financial empires that would direct and dominate world trade by 1850.
It was London, Paris, New York, and other Western capital cities that
would prosper by this commercial and financial growth. These institutions served to assemble the capital funds, the savings of society that
were needed to meet the emerging investment opportunities of the
industrial state. One area of great opportunity was the transportation
industry.

Transportation

Improved means of transportation made possible the exchange of
products on a greatly increased scale as a series of innovations lowered
costs of raw materials and delivered products. Improvements in carriages and the development of overland turnpikes aided the movement
of high-value items. This was complemented by the creation of a canal
network of channels and locks that moved bulky lower-valued items
between rural farm or factory and urban market. Moving goods across
the ocean became cheaper as ship speed and size grew continuously.
This decrease in costs increased potential market size and made possible increased *specialization of labor.*

Many historians look upon the railroad as the crowning achievement of the Industrial Revolution. Symbolically it meant speed, the
conquest of distance, and power. It broke down land barriers just as
sailing ships had vanquished the oceans in the sixteenth and seventeenth centuries. In reality it brought together the new achievements
of the iron, power conversion, metal fabricating, and engineering
sectors. It became the lifeblood of commerce, making possible the
overland shipment of large quantities of goods in any season, at any
time of day. It freed cities from their river locations just as steam
power had freed factories from their swift-flowing stream locations.
It linked people and towns in a network of communications and
interchange and, in a sense, climaxed the period and ushered in the
modern era.

In Europe and the U.S., the scales did not tip in favor of the industrial
system until the 1840's, with the development of a new form of communication, the railway. The railway is the major technical invention that

brought into play the new forms of production and promoted the growth of large urban concentrations. From 1840 on, railway and capitalism were to develop hand in hand . . . causing the new urban type to prevail. (Choay 1969:11)

CHANGES IN POPULATION, INSTITUTIONS, AND IDEAS

Population growth and shifts accompanied the widespread technical changes. These acted to spur demand (the need to satisfy a larger population's wants) and to provide the human resources for growth (the workers to produce the new output came from the same population). The two tables that follow suggest both of these aspects.

Table 2–1 shows the size of the total population and the rate of growth over given periods from 1701 to 1831, indicating an acceleration that was probably due mainly to better nutrition and sanitation (a more widespread use of soap) among the poor. There was also *migration*—a continuous shift from the rural to the urban base. Table 2–2 shows more specifically the net movement from agricultural and mixed areas to urban areas within England. By eliminating the variation due to rates of *natural increase* (births minus deaths) in both areas (and differences between them), it highlights more clearly the net movement between the rural and urban sectors. By examining the

TABLE 2–1 Total Population Change by Area, England and Wales, 1701–1831 (in thousands)

	Rural Counties	Mixed Counties	Urban Counties	Population Size at Start of Period
1701–51	10	8	296	5,826
1751–81	373	401	617	6,140
1781–1801	272	456	897	7,531
1801–31	1,086	1,256	2,553	9,156

SOURCE: Adapted from P. Deane and W.A. Cole, *British Economic Growth,* 1688-1959, 2d. ed. (Cambridge at the University Press, 1969), Tables 24, 25, pp. 103-9.

economic sectors, it points out the agricultural-industrial links to urbanization. Having seen something of industrial and population change, we turn now to a discussion of how these fit into the broader changes in society.

As was pointed out in Chapter One, medieval institutions and ideas were slowly dissolved by a flood of innovations. Gunpowder penetrated the physical walls of the city just as the printing press burst apart the social bonds. Trade expanded as commercial capitalism eroded the power base of the landed aristocracy. The new economic-social order was linked to the growth of the centrally controlled nation state and the roots of modern *bureaucracy* were established in the *rationalization* of business. By 1750 many of these institutions and ideas were being challenged by the first thrusts of industrialization. Adaptation or change was again needed.

New ideas and institutions facilitated and spurred on the urbanization-industrialization process in England in the eighteenth century. An examination of this process is important for several reasons. First, new ideas and institutions provide the framework within which the population shifts and technical changes are adopted and motivated. Second, they represent the new developmental directions that the structure of urban life takes in the nineteenth century. Third, they also suggest a new balance in functions that cities perform in the history

TABLE 2–2   Population Shift by Economic Areas, England and Wales, 1701–1831 (net migration in thousands)

	Agricultural Counties	Mixed Counties	Industrial-Commercial Counties
1701–51	−232	−316	+548
1751–81	−115	−215	+330
1781–1801	−252	−126	+378
1801–31	−379	−341	+720

NOTE: On a per decade basis, the rate is fairly uniform from 1701 to 1801 (about 100,000 every ten years). Then it more than doubles as the full impact of the Industrial Revolution is felt.
SOURCE: Adapted from P. Deane and W. A. Cole, *British Economic Growth, 1688-1959,* 2d. ed. (Cambridge at the University Press, 1969), Tables 24, 25, pp. 103–9.

of mankind. The four developments discussed below show both conflicting and complementary aspects of these new directions and functions.

The Decline of Mercantilism

As seen from the viewpoint of the writers of the sixteenth and seventeenth centuries, the purpose of the economic policy of *mercantilism* was: use the power of the state to help the nation develop its economic potential and population. The policy of mercantilism included protection of merchant interests through the control of trade subsidies, the creation of trade monopolies, and the maintenance of a strong armed force to defend commercial aims.

The early phase of mercantilism originated during the period when Europe experienced an acute shortage of gold and silver bullion. This was critical since it meant there was not enough money to service the rapidly expanding volume of trade. The logic of the mercantile system was based on the desire to promote what was called a favorable balance of trade, which could be achieved only when payments of gold and silver into a country were greater than payments flowing out of the country. This goal caused European governments to encourage a strong commercial trade, to increase exports and restrict imports in the hope of increasing the wealth of the country. Later writers on the subject pointed out that imports were needed so that foreign countries could earn the currency to pay for the homeland's exports. Thus the "favorable balance of trade" evolved into the doctrine of the *balance of payments.*

By 1700 the medieval order had largely broken down. Religion, trade, and politics were now going in different directions and at different rates of speed. Economic power was consolidated under the king's banner. Cities no longer gave privileges to individuals, the monarch did. As the king's capital city dominated, the age of the "free city" ended and mercantilism reflected these shifts. A strong monarch, concerned with strengthening his power, forged economic policies intended to increase the wealth and resources of his country.

However, the monopoly of the crown proved only temporary for the forces of capitalism were changing too rapidly for such a rigid system of control. New industries, new technologies, and new leaders were shifting the whole purpose of society toward the making of money.

While mercantilism was based on new economic ideas and practices, it had one important element in common with medieval beliefs. It restrained and controlled individual merchants in favor of the needs of society. The medieval Christian ethic condemned acquisitive, profit-seeking behavior, upholding instead the ideal of the general welfare and common good. It demanded that the activities of the merchants be checked in the interests of the welfare of the entire community. Society had built-in methods of social control.

In terms of this tradition mercantilism represented a continuity in policy, with the major difference being that the common good was redefined in more material terms. Its protection became the responsibility of king and central government, instead of church and guild. However, the rising new middle class of merchants and industrial capitalists were against any restrictions on their profit making. They opposed economic regulation and used their growing power to demand freedom from state control. In sum they desired an end to mercantilism.

As the power of the capitalists increased, the goal of the economy became expansion with money making the function of city growth. Opportunities for social advancement in the emerging economic and social system were great as craftsmen, yeomen farmers, traders, and members of the lower middle and working classes aspired to the expanding middle class. While the market economy provided a means to social recognition, the social costs were also high. The greatest hardship fell on those receiving the fewest benefits. Poor farmers and and members of the rising industrial working class all suffered during this period.

The Rise of Laissez Faire

The development of new industries in eighteenth-century Great Britain involved a rapid expansion of foreign trade. Phyllis Deane estimates that overseas trade increased fivefold and was of central importance to a doubling of the real standard of living. A second aspect of trade expansion focuses on the relation of prices paid for farm goods. In 1800 agriculture was still the major source of income and jobs. The idea was that a rapidly developing commercial agriculture could support a larger industrial population and complement the kinds of new crops being raised in the colonies of Latin and North America.

Foreign demand for British exports was then the initiating factor in the creation of new leading industries. These led to more jobs, rising wages, and in turn were fueled by expanded agricultural growth after 1750. The growth of population kept money wages low and led to ample business investments. Businesses sought new locations and markets, and new sources of labor and capital. The regulations of the mercantile system (designed for a slow-growing agricultural-commercial era) no longer helped the system's dynamics. Freedom from restraint, mobility, and a relaxation of control were seen as the natural way for society to proceed.

The government was viewed by many as interfering and even hindering national destiny. A nation of small farmers wanted to be a nation of small businessmen, and they could not envision the upper-class aristocracy as agents for change. The halls of Parliament were filled with debate; the countryside was to be won over to a new view of society. In 1776 Adam Smith wrote the bible of the movement, *An Inquiry into the Nature and Causes of the Wealth of Nations.* Labor specialization, expanding markets, and free trade could turn the economy into a great private industrial order where there would be no need for public social control. This assumption was at the heart of the policy of *laissez faire.* Competition and the laws of the market economy would work smoothly together. Each individual seeking his own good would lead to the greatest public benefit in the natural order of things.

The End of Public Social Control

The effects of free capitalism (laissez faire) were a disaster in many ways for city form and structure. It is the authors' premise that the problems of urban growth and change were compounded by the treating of the city as if it were a commodity. The city was viewed as a valuable pie to be cut up by profit-seeking real estate speculators in search of rising land values. As Mumford notes, "from the beginning of the nineteenth century laissez faire meant, municipally speaking, 'Let him who will, speculate on a rise in land values and rents.' "

At the level of the neighborhood, the new city block had no regard for social function, the shape of the land, or historic purposes. The city became an abstract *gridiron*. The idea that the varied purposes of the city—civic, commercial, residential, industrial—require different kinds of block patterns and transportation paths was not even considered. Treating the city as a private capitalistic venture led to overcrowding and pollution on a massive scale. This was compounded in the area of people's social lives by a lack of recreational and open areas, as well as the unneeded extensions of streets and utilities. Unplanned dispersal accompanied congestion. These led to a destruction of old forms and chaos and crowding in both new and established areas.

Capitalism wore away local community strengths by destroying the structure of the old social-political system. And it offered no replacement other than the rule of money. Just as freedom from feudal restrictions had led to the "City of the Middle Ages," freedom from municipal restrictions led in the sixteenth and seventeenth centuries to the "Commercial City." Now in the eighteenth and nineteenth centuries freedom to maximize individual rights led to the "Industrial City."

The motive of personal gain had certainly been present in the medieval and precapitalist mind. Until the industrial period, though, customs, beliefs, and institutions had limited and restrained that impulse in favor of community concerns. Now the social responsibilities imposed by customs and manners, as well as the relations between groups in the society, no longer provided means to alleviate social problems. Only the market replaced the religious concepts of sacrifice and justice. Ideas such as *stewardship* for wealth, community control of land, and guaranteed workmanship for handcrafted goods tended to disappear. The individual was forced to adapt and change in ways not previously experienced at a time when the system's social and political mechanisms for balanced control and stability were destroyed. The rule became growth at all costs; expansion was for its own sake.

The Development of the Private Industrial Order

Until 1800 the activities of men and women in religious, artistic, and recreational endeavors had partially offset the growth of commerce and the turning of land and labor into marketable commodities. Some semblance of the good life remained in the town and city before 1800. Thereafter the full force of laissez-faire capitalism was unleashed in the form of the factory town: the town became a factory and the factory dominated urban life.

The working classes were now without a secure base, for the guilds had been abolished and labor unions had not yet been formed. The coal mine, steam engine, and iron mill provided the needed resources; the growth of foreign trade, the markets; the countryside, the new workers. All were organized and administered under the impersonal laws of the business world. This new industrial order was reflected both in political philosophy and changes in law. Now the only legitimate role of government was to grant protection of the new economic individual, his property, and his freedom of choice.

These new economic and political forces also produced another trend. They deeply shaped the *human ecology* of the industrial towns and cities.

The result of thousands of competing individuals working against each other was urban chaos. Dense, congested residential areas were piled on top of poisonous, belching factories. Slums and pollution dominated, and public facilities simply were not built. One expert lists the various poisonous gases that pervaded the atmosphere and refers to the 200 cancer-producing chemicals that were disseminated into the city's air. There were few innovations in transportation, storage, or port facilities to relieve the spatial congestion of the port and factory until the mid-nineteenth century. And there were few attempts at developing a new political and social order that could redirect the unleashed forces for change.

One significant social change was the creation of two new urban classes—the industrial capitalists and the industrial workers. The growing power of the industrialist and financier and the exploitation of the industrial worker were stamped into urban physical design. Even in this early period sharp physical separation of the classes developed. In his study of Manchester, Friedrich Engels noted the physical demarcation of the living areas between the rich and poor. He suggested there was a planned exclusion of working-class people from the main streets of the city so as not to offend middle-class eyes. Workers' areas became increasingly isolated, while the middle class left the city centers for the newly growing "suburbs." Thus economic divisions reproduced themselves socially and ecologically. Class conflict extended from the work place to the communities where women and men lived to the institutions that regulated their lives.

The effects of economic growth were of mixed benefit to the urban dwellers of eighteenth- and nineteenth-century England. Their chances of surviving to adulthood had probably increased and they, no doubt, had a better standard of living in 1850 than in 1700. However, poverty was still the rule, not the exception. Working conditions were terrible, hours were long, and small children and women were exploited. The city became a dangerous and insecure place in which to live, and the ups and downs of the *business* or *trade cycle* made continuous employment very uncertain.

COMPLETING THE URBAN TRANSFORMATION

The shackles that had limited production or controlled growth were many and included a preindustrial social structure, limited technology, and periodic famine. These had also contained urbanization. Now economic breakthroughs quickly transformed the English countryside.

In 1801 one-fifth of the population of Great Britain lived in cities and towns with 10,000 or more inhabitants. By the middle of the century, the census reported that for the first time the urban population exceeded the rural. Towns of over 100,000 inhabitants increased from six in 1841 to thirty in 1901. Towns of 50,000 to 100,000 population increased from five in 1801 to twenty-two in 1841, to forty-nine in 1901. In 1800 the population of London numbered less than a million people. By 1850 it had increased to two million; at the turn of the century, it reached four million, an unprecedented figure in urban history.

Great Britain began the nineteenth century as another rural society and ended it as the first modern urban industrial society. The whole complex of changes involved in the transition to an industrial, factory system of production pushed peasants off the land and pulled them to the emerging urban areas.

The enclosure movement, mentioned previously, was a powerful push, with corresponding pulls being new factory jobs. Other opportunities in manufacturing, trade, and personal and business services were constantly opening up in the towns and cities. In addition, the great Irish famine had driven people from the countryside into urban areas, from agricultural to industrial jobs. One and a half million people, out of a total Irish population of eight and a half million, migrated between 1835 and 1850—many to Great Britain, more to America.

THE NEW URBAN EXPERIENCE

The industrial cities grew so rapidly, without plan or supervision, that even the most elementary city services could not keep up with population increases. A good example of this was the lack of an adequate water supply. Water, which is taken for granted in contemporary cities, was then a precious commodity, bought and sold at high prices. When it was supplied on a mass basis, it was distributed by private profit-making companies that charged a yearly rate to individuals or communities.

Since city dwellers had to pay privately for water (as well as other services now publically provided), the poor were at the greatest disadvantage. By the time the cost of water passed through a number of middlemen suppliers to reach the poor, it was charged at so much a jugful. As an alternative the houses of the poor were sometimes supplied from public wells. These often were polluted by seepage from sewers, from standpipes turned on only for short periods a day, or from water butts in back courts. One commentator describes what this meant for those in poverty:

> The water of the town wells is acknowledged to be very bad and it is generally avoided. . . . It happens sometimes that persons are obliged to

come out as early as one o'clock in a morning to secure a supply of water for washing day . . . the water must be taken as it issues or it is lost. A large proportion is therefore employed catching water as it flows. . . . The great trouble in bringing water home causes it to be used again and again, until it becomes exceedingly filthy and in this state it is employed at last to wash the floors. . . . (Gauldie 1974:76)

With death rates high, city growth came from migration from the countryside. The rural immigrants who crowded into the towns and cities suffered not only from lack of water, but also from overcrowding, polluted air, long hours of work, disease, and epidemics. The First Report of the Registrar-General of England (1839) showed that about 20 percent of the total death rate was due to tuberculosis, a disease normally associated with poverty and overcrowding. In the first four decades of the nineteenth century, the infant *mortality rate* was often twice as high in the new industrial towns as it was in rural areas. The city that offered its inhabitants the possibility of new jobs also killed them in fairly large numbers. The death rate in modern urban Western countries is now about 12 to 15 per 1,000. During industrialization an urban death rate of about 20 per 1,000 was considered low, and most large cities had rates of 30 to 35 per 1,000.

As one historian of the period comments:

If half the technical skill applied to industry had been applied to the Victorian cities, their record would have been very different. As it was, Victorian cities were places where problems often overwhelmed people. (Briggs 1964:22)

During the nineteenth century, England completed part of her demographic transition, moving from high birth and death rates to moderate birth and lower death rates. Britain's death rate, which peaked around 24 to 25 per 1,000 inhabitants in 1849, fell to 22 to 23 per 1,000 in the later 1860s, and to 17 to 18 per 1,000 at the close of the century. This reflected further advances in medicine, vast expenditures on water systems and sanitation, and gains in living standards due to industrialization.

However, throughout the first half of the century, mortality rates had increased steadily with size and density of population. They were highest in the great cities, such as London, where death rates were consistently above birth rates.

Poor housing, impure water, lack of fresh air and sunlight, dirt, and disease were the common lot of city dwellers, especially the working class. Urban water systems were a natural breeding ground for typhoid and cholera, and real improvements had to await advances in hydraulic engineering and the development of bacteriological science. These occurred in the last quarter of the nineteenth century.

THE ECOLOGY OF THE INDUSTRIAL CITY

Industrialization directly affected the ecology of the growing English towns and cities, that is, their spatial layout, physical structure, and distribution of population. As already noted, the steam engine was the pivotal innovation of the Industrial Revolution in England, supplying power for the railroad and all leading industries. This innovation also deeply affected urbanization in several ways, one being that a single steam engine could run a number of machines. Now both engine and machines could be housed in one building for maximum efficiency. This resulted in a concentration of people during working hours and the growth of workers' housing around the factories, so people could get to work quickly. This arrangement of *factory district* and surrounding residential area was a basic urban physical form of the time. The term "slum" was initially given to just such areas.

Workers chose to live near the noisy, dirty factories for two basic reasons. One was that, for many, employment was on a casual basis, with the number of available jobs fluctuating greatly from day to day. Since many working people had to search for jobs on a daily basis, they were obliged to live within reasonably close walking distance of their work. The second reason was the inadequacy and expense of public transportation. The following is a statement by a worker of the time explaining why he chose to live in the center of the city (London).

I am a working man, I go to my factory every morning at six, and I leave it every night at the same hour. I require, on the average, eight hours sleep, which leaves four hours for recreation and improvements. I have

lived at many palces in the outskirts, according as my work has shifted.
. . . I always live near the factory where I work, and so do all my mates,
no matter how dirty, small and dear the houses may be. . . . One or two
of my uncles have tried the plan of living a few miles out, and walking
to business in the morning, like the clerks do in the city. I don't do it
. . . perhaps because walking exercises at five o'clock in the morning
don't suit men who are hard at work with their bodies all day. As to
railroads and omnibuses, they cost money. (Dyos and Reeder in Dyos
and Wolff 1973:368)

To understand how industrialization affected the location of the
industrial city, we must once again focus on the steam engine. It was
a fuel-consuming machine and required large amounts of coal. England, fortunately, was rich in coal deposits, and coal mining was vital
to this whole phase of industrialization. Therefore, urbanization was
no longer confined to ports, trade centers, and capitals, but extended
to any region with exploitable coal deposits. As the lure of oil now
brings men to small, desolate Alaskan towns, coal propelled formerly
insignificant English regions into national prominence. Small towns
and villages blossomed into large towns and cities within a few
decades. Mine sites joined with the railroad to set whole new patterns
in motion.

Urban growth occurred where factories were built and mines sunk,
and the new towns were unprepared to absorb the people migrating
to them. One reason was that, from a public service and social welfare
view, they were unplanned. As one historian puts it:

The founders and owners of the new industries were first and foremost
businessmen interested in production and profit; they did not see themselves as the founders and planners of the new towns and cities, whose
growth was only incidental to personal business concerns. (Briggs
1964:210)

As the towns and villages grew, the most common regional pattern
was a manufacturing or mining center that served as the hub for a
circle of industrial villages. As the center spread, the villages became
suburbs and the nearby farmlands were absorbed by the great urban
areas. In the nineteenth century urbanization occurred so rapidly that
fewer than one hundred years after the beginning of the Industrial
Revolution England was over 50 percent urbanized.

IMPACT ON THE FAMILY

Industrialization and urbanization fundamentally changed patterns of where people lived and the work they did. These processes also affected a number of other social patterns, with the family being a particularly clear case.

Before industrialization, families were quite stable and cohesive. Since much work was done either in the home or in the fields, the family worked together and its common activities created clear links among family members. In 1619 the bakers of London petitioned the Crown for an increase in the price of bread. In support of their claim, they sent a complete description of a bakery and an account of its weekly costs. This document gives us a good description of how the family functioned as an economic unit in preindustrial England.

A London bakery was a business, a commercial enterprise, baking bread to be sold at market. However, unlike today, the business was carried on in the house of the baker. Thirteen or fourteen people lived in such a house: the baker and his wife, four paid employees, known as journeymen, two apprentices who were learning the trade of baker, two maidservants, and three or four children of the master baker. Everyone ate in the house and, except for the journeymen, they all slept in the house and lived together as a family. In historian Peter Laslett's words:

> The only word used at that time to describe such a group of people was "family." The man at the head of the group, the entrepreneur, the employer, or the manager, was then known as the master or head of the family. He was father to some of the members, and in place of father to the rest. There were no sharp distinctions between his domestic and his economic functions. (Laslett 1966:4)

The family was not only the basic economic unit of society but also the basic educational unit, providing the source of instruction for children. Since the family performed many functions, all family members played many more useful roles than they do today. For example, when grandparents became to old to work, they could spend time regularly educating and caring for their grandchildren. This allowed older family members the opportunity to feel needed and useful and helped to develop strong bonds between generations.

By 1850 these *extended family* patterns were being drastically changed. With the rise of factory production, family members no longer worked together. Instead, they were often employed in differing unrelated occupations and they often had totally different hours of work and leisure. The new mobility made possible by the railroad also operated to disperse families. As a result, many of their members sought out job opportunities wherever the newest industries were expanding. Some became lodgers in the houses of others or servants in the homes of middle-class families.

There were also changes in the size of families and in the rights and authority of family members. Younger people frequently went out on their own. The lure of higher wages, the possibility of greater personal freedom and a wider social life in the towns and cities weakened the authority of the father and the older folk. There is a fair amount of evidence that women from fifteen to twenty years of age and men from twenty to thirty-five formed the great bulk of migrants from the countryside. Although the cities were dirty and dangerous, these young people were attracted by the promise (sometimes unrealized) of work and by what a then contemporary commentator called

> . . . the contagion of numbers, the sense of something going on, the theatres and music-halls, the brightly lighted streets and busy crowds—all, in short, that makes the difference between the Mile End fair on a Saturday night, and a dark and muddy country lane. (Banks in Dyos and Wolff 1973:98)

When these migrants arrived, they were often crowded into inadequate housing, filling the spaces from attic to cellar of old decaying property or flimsy, small, and cheaply built new dwellings. When they began their own families, space was at a premium. Children were no longer an economic asset and as a result the size of families began to shrink slowly.

DEVELOPMENTS IN CITY FUNCTIONS

In the process of developing such a strong generative function, the city failed to balance public and private welfare. Both the older interaction and newer upgrading functions of the urbanization process were overshadowed. Urban life lost much of its social dimension, and the values of community and family were endangered. It was to take another two generations after the close of the Industrial Revolution for many of the benefits of this great expansionary period to reach down into the lives of the average working person. Today's simplest comforts—soap, hot water, glass windows, lights to read by, even books to read—were largely unknown in the mid-nineteenth century, urban, working-class home. Nonetheless conditions in 1850 were less brutish than the life of the casual agricultural laborer of the seventeenth century before it all began. Perhaps most important was the recognition by some leaders in society of two facts: first, the trend away from rural-agricultural ways to urban-industrial ways was irreversible; and, second, the conditions for interaction in cities could be improved. Sanitation, public health and safety were controllable aspects of urban living. In order to continue to upgrade the millions flocking to the cities, the common welfare had to be attended to. Some felt these needs would never be met and decided to venture forth to the New World. Some came to escape; others to find opportunity. All came to better their lives, as they saw it. It is to this perspective—the American experience, rooted in the British past—that we now turn.

CHAPTER THREE

American Cities: An Overview

A MODEL OF AMERICAN CITY DEVELOPMENT

Today most of us live in or around cities, but this was not always the case. In 1789 when our nation adopted the Constitution, only about 5 percent of the population had settled in fewer than twenty-five cities (defined as places of 2,500 persons or more). The largest city of those times was Philadelphia, holding just about 30,000 persons.

Today over 90 percent of Americans live within the orbit of one of over 200 metropolitan areas that contain over 4,000 cities. And each of these areas has at least one city of over 50,000 population within it—thus our smallest urban area today is larger than Philadelphia was at the beginning of our nation's history.

The story of America's urbanization is closely interwoven with the history of its economic growth, just as it was in England. Over the past 200 years, the increases in population and the development of new technologies have interacted to raise our standard of living to unprecedented levels. These forces also shaped us into an urban nation. As our network of cities evolved, it impressed its pattern on the economy. The current complex of interlocking metropolitan areas is the end product of an economic growth-urbanization-economic development-urbanization spiral. This interaction pattern continues today.

This chapter provides an overview of these changes in size and number from colonial times to the present. It explores the whys and

hows of city-spread, the rhythms and patterns of growth and multiplication.

Cities don't just happen; they arrange themselves and are arranged
in physical and social space as a result of the numberless investment
and building decisions of private business and the millions of
household responses to changing economic opportunities. Public policy decisions at all levels of government deeply affect the ebb and flow
of these economic factors, and all of these operate within changing
political and social boundaries.

Economic development in nineteenth-century America altered the
pattern of evolution for the network of cities, multiplied their numbers
sharply, led to increases in their size, and changed their functioning.
Two important facets of economic development were the increasing
size of the income pie generated and the redistribution of its parts
away from agriculture toward industry. The rise in the *real standard
of living* was more rapid in the nonfarm sector as the century wore
on and growth became focused on the urban-industrial interaction
process. As people's incomes rose above subsistence, they had more
money to spend on clothing, homes, house furnishings, more varied
diets, and numerous personal services. The demand for such manufactured goods and services was further stimulated by rapidly expanding
population growth due to declining death rates and massive *immigration.* Both of these were in turn affected by the very process of economic development itself.

As people settled in cities, a series of interactions followed. New
jobs were created both by the demands of the new migrants and by
the responses of business and service specialists to fulfill these demands. Economies resulted from placing together of complementary
enterprises, thus reducing the costs of services. Urban building booms
stimulated the need for private and public investment at high rates.
The close quarters of city interaction led to increased exchanges of
ideas and information and fostered experiments with new products
and innovations. The larger scale of enterprise encouraged mass production techniques and the assembling of substantial capital funds for
investment. Material and human resources grew apace with technology. Natural resources were abundant and high birth rates complemented high immigration rates to provide workers for the expansion

of industry. The challenge and the opportunity of this economic development simultaneously changed and were changed by the American urbanization process.

Let us consider a modern example of the interaction process. In the last half century the domination of metropolitan America has become a reality, and yet the change patterns continue—although with different emphases. Urban life has altered the nature of the family and work. As the immigration component in the labor force declined, the focus of change turned to the urban woman. Social attitudes changed toward women working for pay. The occupational mix of industry moved toward white-collar jobs that depend less on physical strength. The *mechanization* of housework functions through the marketing of electrical appliances and the separation of "housewifely" tasks to outside specialists accelerated these tendencies. The growth of the female component in the urban work force and the development of economic independence for many women led to a revolution in family life. New roles in society changed attitudes toward the bearing and raising of children. Birth rates were affected, further altering family size and fostering demands for new kinds of urban services such as child care centers and community health centers. Although more women workers per household depressed the labor market for older men and teenagers, on balance, family incomes rose dramatically over the past generation. Thus the needs of the economy and the desires of the modern urban woman have intermingled to indicate new directions for our metropolitan life styles.

In the case of the United States then, the private sector dominated while the public sector was continuously supportive, encouraging, and stimulating. For example, our legal framework encouraged land expansion and an exploitation of our abundant natural resources. Our social attitudes focused on the importance and value of hard work and savings. The result has been a harsh, competitive economic system producing ever higher material living standards and continuing inequalities. As the industrialization-urbanization process gathered momentum, the social costs began to mount rapidly, just as they had done in nineteenth-century England. Let us turn backward to these earlier days to discover the distinctive characteristics of the American experience of urbanization.

COMPARISONS WITH ENGLAND

Urbanization in the United States, as in England, was rooted in the commercial and industrial thrust of the nineteenth century. However, English society had been a traditional one, highly structured in its preindustrial forms and wedded to an aristocratic vision of political order. England was also conscious of its role as world leader in trade and finance. American society found little use for such traditions. Ours was an abundant land, open and diverse in its challenges. The frontier was everywhere, and the varied forms of our early settlements, with their rebellious pioneers, set the tone for our entire history. Experimentation with new political forms and a belief that all men should have equal opportunity gradually shaped our special brand of *"free enterprise."* Social structure in the early cities was loose. Although class differences existed, great optimism about the possibilities of economic progress usually swept aside realistic appraisals of the inadequacies in this society of abundance.

Abundance is a key concept in understanding the uniqueness of the American experience. Both the cities and the countryside reflected a richness in resources and an attitude toward the use of land that could not have been envisioned by the European counterpart of the American workingman. This idea should not be thought of in a fixed way, nor should it be associated with only a physically rich resource base. Rather, it should be conceived as the potential of groups from highly diverse backgrounds for productive cultural-physical interactions.

Initially, cheap fertile land, a strong spirit of adventure, a sense of destiny, and a desire to cut loose from European roots were the main ingredients. Slowly, the control of the environment through technology, the growing skills of the work force, and the awareness of the possibility of a continually rising standard of living came to the forefront. By the mid-nineteenth century our standards of behavior were shaped by high economic expectations. Our belief in the private economic benefits of equality and liberty permeated every phase of the early industrial-urban system. Just as our nineteenth-century economic abundance shaped our values, so also did Great Britain's experience of the first Industrial Revolution, in a framework of certain resource scarcities, shape the origins of the modern British welfare state.

But relative abundance does not eliminate the central questions of any modernizing society. How do we allocate available resources among the seemingly limitless wants of a rapidly growing populace that has great expectations for progress? In short, our development produced conflicts. Perhaps the most well known was between the agrarian plantation owners of the southern slave-cotton "kingdoms" and the commercial farmers, merchants, and industrialists of the West and Northeast. This led toward the greatest internal struggle of our history—the Civil War. Some of the effects of that struggle are still with us well into the twentieth century. When, after World War II, all the states found themselves with a majority of their populations in urban areas and nonagricultural jobs, new urban-dominated issues developed in a political framework still overrepresented by rural interests.

A second great series of conflicts arose over the mobility patterns resulting from the redistribution of opportunity accompanying the growth of the economy. It is possible to distinguish four. The westward movement of farmers in the nineteenth century has been matched by the growth of urban centers in the West and South in the mid-twentieth century. Between these were two other major shifts of population. The first was the migration of over 30 million Europeans between 1840 and 1920. They came in great waves, first from northern and western countries such as Ireland and Germany, then from southern and eastern areas such as Italy, Poland, and Russia. This was followed by a massive internal movement of blacks from rural regions and small towns in the South to the industrialized Northeast and Great Lakes regions.

These four movements have led to dramatic collisions in which some cultures (American Indian) were almost wiped out; some were modified (white Christians of German and Irish descent); some were slow to change (southern and eastern Europeans); and some have still been seeking a reasonable path toward the future (the minorities of today). In turn, the white, Anglo-Saxon, Protestant, small-town, individual farmer or businessman dominated nineteenth-century American culture. He tried to adapt to the changing scale and technology of the twentieth century. Neither the attempted homogenization of the plurality of American cultural roots nor the healthy preservation of its vital diversity has been achieved. The tension between these two goals maintains itself today. Economic power differences perpetuate social inequalities, and lack of opportunity and mobility cannot be overcome by a one man-one vote system of government that does not recognize the reality of such power differences.

Since there are unique aspects of the American urban experience, the rates of dispersion and concentration of population were quite distinctive in some ways. Although similar technological forces lead the way in all modernization, the organizational, demographic, and decision-making factors tended to develop here into a more open society. These factors produced an American social system that was more mobile, more individualistic, and more optimistic about solving urban social problems. However, an examination of our history suggests that there are recurrent themes in American urban problems produced by these patterns. In short, we must investigate the trends and the patterns of growth to understand the problems.

TRENDS IN CITIES SINCE 1800

Of the important trends in city growth in the United States since 1800, three are most evident: an increasing percentage of the population residing in urban areas, increasing size and number of large urban areas, and the slowly accelerating spread of activity away from one central city with the creation of many-centered metropolitan regions.

Less obvious, but also important, are three other trends that have had great impact: a pattern of city growth toward metropolitan dominance accompanied by a tendency toward change in the ranking of leading cities (new centers appearing with others rising and still others falling over time), and differential rates of growth for urban areas in various regions of the country.

Data on these trends are presented in the tables below.

Table 3–1 shows that only about 5 percent of the population lived in twenty-four urban areas in 1790 (urban here is defined as 2,500 persons or more). By 1970 almost 75 percent of the population was concentrated in over 6,400 cities. The last column indicates the sharp increases in the percentage of persons living in urbanized areas of over

TABLE 3–1   United States Urban Growth Since Colonial Times

Year	Number of Cities	Total Urban Population (thousands)	Percent of Population Urban	Percent in Urbanized Areas over 500,000
1790	24	202	5	—
1820	61	693	7	—
1850	236	3,544	15	3
1880	939	14,130	28	7
1910	2,262	41,999	46	20
1940	3,464	74,424	57	28
1970	6,435	150,251	74	42

SOURCES: Derived from U.S. Bureau of the Census, *Census of the United States,* 1960 and 1970 (Washington, D.C.: Government Printing Office), and Jerome P. Pickard, "Growth of Urbanized Population in the United States", in *The Modern City,* ed. by David Rasmussen and Charles Haworth (New York: Harper & Row, 1973), p. 10.

500,000. There are twenty-six areas which today contain almost 45 percent of the population. Pickard projects that such large complexes will hold close to 60 percent of the totals by the year 2000.

Table 3–2 looks at size changes in more detail. In 1800 only one city had over 50,000 persons, but today almost 400 are in this category. Of middle-sized cities of 10,000 to 50,000, there were 5 in 1800, today there are almost 2,000. Since 1900 very large cities of over 250,000 grew from 15 in number to almost 60.

Table 3–3 illustrates the growth of metropolitan regions inside and outside their central cities since 1900. It suggests that growth in suburban areas was substantial even in the two decades before World War I. Since 1920 it has exceeded the growth of central cities by significant margins. Another analysis by Kenneth Jackson demonstrates that urban spread was occurring in many areas even before the Civil War. He found that New York, Boston, Philadelphia, Cleveland, and St. Louis followed early paths to deconcentration.

The three tables above dramatically indicate how growing size and the multiplication of urban areas nurtured the urbanization process. The next three tables point toward the evolution of a network of cities

TABLE 3-2   Size Changes—United States Cities, 1800–1970

	1800	1850	1900	1950	1970
1 million +	—	—	3	5	6
500,000–1 million	—	—	3	13	20
250,000–500,000	—	—	9	23	30
100,000–250,000	—	5	23	65	100
50,000–100,000	1	4	40	126	240
25,000–50,000	2	16	82	252	520
10,000–25,000	3	36	280	778	1,385
2,500–10,000	18	175	1,298	2,782	4,134

SOURCE: Derived from U.S. Bureau of the Census, *Census of the United States,* 1960 and 1970 (Washington, D.C.: Government Printing Office).

dominated by a group of metropolitan centers. Table 3–4 suggests the specific city leaders at different times in our history; Table 3–5 points out the relation of the spread of the urban network to regional growth; and Table 3–6 gives a set of guidelines for judging this development at different stages of the process. Together these three tables form the basis for analyzing the theme of the evolution of our urban system toward metropolitan dominance in the rest of the chapter.

TABLE 3-3   Population Growth Rates within SMSA's (in percent)

Years	Central City	Outside Central City
1900–10	37	24
1910–20	28	20
1920–30	24	32
1930–40	6	15
1940–50	15	36
1950–60	11 (2)[*]	49 (62)[*]
1960–70	7 (0.1)[*]	27 (33)[*]

[*]Corrected for annexations.
SOURCES: Derived from Leo F. Schnore, "Metropolitan Growth and Decentralization," in *The Urbanization of America,* ed. Allen M. Wakstein (Boston: Houghton Mifflin, 1970), p. 365, and U.S. Bureau of the Census, *Census of the United States,* 1960 and 1970 (Washington, D.C.: Government Printing Office).

Table 3–4 reveals the regional dispersal of the ten largest urban centers over our history. In 1800 all ten were on the Atlantic Coast. By 1860 half were inland, and by 1900 a West Coast representative had joined the group. In the modern period the continued growth of the West and the emergence of the South are evident. Another striking characteristic of this table is that the absolute size of these areas grows as a group over time—moving toward the dominance of the metropolis in modern urban life. We offer a fuller discussion of the causes of these patterns of changing leadership after Table 3–6 and in Chapter Seven in the sections on the evolution of the system of cities.

TABLE 3–4   Size Ordering of the Nation's Ten Largest Cities

	1800	*1830*	*1860*
1.	Philadelphia	New York	New York
2.	New York	Baltimore	Philadelphia
3.	Baltimore	Philadelphia	Baltimore
4.	Boston	Boston	Boston
5.	Charleston	New Orleans	New Orleans
6.	Salem	Charleston	Cincinnati
7.	Providence	Cincinnati	St. Louis
8.	New Haven	Albany	Chicago
9.	Richmond	Washington, D.C.	Buffalo
10.	Portsmouth	Providence	Newark

	1900	*1930*	*1960*
1.	New York	New York	New York
2.	Chicago	Chicago	Chicago
3.	Philadelphia	Philadelphia	Los Angeles
4.	St. Louis	Detroit	Philadelphia
5.	Boston	Los Angeles	Detroit
6.	Baltimore	Cleveland	Baltimore
7.	Pittsburgh	St. Louis	Houston
8.	Cleveland	Baltimore	Cleveland
9.	Buffalo	Boston	Washington, D.C.
10.	San Francisco	Pittsburgh	St. Louis

SOURCE: Lance E. Davis et al., *American Economic History: The Development of a National Economy* (New York: Richard D. Irwin, 1965), p. 289.

Table 3–4 points out that of the top ten cities in size in 1800, only two, New York and Philadelphia, remain in 1970. It also shows that some of the cities, which were on the list for quite a few decades, have dropped off. This was complemented by newer urban centers. Examples are the decline of New Orleans and Louisville and the rise of Chicago and Detroit. It also suggests that some cities may come back to positions of prominence after having slipped off the list. For example, Washington, D.C., appears, then disappears, then reappears.

Finally, Table 3–5 suggests the timing of the city growth by region. The decade of urban acceleration came first to the Northeast (1820s) and last to the South (1880s). Each area reached its 50 percent urban-50 percent rural break point approximately six decades after acceleration. Today the differences between regions are narrowed to about 15 percentage points (Column 3) and seem to be declining as some of the oldest areas level off (100 percent being the theoretical maximum).

Let us now examine the why and how of these changing patterns in more detail.

TABLE 3–5   Patterns of Urbanization by Region

	Decade of Acceleration	Decade 50 Percent Urban	Percent Urban in 1970
U.S.	1830–40	1910–20	74
Northeast	1820–30	1870–80	80
South	1880–90	1950–60	65
North Central	1840–50	1910–20	72
West	1850–60	1910–20	83

SOURCES: Derived from Eric E. Lampard, "The Evolving System of Cities in the United States," in *Issues in Urban Economics*, eds., Harvey S. Perloff and Lowdon Wing (Baltimore: Johns Hopkins Press, 1968), p. 108, and *U.S. Census of Population, 1970.*

THE EVOLVING SYSTEM OF METROPOLITAN AREAS

Our discussion in the following chapters will show how specific technological changes in transportation, power sources and converters, communications devices, and construction materials all influence the growth of city size and the evolution of the city's physical form toward the end product—a fully "metropolitanized" America.

Perhaps it is useful to conceive of the development of these areas and their increase in number in terms of the technological era in which they were born and the patterns of growth they followed over the last century and a half. The basic data are in Table 3–6.

Table 3–6   Development of Metropolitan Areas, 1790–1960

Year	1 Total Population in "Metro" Areas* (millions)	2 Minimum Central-City Size (thousands)	3 Minimum Metropolitan-Area Size (thousands)	4 Maximum Metropolitan-Area Size (thousands)	5 Total Number of Areas
1790	3.9	1.1	5	over 180	39
1830	12.9	3.6	15	over 530	52
1870	39.8	11.1	30	over 1,300	91
1920	105.7	29.5	60	over 4,750	147
1960	179.3	50.0	80	over 8,000	178

* Counties currently making up metropolitan areas.
SOURCE: John R. Borchert, "American Metropolitan Evolution," *Geographical Review* 57 (1967):301–23.

Columns 5 and 1 indicate respectively the number of metropolitan areas and their populations at different points in time. Columns 2 and 3 show the critical size or threshold needed at these points to join the metropolitan family. Column 4 shows the size of the largest centers.

Several conclusions emerge from a close analysis of the data. There has been a sixfold increase in the number of metropolitan areas since 1790 and a sixtyfold increase in the total metropolitan population. Also, the minimal central city has grown in importance over the long run in relation to the entire metropolitan area. These conclusions further point toward a central theme of this chapter—that of metropolitan dominance and the importance of the leading cities in shaping the entire urban network.

It is the viewpoint of writers such as N. S. B. Gras and L. Schnore that major metropolitan areas have tended to dominate our urban system since its very beginnings. As the needs of the total economic system for more and larger centers for production and trade grew, the older regions expanded and moved up the scale as newer centers were added on at the bottom.

Our enumeration above of the long-range trends since 1800 suggested somewhat this idea of metropolitan dominance. This concept implies the exercise of control not by any law, authority, or right, but rather by ability to shape the conditions fundamental to life. Such centers adjusted to the wide variations in the history of our social, technical, and political changes. These dominant regions acted upon and altered their environments to benefit themselves. Dependent urban areas gained in two ways. As industries spun off from the largest areas, they settled into middle-sized and smaller locales. These could then continue to generate high living standards while climbing the size ladder. In addition, the potential for human interaction increased geometrically as the urban network of communication and transportation grew rapidly. Since World War II the agricultural countryside has blended these urban industrial influences into its work and life patterns.

The growing dominance of the largest metropolitan areas in twentieth-century America is attested to by the following facts: the growth of their share of the total populace; the increase in economic and social interdependence; the narrowing in our concepts of the meaning of time and distance; the expansion control of the physical environment and work place; and the adjustment of all parts of the network of cities to the activities generated at these points of focus.

Let us examine what led to the emergence of such dominant metropolitan centers. Dominance means control at all geographic levels (individual regions, groups of states, and national) and in all aspects (political, economic, and social). Control increases in proportion to knowledge of the environment. These urban areas played important roles in initiating increases in that knowledge and in diffusing it throughout the society. The concentration of population into dominant metropolitan centers increased both interdependence and the amount of interaction. This furthered the generative function of cities by increasing the rate of technical and economic innovation, and provided opportunities for upgrading.

Let us now review the growing pattern of metropolitan dominance, the major regional shifts within this pattern, and some of the changes causing these shifts.

1770–1820

Cities in 1790 were in about the same position as in 1770, since it took almost ten years for trade to be restored after the Revolution. At the first census (1790) the nation had eleven cities that were considered of second- or third-order size (40,000+).* Only two, Pittsburgh, Pennsylvania, and Worcester, Massachusetts, were not situated on a river that emptied into the Atlantic Ocean. There was no dominant East Coast seaport of first-order size. And all the major cities, Boston, Philadelphia, New York, and Charleston, had relatively undeveloped local trading areas. Until 1820 change was slow and those places that grew faster that the average national urban growth rate were in the areas of westward expansion: western New York and Ohio valleys and the blue grass region in Kentucky and Tennessee.

This growth rested upon the development of water, power, timber, and potential anthracite coal resources, all of which complemented the new lands that were cleared and the farms that were built. The local overland road network supplemented the system of interdependent production and trade.

The boom cities were those located at inland harbor sites and at the intersections of terminal points of rivers. Thus a Louisville, Cincinnati, or New Orleans jumped upward sharply in the rankings. However, all of these cities slipped dramatically later, when they failed to adapt to changes in society or were bypassed by new technologies or resource discoveries.

1820–70

The next period is marked by what scholars call a transportation revolution. It began with the construction of primitive roadways and continued with an extensive canal system that completed the natural overland and waterway interconnections by 1840. This was followed by the development of a market-expanding railroad and telegraph system that was the world's largest by 1870 although restricted to the Midwest and eastern seaboard.

*Standardization of size by time period has been done by Borchert, and this discussion relies on his work.

The results for city growth patterns were complex. First the canal terminals and exchange points grew and then the railroad centers developed. Both were impressed on top of the natural water system which, in turn, saw the steamboat change its basic cost picture.

The net effect was that, inland, new cities such as St. Louis, Buffalo, and Chicago joined the earlier group of leaders. These tended to incorporate extensively two or three of the major transportation innovations into their trade structures. Earlier standouts such as Louisville, Albany, Charleston, and Providence saw the growth of manufacturing and commerce bypass them and cause them to slip downward in the rankings.

The largest eastern seaboard ports prospered dramatically. Boston and Philadelphia held their own as *second-order cities* and were joined by Baltimore. Cities of such size would have populations of 150,000 in 1830 and 400,000 in 1890 as minimums. New York led the way not only in all transportation developments but also in many innovations in foreign trade and manufacturing as it attained the distinction of becoming a first-order region. By 1870, as the national metropolis of over 1,300,000, it was a true pioneer in large-scale urbanization. Such leadership led not only to the benefits of very rapid growth but also to the collection of serious social and political problems. Containing over 10 percent of the total population of the nation, 15 percent of the manufacturing employment, and 50 percent of the banking, finance, and foreign trade, New York was also the leading processor for immigrant groups and a source for new technologies and industries.

New Orleans kept its prime position in the South, but other new areas did not develop under the plantation system. Some of the older seaboard centers, such as Savannah and Charleston, suffered declines in rank order. The only other areas of urban decline were some of the smaller inland centers in the Mid-Atlantic and New England states.

1870–1920

By 1870 a few metropolitan centers arose as far west as the Missouri Valley. Yet only a low-cost transportation system could make full use of the many natural resources of mining and the fertile farmlands of the interior plateaus and valleys. The completion of the national steel rail network made such access possible by World War I. Accompanying this was the switch in power sources from water to coal and from wind to steam. New energy conversion mechanisms led to larger city size and made possible more flexible internal structure.

What were the main patterns of growth and decline during this full blossoming of the industrial era? These five decades saw the leading five metropolitan areas increase their share of the nation's population from about one-eighth to almost one-fifth. It was their most rapid growth period. Medium-sized cities, which had grown most rapidly in the pre-Civil War era, stabilized their numbers and increased their share from 10 percent to 14 percent of the total population. It was the smaller metropolitan centers that proliferated most quickly (from 70 to 126) probably partly due to the larger centers' generating new industries and products. This accompanied the discovery of new mineral deposits and better use of previous discoveries. As a result of these changes between 1870 and 1920, metropolitan population had increased about fourfold from 13 to 53 million, thus maintaining the growth rate of the earlier part of the nineteenth century.

Two other kinds of growth and decline were important. One was the rise of specialized manufacturing cities of major size. These were usually situated close to adequate coal supplies as the shift to steam and later electric power became more significant. Examples were Pittsburgh, Toledo, and Birmingham. All were located in the wedge around the lower eastern Great Lakes region and part of the Appalachian Mountains. In contrast was the decline of water power sites in New England and in the Mohawk River Valley in New York. In addition, some inland ports of the pre-Civil War period of the Ohio, Mississippi, and Missouri rivers saw sharp slowdowns in the expansion of their commerce and populations. Chief among the losers were New Orleans, Cincinnati, Louisville, and Wheeling.

1920–70

By 1920 the first threads of new patterns of metropolitan development could be seen. These were caused by substantial changes in the technological capabilities of mining, manufacturing, and service industries. Among the most important were new power sources (electricity and internal combustion); new resource *inputs* (chemicals, aluminum, plastics, petroleum, synthetics, and so on); the building of a nationwide highway and airport system; and a public and private communications network that moved vast amounts of information between cities almost instantaneously. These factors operated to create massive movements and cross-movements of industry and population.

Which parts of the system grew most rapidly? New York and second-order centers (that now included Chicago, Detroit, Los Angeles, and San Francisco) increased their share to 25 percent of the total population and to 38 percent of the urban sector. Smaller SMSAs (those under 820,000 in 1960) held their own at about 60 percent of all metropolitan areas. One of the most important shifts was geographic. The West and South became the leading growth centers. Specifically, the West Coast and scattered sites in the Southwest and the Gulf Coast crescent from Texas to Florida saw the most rapid increases. Among the leaders were: Los Angeles, San Francisco, Oakland, San Jose in California; Dallas, Fort Worth, Houston, and Corpus Christi in Texas; Miami, Fort Lauderdale in Florida; Atlanta, Georgia; Las Vegas, Nevada; Phoenix, Arizona; Denver, Colorado; and Seattle-Tacoma in Washington. Many of these were associated with the growth of new leading industries such as automobiles, oil, chemicals, aerospace, agribusiness, and tourism.

Within these newer centers, as in the older areas of the Northeast and North Central states, there was a common, threefold change pattern in the internal, physical structure. This consisted of a strong dispersal function (called suburbanization) of both residences and jobs; a multiplication of smaller ring satellite centers; and the expansion of metropolitan control into the rural fringes from the larger dominant centers. This physical change pattern interacted with the other variables and created changes in socioeconomic patterns both within and between cities.

If the trends in American urbanization are now outlined, they are still not explained. The intricate patterns of interaction between the socio-technical and politico-economic spheres have to be illuminated. In the last chapter we left the story in Great Britain at the end of the Industrial Revolution. In the next chapter we step back chronologically to examine colonial America. We then trace our story here in the United States up to the time of the Civil War and the thrust toward industrialization.

CHAPTER FOUR

Colonial and Pre-Civil War Cities

THE LOCATION OF COLONIAL CITIES

The first European colonies were strung along the Eastern Seaboard in the early seventeenth century and provided the base upon which many of the cities of colonial America were built by the end of the eighteenth century. By 1776 Philadelphia, the largest urban area in America, was one of a small class of centers, second in size only to London, in the entire British Empire. The other major urban areas were New York, Boston, Charleston, Newport, and Baltimore. All owed their growth to their function as commercial headquarters. They served as trading, storing, and shipping points between the Old World and the New, and all had safe and secure harbors to berth the ships of the Atlantic trade.

Other smaller settlements along the coast and in the interior served different and more specialized purposes. Fishing ports, trapping and hunting centers, forts for defense, and way stations for trade and barter were found in towns such as Portsmouth, Salem, Pittsburgh, Lexington, and Albany. Without exception, these major and minor urban areas had one thing in common: they were located on rivers that served as their essential means of transport. Even the farm centers of the interior valleys such as Lancaster and York usually had access to navigable waterways. The cities used these rivers as trade routes to export their farm products and to import needed manufactured goods and raw products, such as textiles and tea, that were not locally produced.

"City air makes men free." Nothing could better express the relation of the cities to the American Revolution. Though fewer than 5 percent of the populace lived in urban areas, it was there that the nation's leaders first considered seriously the ideas of independence. The people and events of that period centered on Boston, Philadelphia, and other urban settlements along the coast. It was in their coffeehouses and taverns that the radical ideas of men such as Thomas Paine and Samuel Adams found their best audiences.

Though the battles of the war had damaged the cities, by 1790 the population had returned and rebuilt in a new spirit. By 1800 the lifeblood of trade had been revived, and even trade with England had grown rapidly. In 1775 it had been about 3.8 million pounds sterling annually. By 1800 trade valued at 10 million pounds sterling flowed between the former mother country and the United States, but it was now *free trade*. The cities revived with the rebirth of commerce. The major ports of New York, Philadelphia, and Boston, which had lost over two-thirds of their populations during the war, almost doubled their prewar peaks by 1800. They expanded their influence and attraction into the surrounding regions and the areas across the Appalachians.

CITY STRUCTURE AND SOCIAL PATTERNS, 1750–1800

The cities were compact enough for a man to walk to work in less than half an hour or to stroll from end to end in less than two hours' time. Although they could be considered preindustrial in physical shape, simple manufactures were produced for local consumption. And extensive foreign trade brought the latest fashions and ideas from the Old World. The dominant *merchant elite* attempted to spread the influence of their cities into the interior. Sometimes they competed and at other times they cooperated in their efforts to increase their wealth and power. In contrast to the early eighteenth-century upper class of religious affiliation and nobility, this new group was focused on the free operation of private economic interests. In the pursuit of these economic goals, serious doubts developed as to a person's place in society. Insecurity and uncertainty in all spheres—social, economic, political, and religious—tended to produce unrest and conflict.

An overview of colonial American cities is complicated because each region had a unique economic pattern that strongly differentiated *social structures.* Virginia and Maryland were plantation economies whose growth was fueled by the English demand for tobacco. Their social and political structures were dominated by wealthy planters. With their plantations covering many acres, their exploitation of slaves, and their land speculation, they amassed great fortunes which they quickly translated into political power.

The Carolinas grew more slowly, but eventually found a profitable export crop in rice. It was difficult to attract immigrants for the dull, hard work in the rice fields and, as in Virginia and Maryland, the slave-worked plantation eventually took over. This created a social structure also controlled by a planter class.

The economic development of the northern colonies was wholly different than in the South, producing quite different social and political structures. New England, rather than being a single-crop economy, was based on a variety of crops and a sizable household manufacture. Pennsylvania, New York, and New Jersey were the heart of farming America, having a variety of richer soils and a less harsh climate than New England.

At least during their early phase of growth, the New England and Mid-Atlantic communities had more open social and political structures than the southern colonies. Farms of many sizes prospered, and many segments of the population were involved in commerce. New England developed the political tradition of the town meeting, where politics was democratic and direct, and decisions required agreement among the participants. There was also a greater ethnic and religious diversity among the New England population that some historians believe helped to stimulate more economic and social innovation than occurred in the southern colonies.

COMMON FEATURES OF COLONIAL CITIES

Although the patterns of economic development were quite different among the regions, the cities of this period shared many common features. The consequences of economic growth had a similar impact on urban social structures, making cities more wealthy, more diverse, and more complex, in short more "modern" than rural areas.

One common feature was that most cities had more men and women at each level of the economic scale. In sociological terms they had a more complex social structure and a more elaborate *stratification* system, that is, distinctions based on wealth and income, power and prestige.

At the top were the wealthy merchants, landowners, and those planters who chose to live in urban areas. Their wealth was generated by the pattern of economic life. The merchants profited from trade with Europe, which was a basic feature of all the colonial cities, and the landlords benefited from the growth of the cities. Although, in general, America was a land of abundance, good urban locations were always at a premium. This encouraged land speculation and drove real estate values upward.

Below the merchant class were a wide variety of small shopkeepers, tradesmen, and artisans. This stratum was quite large and was produced by basic features of urban life already discussed—specialization and growth of the market. As urban economies grew, many of the master artisans, journeymen, apprentices, and small shopkeepers who had made the journey from Europe began to accumulate wealth. Their living standards rose as demands for their varied goods and services expanded. This, in turn, led to an increase in crafts that divided and subdivided, permitting greater specialization. Historian Carl Bridenbaugh gives a particularly clear example:

> No longer did the carpenter perform all the operations in woodworking; in each city he had the assistance of joiners, turners, cabinetmakers, chairmakers, carvers, upholsterers, coachmakers, and half a dozen more artisans. In the busy building trades, housewrights, bricklayers, and stonemasons were joined by roofers, slate roofers, glaziers, painters, plasterers, and paperhangers. Likewise in the metal trades the labor of the village blacksmith split into a dozen or more skills. (Bridenbaugh 1964:272)

At the bottom of the urban social structure were the poor, slaves, and indentured servants. While differing in many ways, the groups at the bottom shared one characteristic—they owned no property. At this time property was the basis of secure employment and political standing. Its lack placed one at the margin of colonial society. However, the urban social structure was more fluid than that of England and during good economic times those at the bottom could hope for a better life. Lacking the craft guilds of Europe to control trade, anyone, newcomer or long-time resident, could take up any craft or business he wished. As Sam Bass Warner notes, this meant for the common man that there was always an opportunity to make a fresh start.

URBAN STRUCTURE AND NETWORK IN 1800

By 1800 American cities already exhibited unique features in their social structure. On the one hand the fruits of economic progress were unequally divided, producing disparities in wealth and property. Merchant and landowner profited from growth and used the emerging political institutions to aid the upward spiral through promoting port facilities, roads, and other public investments. On the other hand specialization and complexity of social structure also produced a large group of small businessmen and artisans that was an expression of the middle-class nature of the new nation. Finally, a permanent stratum of the poor emerged who were not fully integrated into urban society, but were buffeted about by economic forces they did not control. During times of prosperity, the poor could find work and hope for advancement. During periods of recession, they depended on the aid of individuals and private charitable groups.

At the beginning of the nineteenth century, the cities of the recently formed United States of America could be grouped into three classes. There were the dominant Atlantic trade cities of the Eastern Seaboard mentioned above. They were the second-order cities of the time. No absolute leader of first-order size had appeared. In third- and fourth-order were the smaller river-trading-specialty cities such as Marblehead in New England of fishing, shipbuilding, and maritime trade; or southern tobacco and milling centers such as Savannah. Among the smaller centers were also the inland middle state centers built on the river trade of the Ohio and Mississippi valleys. These were places such as Louisville, St. Louis, Cincinnati. In 1805 the largest of these was Lexington, Kentucky (2,800 population). Their major export point was New Orleans at the Mississippi's mouth. These were still very small urban settlements by modern standards. In all, only thirty-three had populations over 2,500. The total urban population was about 322,000, or 6 percent of the nation.

Between 1800 and 1820 opportunities in the opening of new lands attracted many new settlers into farming. On the one hand disease and fire plagued many urban areas, while poor internal transport and the high costs of fuel limited the growth of others. Despite such problems, by 1820, there was a slight increase in the urban sector to 7 percent of the total. Of the about 693,000 city dwellers, two-thirds lived in twelve cities, with one-third in the two largest, Philadelphia and New York. Since average city size increased only slightly, much of this could be viewed simply as an expansion of the network of cities accompanying the spread of farming and international commerce. In fact, the process was more complex. Some of the older cities grew more rapidly than the average, while others declined in importance. Examples of the former were the foreign trade centers of New York and Baltimore and the opening of the Appalachian frontier near Lexington, Kentucky. Slow growth was the experience of other centers such as Norfolk, Virginia, and the fishing centers of New England. Still others, later to be of great importance, had not even reached the threshold of citydom; examples were Cleveland, Chicago, and Detroit.

Finally, hundreds of towns, planned on paper, were never realized. Among the factors that determined the success or failure of town growth, a good natural location was important. But it was not all. At the junction of the two great interior rivers the Ohio and the Mississippi, plans were made for the town of America, but they were never realized in that form. This suggests that local abilities and energies, the decisions made in eastern cities, and the direction of events in the outside world all determined a city's success or failure.

Let us examine these interactions more closely over the next four decades when urban growth outstripped rural growth, when the shift from *extractive* to manufacturing industries began, and when the patterns of trade focused more on domestic markets than on foreign markets.

CAUSES AND EFFECTS OF ACCELERATED URBANIZATION, 1820–60

Between 1820 and 1860 there were a series of sharp, pulsating accelerations in city growth in three sections of the nation: first, it started in the Northeast in the 1820s; then, the North Central region in the decade 1840–50; and finally, in the West between 1850 and 1860. Only the South did not start to urbanize before the Civil War.

By 1860, 20 percent of the nation's people lived in cities; in total, over 6,200,000 lived in 392 cities. There were 101 cities over 10,000 population, eight over 100,000, and one, New York, had passed the one million mark.

Urbanization accelerated along with the increased pace of economic growth. There was an intensification and spread of the changes previously labeled as an "industrial revolution." When combined with a growing commercial-agricultural sector of wheat and cotton, this created a need for new centers of trade and business. Led by changes in certain manufacturing industries and new means of transportation, western cities appeared at a record rate. And the older coastal cities, fueled both by the Atlantic and the new western trade, grew apace.

The cities and states themselves sponsored much of this growth through governmental support and subsidy of investment projects. Of course, bitter rivalries occasionally marked such attempts at new ventures. However, the nation was still rural in character, farm-oriented, and some sections, such as the plantation South, saw no urban growth of any consequence outside of New Orleans, the focus for the cotton trade.

There were three major aspects of economic growth during this period that influenced city development.

1. A series of major innovations in farming, manufacturing, and transportation. Many of these originated in one city and then spread to others.
2. Rapid overall growth in the market. Population and income levels surged, providing opportunities for investment in the areas of farming, manufacturing, and transportation.
3. Important changes in the internal economic, social, and political organization of cities. These were affected by the interaction of the first two factors.

Major innovations tend to increase the ability of the society to provide more goods and services (increasing the quantities supplied at all price levels). Some of the most powerful innovations throughout our history have been in the farming sector, where a continuously expanding ability to feed more and more people with fewer and fewer workers has provided a huge labor source for the urban sector and a basic market for industrial output. Other innovations having equally strong effects would be the discovery of new natural resources, especially metals, synthetics, and chemicals; new power sources or converters (oil, electricity, nuclear power, internal combustion); and improved means of transportation (steamboats to railroads to automobiles, airplanes, and spaceships).

The effects of such innovations are manifold. They may release workers from one industry for another (rural to urban jobs). They may also lower prices (the nineteenth century saw consistent price declines in most constant quality goods). They lead to substitution of one good for another, create new jobs, stimulate sales, and initiate profit opportunities. This market growth in turn has numerous effects on households, businesses, and government.

The growth in the demand for labor leads to extended working hours, less unemployment, and increased migration to the growing regions. Wages go up and rising incomes lead to more sales and demands for services. Business invests more, purchases machines to further increase productivity, and seeks out more innovations to lower costs. Government invests in services; transportation, education, safety, and public utilities expand. As land and human resources are developed, more migrants and industry are attracted, and the process continues until bottlenecks are reached in supply or growth swamps the organizational capacity of the area.

FACTORS SHAPING PRE-CIVIL WAR INNOVATION

Shaping the specific innovations of the pre-Civil War period were many inventions borrowed from Europe and domestic ones that developed slowly; rapid market growth providing investment opportunities; and the existence of abundant natural resources.

Although we tend to think of inventions as the work of one individual, in reality most of them evolve slowly over a period of years or decades from first idea to salable product. It was so in this period, particularly since innovations were borrowed from Europe (especially from England). Textiles, iron, transportation, and power sources were key areas of borrowing.

On the nature of the market—its size and the complexity of its organization increased very rapidly due to high *fertility* rates, a high value placed on children as workers, expanding economic opportunities, rising incomes, and lowered transportation costs. This rapid market growth directed new innovations into areas that would maximize profit opportunities—especially in good times. These first two factors were shaped by a third, the nature of the resource environment.

The most outstanding feature of the resource base was the relative abundance of natural products. From fertile soil to hardwood forests to numerous navigable rivers to temperate climate—these factors led to labor-saving innovations that made best use of available materials. Four examples of the way the resource base shaped innovation were (1) the slow transition of the machine tool industry to iron; (2) the rapid adaptation of steam to inland shipping; (3) the slow development of coal-burning techniques in railroad boilers, iron foundries, and home heating; and (4) the slow diffusion of steam to manufacturing. These patterns reflected the plenitude of wood and wood products and the ever present stream or river providing abundant water.

SPECIFIC INNOVATIONS IN FARMING AND MANUFACTURING

In farming there were numerous developments that increased *output* and *productivity.* The bottlenecks at the time of planting and harvesting were partially overcome, the first through the invention of the steel plow and the harnessing of the horse and mule in speeding soil preparation:

> The wooden and cast-iron plows of the eighteenth and early nineteenth centuries were scarcely adequate to break the tough prairie sod. . . . In Europe iron plows had been at work for many centuries, but the prairie needed a heavy plow with a long, sloping moldboard. Labor shortage

and growing markets stimulated many Americans like Thomas Jefferson and Daniel Webster to make experiments. Heavy, clinging western soil stuck to pitted iron plowshares; sharp, smoothly polished steel was the answer . . . the first successful all-steel plow was made by John Deere in 1847. (Jones 1960:73)

The use of the cotton gin and reaper in harvesting and final processing of the two major cash crops, cotton and wheat, overcame the second obstacle. Less obvious were the improvements in tools such as axes and saws which helped the farmer in his two other critical tasks of land clearing and improvement and the construction of farm buildings. These activities normally took up a large portion of the farmer's time outside of tilling the soil and represented major investment decisions.

It should be noted that these were not borrowed innovations but rather American responses to the frontier abundances of nature and the shortages of labor. In England land shortages and labor surpluses had generated a completely different innovation mix.

The results of such innovations led to greater product variety and lower food and textile prices for all consumers. They especially aided village and city dwellers who spent proportionately about twice as much cash income on food and clothing as did the typical farm family. However, as Dorothy Brady notes, the noncity market dominated American distribution before 1860. Housing and fuel aside, farms consumed about 45 percent of the purchased goods, villages 31 percent, and cities 24 percent in 1830. Considering the low level of a rural family's cash income at this time (about $150 per year), is it any wonder that simple, colonial designs were adopted and led to a nationwide *mass consumption* market? This paved the way for the acceptance of standardized *consumer durables* later in the century.

These inventions also released labor for manufacturing and services, thus lowering the labor and final product costs of these sectors. As sales of many capital goods rose, the interdependence of the farm output and nonfarm input accelerated. From 1850 to 1860 reaper sales grew rapidly. In a complementary way half or more of the ten largest manufacturing industries in 1860 used directly as their input the material output of farms, mines, and forests in producing their final products.

Manufacturing grew from fewer than 75,000 employees in 1800 to over 1,500,000 in 1860. The sources of nonagricultural goods in the early decades of the century, imports from England and the products of local American smiths, wrights, or makers (as they were called in the varied handicrafts), were replaced by factory output. In small plants, specialized labor, using machines, replaced home workshops at a rapid rate.

Specific industries led the way in this regard. Of the ten leading industries in 1860, four—cotton goods, boots and shoes, men's clothing, and woolen goods—were in the apparel field. This growth created thousands of jobs over the period 1820–60 and affected the average urban consumer.

Zevin notes that textile cotton output per capita grew at about 13 percent per annum till 1833 and at about 2 percent per annum between 1833 and 1860. Meanwhile the price of cotton textiles fell on the average about 1 percent per year over the entire period. This meant that people could buy more and cheaper cotton clothing, which was more comfortable and washable than former blends of wool and linen. In this period the typical American household spent between $50 and $200 per year (about 20 percent of real income) for clothing. Better, cheaper clothing was a real advance in living standards for many American families.

If cotton textiles helped to push American industry free of European imports, the iron industry helped to pull it into the age of machines and mass production. Making allowances for the different resource base from England (more wood—cheaper charcoal—less use of coal), American iron making, like American textiles, closely resembled the British experience.

In the iron industry, lower costs and a greater variety of products provided better plows, reapers, and kitchen utensils, stronger wheels (for wagons and buggies), longer-lasting stoves, and more comfortable bedsprings. Even something as simple as cheap nails was important since they made possible the *balloon frame house* that provided a breakthrough in low-cost urban housing in the decades before the Civil War. For the businessman, iron was used for the rails to carry the goods and the locomotives to pull them. Last, but not least, iron was the key element at points of stress in the machine tools that helped to manufacture and transport a variety of consumer goods.

THE AMERICAN SYSTEM—NATURE AND EFFECTS ON URBAN LIFE

Among the changes in manufacturing, those that have been called the "American system" had important long-run effects in the shaping of American urban ways.

The American system of manufactures evolved between 1800 and 1860, having originated with Eli Whitney's application of the idea of interchangeable parts to the manufacture of firearms. Prior to 1800 all muskets had been individually handcrafted and fitted together, with the shaping, chiseling, and filing of wooden parts and the hardening, grinding, and polishing of metal parts all done by hand labor. Whitney and others who followed him, such as Elihu Root and Samuel Colt, standardized the parts and jobs, specializing each task for one man and devising specific tools for the machining and finishing operations. Such changes required new, more precise measuring tools and gauges which led to the establishment of an infant machine tool industry by the 1830s. These changes also elicited developments in the iron and steel industry as the new machine tools required greater strength, durability, and resistance to stress and speed.

The practices of interchangeability and standardization centered around a production line and helped to shape the restructuring of industry from home craftsmen to the factory system. In watches, clocks, locks, sewing machines, farm implements, typewriters, rifles, and locomotives, the names of Waltham, Jerome, Yale, Singer, McCormick, Underwood, Remington, and Baldwin mark the beginnings of big business, using the American system as its basis. By the second half of the nineteenth century, the assembly line and conveyor belts run by power, the mass-produced consumer and producer goods were already realities.

The diffusion of the American system had immediate results for the urban dweller since there were sharp reductions in the prices of the final products, consumer durables. Specifically, household items such as furniture, housewares, and stoves dropped in price. Clocks, for example, that had sold for $5 to $10 as late as 1830 were down to $.50 by 1850. There were improvements in methods and devices for preparing, storing, and preserving of foodstuffs. This made for more variety in the urban diet, helped prevent food contamination, and led to better nutrition and health especially among young children. Life for the working person was made more comfortable in the city by the proliferation of household equipment. Heating, lighting, cooking, recreational devices multiplied at low cost. In addition the methods of the system were widely copied in the making of producer goods (capital equipment) that lowered, in turn, the costs of all other goods. In the long run the fundamental shift from home craft to factory was accelerated. The pattern of mass production—use of machine tools, standardization, and ease of repair—became fixed in the American way of life. The luxury market concepts of Europe gave way to the middle-class, high-volume, low-markup, mass distribution approach of American business.

THE PIVOTAL ROLE OF TRANSPORTATION IN URBANIZATION

The costs of distributing this growing output to farflung markets would have presented a serious barrier to growth had they not been accompanied by radical improvements in the transportation industries.

Turnpike, canal, steamboat, railroad—this succession of innovations between 1800 and 1860 was so widespread in its effects upon economic and social patterns that it has been referred to by historians such as George R. Taylor as the "transporation revolution."

From the 1830s onward, there was a gradual redirection of western produce toward the eastern seaboard. The "transportation revolution," the rise of canals and railroads, solved the problem of cross-mountain haulage, making possible a new outlet for western farm products. . . . The demand for farm products gradually transformed the social structure and psychological attitudes of the West. The outlook of the early individualist and small-scale capitalist, characteristic of the Northeast, spread to the dominant upper stratum of the western farmers. (Moore 1966:128–29)

The timing of these innovations overlapped. They were roughly as follows:

turnpike	1800–20
canal	1820–45
steamboat	1815–55
railroad	1830–60 and beyond

Each represented a major investment effort and had substantial expansive effects on the economy in general and the process of urbanization in particular. A number of common characteristics were shared by all four.

First, all were borrowed innovations. Each had been under development in Europe, especially in England, for a number of decades before being imported to the United States. When each innovation was brought over, it was adapted to the special American resource mix of abundant natural products. Turnpikes and canals used more wood and less stone; special high-pressure steam engines were developed for the big riverboats; early railroads had light aggregate roadbeds and boilers designed to burn wood instead of coal.

Second, in both the construction and operation stages, each stimulated industries linked to it in many ways; lumber and iron as *backward linkages* and trade and services as *forward linkages* are examples.

Third, the canal and railroad demonstrated the interaction of private and public (governmental) interests, while the steamboat and turnpike were almost exclusively privately capitalized.

Fourth, all tended toward overexpansion of capacity, which reduced short-run profits, although the long-run social benefits of such capital investment were probably more substantial as the major cities competed with one another for new routes to attain advantages in trade patterns and expand their commercial influence into the hinterlands.

This revolution in transportation had important effects on the rate and pattern of urbanization. Directly, it reduced the costs of shipping goods to the customer and expanded the radius of the market. It also reduced the costs of raw materials for the production process. On the one hand, businesses using large amounts of raw materials were freed from locations close to their sources in nature. On the other hand, workers could move more easily between and within urban areas from areas of low to areas of high economic opportunity. Thus, costs in money and time were diminished, trade and migration flows increased, and residential patterns changed.

New cities sprang up all along the main routes; Syracuse, Rochester, and Buffalo along the Erie Canal; Louisville, Cincinnati, St. Louis, and Memphis along the major river systems. Meanwhile the largest eastern ports (Baltimore, Philadelphia, New York, and Boston) profited from the complementary nature of all of these transportation systems operating as one giant network.

GOVERNMENT POLICY AND CITY GROWTH

As in England, urbanization in America was closely intertwined with industrialization and economic growth. The goal of economic growth was consciously and vigorously pursued as government policy on the national, state, and local levels.

In our discussion of English political and economic theory during this period, the role of laissez faire was stressed. This policy advocated a limited role for government, believing that the economy functioned best through the influence of normal market forces. However, in reality there was considerable government intervention to aid business interests and fuel economic growth.

This intervention of government to aid economic growth by assisting private enterprises can be seen as the "bias of the political system" in a capitalist society. During the early phase of industrialization, government was willing to intervene on behalf of business interests. It was unwilling to intervene equally either in expanding the supply of public services or in providing benefits during hard times for the working classes and the poor.

This was evident in many kinds of government activity. Some of the areas and the kinds of support are listed below in tabular form.

Area	*Type of Activity and Support*
LAND POLICY	Survey and layout of western lands; constant liberalization of land-purchasing terms; purchase of huge

	new tracts; establishment of the Department of Agriculture
FOREIGN TRADE	Support to shipbuilding and commerce; building of port facilities; clearing rivers and harbors
TRANSPORTATION	Huge land grants to different systems; state development of canals through bond sales; local and state aid to railroads and turnpikes; state subsidy to merchant marine
FINANCE	Development of First and Second Banks of the United States; providing sources for short- and long-term capital funds; state control of local banking began coinage and treasury functions
MANUFACTURING	Development of patents system; raising of protective tariffs on key items; selected local subsidies and encouragement of incorporation

Such a picture clearly does not support the classic interpretation of this period, that of laissez faire. Market forces certainly dominated, but the government saw itself as a partner with all economic sectors in promoting economic development and fostering expansion.

CITY DEVELOPMENT AND THE EXPANSION OF CITY SERVICES

The economic growth that such government activity fostered had a profound impact on the nature of pre-Civil War urbanization. As historical examples repeatedly show, very rapid industrial and commercial expansion can create as many urban problems as can very slow growth. This section sketches how conditions in the cities changed under the impact of innovations and expanding markets, focusing on the expansion of city services as one response to the problems generated by the very rapid urban growth of the pre-Civil War period.

Innovation and market growth changed spatial relations within the cities. They rearranged the plus and minus values attached by businessmen and residents to their then current locations, enabling some to locate more densely in space and others to disperse if they so wished. These changes in valuation and choices led to dramatic relocations of business and trade in efforts to increase profits. The formation of new economic organizations and the mass migrations into the cities led to increased conflicts between established groups and newcomers. Interests were divided by income level, ethnic and occupational classes. Private individual problems became public when attached to group interests.

Attempts at solutions to such public problems led in a number of directions. Government services were made more formal. Professional "for hire" police and fire departments replaced volunteers. Committees for social reform sought to provide for common needs such as public health and sanitation. Local government, in trying to respond to varied group needs, found itself assuming new tasks and services, thus opening itself to all kinds of political pressures associated with rapid changes in economic opportunities and growing social unrest. In this age modern American "urban problems" were born.

CITY GROWTH RATES, SIZE, AND AGE— THE SETTING FOR URBAN PROBLEMS

Before discussing the general pattern of urban response, one question is in order. Are there any factors that can explain the great diversity in the ways in which cities respond to changing socioeconomic forces? Three characteristics are rate of growth, size, and age. City size and age are discussed in more detail in later chapters. Here we relate these to city growth rates. We can think of all cities going through a growth curve shaped as below. Some cities would be born in the early period, some in the middle, some in the later. The steeper

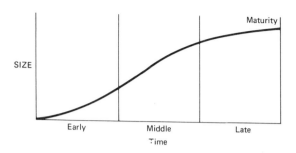

the curve, the higher the growth rate. Some cities take 100 years to reach maturity of size, some 200 years, while still others may take longer. A sample is shown below, of the cities of the early nineteenth century.

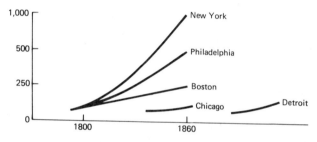

Different cities grow at differing rates of speed, and at different times in their history they reach different sizes. Therefore, age and "date of birth," as well as size, affect the need for certain city services. In 1800 the three largest cities (New York, Philadelphia, and Boston) were about the same size, and all were significantly larger than any other cities of that time. By 1860 New York's population was over 1,000,000, Philadelphia's about 500,000, and Boston's about 250,000. These different growth rates meant that the different service problems had varied impact in the intervening fifty years, with the result that different efforts were made to meet these problems.

In general, larger cities and older cities seem to have more problems than smaller, newer ones. These latter are usually less densely settled with people and structures, and the layers of history have not been built onto them. Since most changes in city services require both human reorganization and some physical building, conflicts of interest typically arise when such changes are proposed.

The older the city the more entrenched the interests in both physical plant and human institutions. The larger the size the more complex the interactions when changes require new financing and economic decision making. Finally, the most rapidly growing cities typically face the toughest service problems due to the relatively large numbers of new migrants and amount of new building they stimulate and require. Even if cities are relatively similar regarding the characteristics of age, size, and growth rate, there may be other restraints besides financial and economic decisions on the public service sector. These can be called technical, political, and social restraints.

Some services could not develop until the technical knowledge became available. For example, the art of street lighting and paving never got beyond the techniques of medieval times until gas lighting, electricity, asphalt, and macadam became technically available in the late nineteenth century. Other services required political cooperation of a high degree. Water, sewerage, and police services were still on a very individualistic basis in American cities until the Civil War, despite the fact that the techniques of providing good public sanitation and organizing police forces were available since Roman times. One last restraint on city services might be called social. For much of our urban history, societal beliefs and values did not consider that caring for the poor, aged, sick, and needy of the city was a public matter. Welfare was only a private responsibility of well-to-do benefactors of charities. Another example is in the area of recreation, culture, and esthetics. Public parks, libraries, playgrounds were not needed in cities. Community control over land use through zoning was the exception rather than the rule in most of our cities until well into the twentieth century.

What were the failures and successes of the city as a place to live, and how well did it provide services and opportunities to the pre-Civil War urbanite?

PERSISTENT URBAN PROBLEMS

One fear that had always been present in urban areas was death from communicable diseases—not only the ever present tuberculosis and typhus but also, periodically, the deadly yellow fever, cholera, and smallpox took their toll. A second old problem was death and destruction from fire. This was handled better by the introduction of steam power to pumping to replace bucket brigades and by the more extensive use of permanent, nonflammable building materials in some cities. These innovations, when coupled with adequate water supplies, made most fires by 1860 much more of an individual catastrophe than a collective one. There were, of course, famous exceptions where, in some of the western cities, wood residences and lack of well-organized fire brigades led to disastrous city-wide destruction.

However, the first problem of epidemic disease was not solved. The urban death rate remained very high as the problem of waste disposal and water supply contamination reached critical proportions by the late 1840s and early 1850s. Until the Civil War, most city streets were open sewers with garbage as well as human and animal waste flushed away only by the heaviest rains. Sewerage systems were primitive and ineffective, and pollution was rampant.

Provisions for clean, abundant water and separate, effective waste disposal systems were not built. Since the technics were available, this lack was partially due to ignorance and partially because such services were very expensive in older parts of the city. In addition, tax increases to pay for such improvements were then (as now) difficult to justify. By 1900, when the origins of many of the deadly diseases of the times were traced to these causes, one city followed another in quickly improving both public sanitation and water supplies.

Poverty and Crime

Poverty and crime certainly existed prior to American industrialization and urbanization. However, these problems came into sharper focus during the decades 1840 to 1860. People's views on their importance also began to change during this time.

It is difficult to determine the number of poor people that existed during this period. However, if we try to estimate how many could not provide for basic necessities and had to depend upon charitable organizations for relief, a reasonable guess would be 5 to 10 percent in normal times and 15 to 20 percent in depressions.

There is available a fair amount of information on the life styles and consumption patterns of different groups of the period. From Dorothy Brady's data it seems that poor families spent 70 to 80 percent of their income on food and shelter (depending on family size). The middle class spent about 60 to 65 percent and the upper class about 40 to 50 percent. Typically, another 15 to 20 percent was paid for clothing. This left *discretionary income* of about 10 percent, 20 percent, and 35 percent respectively for each group. Since such a large percentage of the poor's income went for necessities, and their ability to save was almost impossible, the loss of a job was an immediate economic catastrophe.

In smaller cities voluntary organizations could help the small number of poor. But by the 1850s many middle- and large-sized urban areas were confronted with large and growing slums inhabited by the first poverty class who saw little hope of bettering the quality of their lives.

In those days many people thought that poverty resulted from an individual's moral failure. Historian Robert Bremmer quotes a typical upper-class view of the times.

Robert M. Hartley, founder of the New York Association for improving the Condition of the Poor, denied that the "debased poor" were deserving of sympathy. "They love to clan together in some out-of-the-way place," he reported, "are content to live in filth and disorder with a bare subsistence, provided they can drink, and smoke, and enjoy their balls, and wakes, and frolics, without molestation." (Bremmer in Wakstein 1970:239)

Today more modern explanations stress the role of depressions, especially those of 1819, 1837, and 1857, which were especially deep and long. These were complicated by the lack of government welfare programs for the swelling tides of newcomers, inadequate banking and financial institutions, and the breakdowns in foreign trade. Poor harvests, rapid shifts in business opportunities, and other such economic forces also contributed to unemployment and poverty. The individual worker could not be responsible for such changes, nor could he or she find ways of adjusting to such disastrous situations.

Poverty might have been dismissed as a personal matter, but slums bred riots and crime. This hostile atmosphere with its dangerous inhabitants was only a few blocks from "nice" residences and busy business districts. Because the masses of poor and unemployed threatened the peace and safety of the prosperous, new attitudes and policies slowly emerged. It was in the self-interest of "public health" to improve conditions of the poor. As the poor in turn became victims of their environment, they looked with envy on the rich who had the power and resources to change that environment. If the full causes of poverty were hidden, one of its major visible effects was not—the rise of crime. The accounts of city life suggest that it was mainly in cities of large size that crime increased in variety and intensity. Until the 1830s a night watch had served to protect property. To stop riots, the leading citizens called upon volunteer firemen.

The depression of 1837–43 had increased the problems of caring for the poor, especially the ill, the malnourished, and abandoned children. While the influx of immigrants in the forties and fifties was absorbed mainly by expanding employment opportunities, it did put further stress on the police function. In Boston it was an "Irish problem," in Milwaukee a "German problem," and in New York a mixture of all immigrant groups. Most cities responded to rising juvenile delinquency, thievery, the growth of gangs and criminal districts by establishing a police department of sorts. The average ratio was about one patrolman per one thousand inhabitants. Unfortunately, some departments pursued their tasks too energetically. Others were shot through with corruption, while still others enforced the law at their convenience. This frequently meant chasing down sources of vice, prostitution, and gambling. In the process it led to persecuting the ignorant immigrant, visitors looking for a good time, or any less fortunate citizen who happened to be at hand.

Inevitably the power over public health and safety became involved in politics as all these new municipal functions had to be paid for and taxes voted on. Partly as a result, the movement away from semiprivate, voluntary, and informal traditions of the eighteenth century was still not completed by the Civil War. Poor sanitation, fires, crime, and poverty were yet to be solved by the public action of city residents through their government organizations.

TRAFFIC, EDUCATION, AND EMPLOYMENT

In a few ways the city was more successful than in the health, public safety, and welfare sectors. These were traffic circulation, education, and employment generation.

The city was still, as it always had been, a "walking city." Until 1840 the largest cities contained no more than two to four square miles of densely populated business and residential areas mixed together. In 1840 Boston and Philadelphia had total areas of only about two square miles, while New York extended about two miles northward from City Hall. This close settlement was necessary for two reasons. First, there was no way other than walking for the average workingman to get to work. Second, the movement of raw material inputs and marketable finished products would have faced the problem of narrow, rutted, muddy streets as soon as one left the port or transport hub of the city. As an increasing density of population and manufacturing growth added on to an expanding foreign trade, the great eastern cities spread out rapidly. After 1840 this was made possible by the omnibus or city stage coach, the steam ferry, the horse car or horse railway, and the steam railroad. Beginning with New York in the 1830s and spreading to the other large and middle-sized cities in the forties, fifties, and sixties, these innovations doubled and tripled the effective *work-residence radius*. The age of the walking city was drawing to a close.

The story of public education is one of the success stories of the early nineteenth-century city. Expanding on the state laws and state monies of colonial times, most cities had formalized their boards of education, appointed superintendents, and set up separate taxing and bonding powers by the 1840s. With the occasional exception of school construction contracts, most of these organizations were kept free of partisan politics. Typically there were very few illiterates outside of newly arrived foreign-born and slaves in most American cities prior to the Civil War. Between 1800 and 1860 the number of days of schooling of the typical student had doubled, and the number of teachers had risen from 5,000 to 115,000. Expenditures for education between 1840 and 1870 rose tenfold from less than $10 million to over $95 million per year.

Another important aspect of education for urban living flowed from the impact of the changing job conditions of the pre-Civil War city. The commercialization of the labor market, payment of money wages, more regular hours, and the beginnings of a few labor organizations marked this period. There was also the separation of industrial functions by area, and the clustering of residences and work place was common. As Sam Bass Warner describes, there was little or no spatial segregation as housing was mixed almost everywhere. People of different income and ethnicity and occupational class were scattered all over the landscape by industrial groupings. New work groups were formed through the rationalization of tasks, and people began to work in shops and factories rather than as families in households. Finally a decline in imports from Europe matched a growing diversification and sophistication in American manufactures and services, thereby creating thousands of new occupations and opportunities for upward mobility.

SOCIAL LIFE AND NEIGHBORHOODS

As the nature of work was reorganized, a new network of loyalties and interests was generated along with other changes that occurred in urban social relationships. Workers tended to slowly shift from the older ways to new ones. Each generation saw new means of reducing conflict and harassment in their daily struggles to survive and prosper. This was not painless, as the many violent strikes and anti-Catholic, anti-Negro riots of the 1830s and 1840s give witness. But the mixing of income levels and the lack of politically or technologically imposed housing-zoned segregation had one great advantage. As long as the middle class could not escape the costs of city living, they wanted to live to enjoy its benefits. This meant that there was substantial private support among craftsmen, small businessmen, shopkeepers, mechanics, and all who aspired to success to bring about changes in the ways the city served the public needs. That they were not completely successful indicates the difficulty of the problems as well as their ignorance of the causes.

These years were a time of transition. Cities were more like those of the previous century than those after this period, the major reason being that American cities were not yet fully industrialized. Much of the manufacturing was still done in small shops operated by crafts-men-proprietors.

As a consequence, cities prior to the Civil War lacked a basic feature of modern spatial structure—segregation. Contemporary cities are highly segregated, with residents grouped by race and income level. In the 1830–60 period neighborhoods were much more diverse, with the overall spatial pattern socially and economically heterogeneous. Today most large cities contain an urban core of poverty, with affluent families living in the outer urban ring. Then rich and poor, working class and middle class were distributed fairly evenly throughout most neighborhoods. The rich and well-to-do lived in better houses and enjoyed a more comfortable life style, but they shared the city, and often the same block, with middle-class and poor families. There were some exclusively black sections, but these were not the large racial ghettos typical of modern cities.

These conditions produced a vital, lively neighborhood social life and also encouraged small-scale communities, since homes, shops, stores, and work places were all in close proximity. There were tensions, but neighbors of diverse backgrounds and occupations interacted together, faced common community problems, and shared something of a common culture. However, *social distance* was always maintained. Classes may have mixed in the work place, but permanent changes such as marriage across racial, religious, or even economic classes were rare.

By 1860, however, such patterns were breaking down under the effects of growth and industrialization. In fact, one could argue that the destruction of the small-scale, heterogeneous neighborhood and informal work atmosphere of this period was a major social cost of growth and industrialization. Growth meant an increase in the sheer size, scale, and pace of life in the cities. Industrialization meant the rise of factories and manufacturing districts, the separation of home and work, the need to commute. Since the benefits of industrialization were unequally distributed, it meant continued distinction between rich and poor. This prompted a desire by prosperous families to live in exclusive districts when transport was available. Such movement in turn promoted residential segregation by income.

However, the cities were lively places of great interaction. Such interaction tended to produce a strong generative effect that led to a healthy atmosphere of innovation and specialization. In turn this created the ability, in an open and abundant era, to upgrade the thousands of rural migrants who became the new urban citizens. It has been suggested that the communities of the pre-Civil War period represented a good balance among the three city functions. Nonetheless, it was the industrial-agricultural, slave-free, North-South tensions that built during these decades to the greatest internal struggle in our history, the Civil War. This catastrophe formed a watershed in our modernization, and it took many more decades to forge an urban-industrial nation.

CHAPTER FIVE

Urban Change in the United States, 1860 - 1920

Between the Civil War and World War I, the process of American industrialization accelerated. At the heart of this acceleration was the rise of the city. Some saw urbanization as the result of the completion of the shift away from the farm. Others saw it as a main propulsive force of this maturing period. We see it as both. In the decades of most rapid expansion, 1880–90 and 1900–10, increases in population and investment strongly reinforced national economic expansion. In the decades of slower industrialization, the 1870s and 1890s, city building exhibited a less swift rhythm, dampening the overall trends.

Within these national pulsations, all aspects of industry mechanized. It was an era of great capital accumulation—of iron and steel, coal and steam. Cities participated, as larger and more permanent structures in housing and public facilities were built. They were necessary to support the additional tens of millions of urban residents and to service the needs of business and industry. Together the interaction of new technology and the redistribution of industry helped to shape the evolutionary changes within the network of cities.

The data in Table 5–1 reflect the changes in the leading manufacturing industries between 1860 and 1910.

These dramatic shifts affected the ascendency and decline of many cities. For example, the rise in iron, steel, machinery, and railroad cars accompanied the growth of Pittsburgh, Chicago, and Cleveland, while the decline of flour milling, boots, shoes, and cotton goods underscored the downward movement of Buffalo, Cincinnati, and New Orleans.

TABLE 5–1   Manufacturing Shifts (value added by manufacturing)

1860	*1910*
Cotton goods	Machinery
Lumber	Lumber
Boots and shoes	Printing and publishing
Flour and meal	Malt liquors
Men's clothing	Iron and steel
Iron	Men's clothing
Machinery	Cotton goods
Woolen goods	Tobacco goods
Carriages and wagons	Railroad cars
Leather	Boots and shoes

SOURCE: U.S. Bureau of the Census, *Census of the United States,* 1860, vol. 3; 1910, vol. 8 (Washington, D.C.: Government Printing Office).

Most evident is the decline in industries associated with clothing (cottons, woolens, boots, shoes, and leather) and flour and meal production. Rising incomes are reflected in the increase in working people's luxuries, tobacco and malt liquors, and the appearance of printing and publishing. The replacement of carriages and wagons by railroad cars was also significant. Most symbolic of the era, however, was the rise of machinery from seventh to first position. These shifts were made concrete in urban terms in the relative decline of cities such as Buffalo, Cincinnati, and New Orleans and the relative rise in the rankings of Chicago, Pittsburgh, and Detroit.

Some of the older great port cities prospered by adding new growth industries to old leadership patterns; for example, New York added publishing to apparel. The dispersion of industry away from the river system occurred in all sections of the country as the completion of the national railroad network set in motion an entirely new set of location possibilities.

Within individual cities, the application of new technics resulted in the separation of place of residence from place of work. This restructuring led to a complete rearrangement of the physical and social relationships among urban groups, which changes, in turn, led to a deepening of the problems of land use, housing, congestion, and pollution. This prompted major reorganization of city government when the social and political responses of pre-1860 volunteer-type urban institutions were not adequate.

INNOVATIONS LEADING TO CITY DEVELOPMENT

By 1920 just over one-half of the American people (54,000,000) lived in cities as opposed to 20 percent in 1860. This was due in part to increasing average size. In 1850 no metropolis exceeded one-quarter of a million people; by 1900 there were 15 cities over that size, and the three largest—New York, Chicago, and Philadelphia—each exceeded one million inhabitants. Another reason is that much of this growth was from new centers. Considering all the cities over 25,000 population in 1850, there were 25. These would not have filled the over 100,000 class in 1900 (38).

As in the British Industrial Revolution and the American pre-Civil War expansion, major innovations affected all aspects of the society. Most important were those that cut across other fields of endeavor and had wide impact on costs of production and the growth of the market. Again, cities were both the major source and primary recipient of these innovations. Cities grow when they successfully perform their generative function. Innovative urban economies expand by generating new kinds of work. This impacts on the national economy and attracts new job-seeking migrants, producing the patterns to be discussed in this chapter.

Innovations in Energy and Communication

Two areas that made remarkable progress were power sources and transportation. New kinds of energy were developed and new methods of converting fuel into useful mechanical forms were pioneered. As Tibbitts points out, between 1850 and 1950 energy sources and output changed dramatically.

Each dramatically increased output per worker and per machine and each facilitated or forced new locations on industry. This led to the development of new machines and machine tools and required new materials or new forms for old materials. Let us take electricity

Year	Horsepower Hours per Person	Percent Energy, Nonliving Sources
1850	440	35
1900	1,030	73
1950	4,470	98

SOURCE: C. Tibbitts, "Aging as a Modern Social Achievement," in *Aging in Today's Society*, eds. C. Tibbits and W. Donahue (Englewood Cliffs, N.J.: Prentice-Hall, 1960).

as an example. From Edison's direct current lighting of parts of New York in the 1880s, it was only a short step to Westinghouse's alternating current which provided the first commercial electric power in Niagara Falls in 1895. Such changes would not have been possible without developments in the copper, steel, rubber, and glass manufacturing industries. Ways were found to supply the motors, generators, cables, insulators, and other supporting capital equipment needed to electrify cities and factories across the land.

The impact of electrification was felt in the household—growing in importance with every decade. Food processing and preparation, control devices for central heating, fans and motors for cooling and refrigeration, machines for the home sewing of apparel, cleaning, washing; all aspects of home care were being changed. From these beginnings today's women have been liberated from household drudgery and assumed positions of importance in the nation's work force.

Communication also underwent an electric-powered revolution: telephone, phonograph, radio, movies, recordings, teletype-information; news and mass culture could flow at the speed of light—and the electric light itself extended man's ability to conquer the barriers of time. Recreation, education, public safety, and commerce expanded.

Electrical machinery also meant that the conveyor belts and multistory lofts that had been necessary to take advantage of steam-powered factories no longer were needed. The factory could spread out over the countryside since it was no longer tied to the rail siding or port facilities where coal was brought in to generate steam power. Now, the electric cable gave the businessman much more flexibility in his choice of locations. Revolutionary changes in transportation completed this relocation process.

While the effects of electrification permeated the entire society during the later decades of this period, it was the railroad that received the most attention prior to 1900. Although the railroad networks were begun in the 1840s, it was not until after 1860 that the great booms occurred. In 1860 the 30,000 miles of American railroad were one-half the world's total; by World War I over 250,000 miles of track were in place. The story is filled with "robber barons"; men such as Cooke, Morgan, Gould, Fisk, and Vanderbilt were involved in government land grants, labor strikes, watered stocks, and the boom and bust of the money market. Although an interesting story, here we point out the impact of the railroad in more aggregate terms on the course and pattern of industrialization and urbanization.

Ton mileage grew almost a hundredfold between 1859 and 1910, passenger miles multiplied over sixteen times; in short, output doubled every decade between the two wars—faster than any other major industrial sector. Railroad employment grew from 80,000 to 2,236,-000 between 1860 and 1920.

The railroad can be viewed as a construction enterprise, as a transportation service, and as a source of new innovations. Each of these aspects had an impact on the course of the industrialization-urbanization process of this period. As a construction enterprise it made great demands upon the timber, steel, coal, and locomotive–rolling-stock manufacturing industries. It stimulated repair facilities, engineering skills, and long-term foreign investments. As a service industry it lowered the price of transportation to all businesses, especially direct resource users, saving time and money and thus shaping the location decisions of users and potential users of its services. Finally, the railroad directly and indirectly created innovations. Steel rails, air brakes, steel boxcars, more efficient locomotives were developed to serve this new form of transport. It also led toward the perfection of trolleys, the telegraph, refrigeration, and even the standardization of time zones as indirect benefits.

Innovations in Transport and Construction

Further facilitating city growth during this sixty-year period were a series of innovations in transport and construction technology. These permitted the concentration of certain functions such as light manufacturing, office work, commerce, and services in *central business districts* (CBDs). They also led to the decentralization of residences and the relocation of heavy manufacturing and the processing of raw materials into the rural fringes of the urban areas.

The urban counterpart of the railroad was the electric trolley. After thirty years of horse-drawn, steam-powered, or cable-pulled cars, the late 1880s saw Julian Sprague build the first electrified street railway. The growth was dramatic. In 1890 about 70 percent of the total system was horse-drawn, by 1902 only 1 percent was horse-drawn and 97 percent was electric. Sprague also developed the control system that made possible the subway and elevated lines of the largest cities. As tunnels, bridges, roadbeds, and train depots were improved, the electric railway enabled the cities to expand in space and still work as a unified system. The great residential densities could be partially relieved and the journey to work could be shortened.

While these innovations permitted the decentralization of residences and industry, other innovations facilitated increased face-to-face contact. As cities spread out in space, their central business districts remained vital. CBDs are a prime example of the interactive function of cities since they contain activities requiring frequent personal contact. In the CBDs the key innovations were the skyscraper, the elevator, and the telephone. All were essential to the concentration of workers and information. Business could thus take advantage of the low costs of *agglomeration* and highly specialized services that such districts could provide.

Multistory cast-iron (later steel) framed warehouses sprang up in the commercial districts, and department stores and loft factories dotted every downtown. Steam supplied the power and heat for this vertically expanding central core in all the larger cities. In residential areas the tenement design joined the balloon frame. Semiskilled workers using machines and the simplest of hand tools could spread the city across the map at unbelievable speeds. Improvements in paving materials and in street lighting smoothed traffic flow and increased street safety.

Public health became another important goal in the attempt to bring more order into the disarray of the Victorian city. As the causes of the major diseases were better understood, public support grew for zoning, health departments, and control of sanitation. Between 1880 and 1920 urban death rates dropped sharply as clear filtered water began to flow from sites distant from sewage disposal areas. Refuse in turn was now channeled into underground pipes and conduits of clay and cast-iron and then dumped into nearby rivers.

THE ECONOMIC GAINS OF INCREASED SIZE

The major innovations facilitating the growth in city size and the expansion of the urban network have been detailed. Two concepts by which social scientists link together successive increases in city size are *scale economies* and agglomeration. These require additional comments and illustration since they become more essential to the spread of urbanization the closer we come to the present.

The concept of scale economies emerges in the case of the canals or railroads. As more and more barges or railroad cars are put into use, the average cost of transportation goes down. Essentially this shows the very high capacity and high fixed costs of such operations. A continuous stream of new innovations in railroading between 1870 and 1900 made possible longer and longer trains. Braking, coupling, signaling, switching devices, new drive gears in steam engines, standardization of rail size, steel cars—the list is long and impressive. In addition, businesses tended to concentrate around rail yards to share freight cars and loading facilities, thus matching loads and cars to the best length trains for given trips. Railroads also concentrated their main yards in a few locations to reduce repair, storage, and maintenance costs. Chicago is the most outstanding example; there the yards extend for miles.

Chicago can also be used to illustrate the concept of agglomeration economies (a gathering together of complementary aspects of industry). As it became the railroad hub of the Midwest, the growing meat packing industry was attracted to it. Lower transportation costs for both inputs (animals) and outputs (slaughtered meat) were the first reason. This industry in turn attracted the by-product industries, tanneries and leather goods, soap and glue manufactures, canning and preserving. The development of refrigeration also aided this centralization of meat packing and its satellites. In the area of grain processing, Chicago also forged ahead as the agricultural products of Iowa, Kansas, and Nebraska were funneled to the east.

The final touch was the establishment of the service industries of finance and commodity exchanges. These lowered the costs of information, sharply reducing the risks of the shipper, farmer, and processor, by spreading them out over a time period and to groups of buyers and sellers. This nationwide network of markets helped to create the interlocking system of cities of all sizes.

THE ECONOMIC GAINS OF SPECIALIZATION

Many of these cities grew through the increase in demand for one product or line of products. One way of measuring the effect that specialization has on a city's growth relative to other cities is to examine changes in rank. As was pointed out in Chapter Three, between 1860 and 1930 there were dramatic changes and important shifts in the top ten urban areas.

There were five new cities in this group: Chicago, Detroit, Los Angeles, Cleveland, and Pittsburgh. Four from 1860 had dropped out of the top ten: these were New Orleans, Cincinnati, Buffalo, and Newark. Two of the top four, Boston and Baltimore, had slid sharply downward five ranks each.

Which city specialized in what? Omaha, livestock; Minneapolis, grain milling; Milwaukee, beer; Dayton, cash registers; Schenectady, electrical goods; Hershey, chocolate; Birmingham and Gary, steel; Butte, copper—the list is long and varied.

Some grew because of their selection as terminals or junctions for the great transcontinental railroads. Frequently this process was filled with political corruption and conflict as the owners of the railroads sought to choose second-order sites near which the land was cheaper and where greater speculative profits were to be made. Examples were the rivalries between Tacoma and Seattle, Kansas City and Leavenworth, Wichita and Abilene, Houston and Galveston. Each of these cases presents evidence of competition between urban entrepreneurs in real estate developments and transportation routes. In some cases the early leader won, while in others the latecomer was victorious.

We have been discussing the factors underlying urban growth in this period. However, growth was usually uneven, with some cities and regions not participating fully in the process. Only the cotton states of the "Old South" did not urbanize rapidly during this period.

There were some individual exceptions such as Atlanta, Nashville, Memphis, and Dallas. However, the South remained about fifty years behind the nation as a whole in its degree of urbanization. Of the varied explanations for this phenomenon, among the most interesting and plausible are those concerning the lack of *social overhead capital.* This meant that inadequate educational facilities limited the skills of the work force, poor transportation slowed market growth, and lack of supportive government activity hindered industrial development. The above, when combined with patterns of southern wealth distribution, the devastations of the Civil War, and the cultural remains of the slave-plantation society, account for the fact that urbanization in the South was well behind the rest of the nation.

There also were many urban failures. As in earlier periods of American history, growth promoters overextended themselves and made unsupportable claims for their land schemes. As a result thousands of investors lost money.

Between the failures and the many successes of the post-Civil War industrialization lay large numbers of slow-growing urban areas. Some had been successful in earlier times and now settled down to maturity and a movement toward stable equilibrium. Examples of slow growth would be Savannah, New Orleans, Albany, and Providence. On the other hand, places such as Miami, Oak Ridge, Las Vegas, and Marietta had not yet been smiled on by historical circumstances and still awaited their adolescent spurt to adulthood.

CHANGES IN THE NATURE AND SHAPE
OF URBAN AREAS

During these six decades the links between industrialization and urbanization were completely forged. And this rise of industry changed the nature and shape of the city, its relation to surrounding territory, and its internal socio-political structure.

Manufacturing tended to concentrate in the city, while people tended to live at greater distances from work. As we shall see, the shape of the city itself began to influence location decisions of both businessmen and householders. Distinct districts appeared, yet they were unplanned and chaotic because the old systems built under pre-Civil War technological limitations did not blend into the newer industrial metropolitan pattern.

Of the 70 million Americans added to the population between the two wars, about 70 percent, or 50 million persons, were drawn to urban areas. Where did these people come from? We cannot precisely pinpoint their origins, but some possible answers follow. The vast majority were migrants from the countryside. The villages of Europe probably were the main source (about 40 percent), while America's rural areas provided about 30 percent of the total. Natural increase, the excess of births over deaths in the cities, probably accounted for another 20 percent of the increase, and the remainder (less than 10 percent) came from city annexation of nearby suburban areas.

Of the natural increase, some came from the children of earlier foreign-born residents. Thus, most of the grandchildren of the Irish immigrants of the 1840s were native Americans by 1900. The full role of immigrants in urban growth is indicated by the fact that in 1890, while foreign-born and their immediate descendants (*foreign stock*) comprised one-third of the nation, they made up 53 percent of the urban population. Accounting for grandchildren, the figure goes to two-thirds. Because of their age distribution (migrants tended to concentrate in the fifteen-to-thirty-four-year-old brackets), the share of young adults in cities greatly exceeded the national norms. This tendency stabilized average age in cities over our entire history, while the average age in the nation went from around sixteen in 1800 to thirty by World War II. In turn, this stability affected the relation among dependent young, aged, and working age people. The most important historical sequences revolve around mass migration, *ethnicity,* and new employment patterns. The steady flow of migrants, while putting burdens on cities, also provided the essential labor force and consuming public for continued growth and development.

PUSH-AND-PULL CAUSES OF URBAN MIGRATION

Throughout the nineteenth century there were improvements in transportation and reductions in information and search costs that made the movement easier from the Old World to this country. To understand the fundamental causes behind such mass migration, we must examine changes in the demographic, technological, and institutional settings in both the origin and destination areas.

While we have stressed the factors pulling the migrants to the cities (new employment opportunities and low urban rates of natural increase), many forces also worked to push them in their origin areas. We can think of the latter as consisting of changes in rates of natural increase (affecting the supply of labor), changes in technology (affecting the demand for labor), and changes in law and political institutions (affecting both).

Briefly, rates of natural increase rose in country after country in Europe in the nineteenth century due to better nutrition and sanitation reducing the death rates with no immediate corresponding downturn in the birth rates. As a result labor supplies increased in following generations. If there had been corresponding changes in labor demands giving these additional workers employment, pressures to migrate might not have built up. However, the industrialization of the European continent was slower than in America and more sharply localized by geography and ethnic grouping. The resultant situation was made worse by social and political measures that were not equally enforced. Examples contrasting the migration push-and-pull forces for northern and southern Italians and Jews and non-Jews in Eastern Europe seem to fit this pattern quite well.

Furthermore, advances in education and the decline of subsistence-type agriculture due to the opening of farming to world competition operated to make the situation more critical. It was in the same areas where there was little industrial growth and where labor supplies were swelling that farming remained in a primitive state. How could one not expect that newly literate minorities, given the triggering catastrophes of famine, war, persecution, and civil strife, would choose to take their chances in the world across the ocean—a world where they could build a better life based upon growing economic opportunities?

After the 1880s labor supply and demand were in such poor balance in Southern and Eastern Europe that any triggering device set off a mass outward movement. The cutoff of these sources in the 1920s was not due to the restoration of equilibrium but rather the establishment of the immigration restriction laws, or the quota system—a variation of which exists today.

After 1920 blacks from the southern states and Spanish-Americans from Puerto Rico began to come north in large numbers. After World War II these became main sources of migration. In the 1960s other islands and South and Central America became the additional origin areas for migrants. The above pattern of push conditions has seemed to repeat itself in most of these areas since World War I in a complementary way. The pull conditions of the major metropolitan destinations have continued to generate a wavelike pattern for this internal migration.

In sum, in the full picture of our history as a mobile people, the pull, or conditions in destination areas, refers to those both on the eastern seaboard and in the western part (interior) of the Americas. The push, or conditions in origin areas, refers to those in the European or internal American rural sources for migrants. The long-run pattern and volume of migration are seen as results of dynamic disequilibrium between origin and destination areas. The factors are organized around the demand and supply of labor and the forces behind them in each area. These are ultimately the determinants of changes in population growth rates and the rate and spread of the diffusion of industrial and farming opportunities among different social groups at different points in time.

ROLES PLAYED BY VARIOUS GROUPS

The combination of urban growth and large-scale migration led to an ever changing population mix. The mingling of groups with diverse social and cultural patterns produced a more vital urban culture. The city also performed an upgrading function for these groups, although the degree of opportunity and mobility varied considerably.

In the nineteenth century the native white stock dominated rural, village, small-town America, while the foreign stock concentrated in the cities. The proportions were about 2 to 1 for these groups in each of these areas. The nonwhite (essentially black) populations were still tied to farms in the South (nine out of ten lived in that region and eight of those nine lived in the rural, village economy). The data below show a summary for 1890 for native white and foreign stock.

1890	Percent Native White	Percent Foreign	Percent Nonwhite
U.S.	55	33	12
Urban	40	53	7

Examined in a more specific way, we can see below the differences between cities by size and between urban and rural areas.

1890	Percent of Cities, More than 100,000	Percent of Cities, Less than 100,000	Percent Urban	Percent Rural
Native white	8	17	25	75
Foreign	35	23	58	42

This mix was brought about mainly by the demands of the industrialization-urbanization process. The occupational roles of each of these groups reflect how they contributed to the cities' growth. To show upward mobility patterns, we can visualize a three-generational pattern of foreign born–foreign parentage–native parentage. Table 5–2 shows the roles of the occupations in terms of these groups (lines 1 through 6) and how important these groups were to each occupation (lines 7 through 12) for the year 1910.

JOBS, NATIVITY, AND RACE

Lines 1 through 6 answer the question of how important each of these job categories was to each ethnic group. Lines 1 and 2 suggest that native Americans, whether white or nonwhite, were about equally likely to be farmers or nonfarmers, while among the foreign stock the chances were between 4 and 5 to 1 that they would be in nonfarm occupations. Overall this meant that a worker's chances in 1910 (last column) were 2 to 1 that he would be found in a nonfarm job.

Lines 3 and 4 show a clear similarity for the native white stock and the second generation foreign stock of the growing white-collar category. The foreign-born are in an intermediate position while the non-

TABLE 5–2 Occupational and Industrial Ranking of Native and Migrant Groups, 1910

| | Foreign Stock | | Foreign-born | Nonwhite | All Classes |
	Native White	Foreign Parentage			
1. Farm	49	19	13	46	31
2. Nonfarm	51	81	87	54	69
Total all	100	100	100	100	100
Total nonfarm	100	100	100	100	100
3. White collar	41	38	20	2	31
4. Blue collar	59	62	80	98	69
5. Skilled	36	41	43	22	38
6. Unskilled	23	21	37	76	31
7. Farm	61	12	9	18	100
8. Nonfarm	42	22	26	10	100
9. White collar	56	27	16	1	100
10. Blue collar	36	20	30	14	100
11. Skilled	40	24	30	6	100
12. Unskilled	31	15	30	24	100
13. All occupations	48	19	21	12	100

NOTE: The white-collar category consists of professional, technical, and related managers, officials, and proprietors, and sales and clerical workers. Craftsmen, foremen, and like workers, as well as operators of machines, make up the skilled category. Laborers and service workers make up the unskilled category.
SOURCE: Derived from Lance Davis, Richard Easterlin, and W. Parker, *American Economic Growth: An Economist's History of the United States* (New York: Harper & Row, 1972), pp. 138–39.

white have failed to break into the white-collar grouping (2 percent). Overall blue-collar workers still dominated the urban industrial, non-farm job market by better than a 2 to 1 ratio in 1910.

Lines 5 and 6 indicate that native whites and those of foreign parentage were about equally likely to have reached the more skilled job areas in the blue-collar sector (about a 2 to 1 ratio). Foreign-born workers were as likely to have been skilled as unskilled, while the nonwhite was again at the bottom of the pyramid with almost a 4 to 1 chance that he was in an unskilled category if he was an urban worker.

As historian Steven Thernstrom notes, the bulk of workers at the lower end of the occupational ladder, the unskilled and semiskilled, were migrants. Few were what sociologists call downwardly mobile, that is, drifting downward from a higher beginning point. Instead, they were the newcomers to the urban world, beginning at low-level jobs and often able to advance a notch or two occupationally by the next generation.

In summary, despite their underrepresentation in the cities, the native whites clearly were at the top of the occupational pyramid. This suggests the role they played in key urban decision making and innovating. Those of foreign parentage were quite upwardly mobile, while the foreign-born filled in the remaining manual jobs. At the bottom were the relatively minor (in terms of urban work force, less than 10 percent) roles played by nonwhites, mainly in unskilled jobs.

ETHNIC GROUPS THAT FILLED JOBS

Lines 7 through 12 give us a different perspective by answering the question of how important each ethnic group was in filling certain needs of the economy.

In the farm sector (line 7) the native white dominated, but in the nonfarm area the foreign elements were larger (line 8). The native white and those of foreign parentage were overrepresented in the white-collar category, while the foreign-born were more numerous in the blue-collar grouping (lines 9 and 10).

The lack of upward job mobility for the nonnative white comes through quite clearly in lines 9 and 12. They were twice as likely to be in unskilled jobs as their proportion of the work force would indicate (line 12 versus line 13, last column), and they were far, far less likely to be in white-collar jobs or blue-collar skilled jobs (lines 9 and 11, last column). Of the total unskilled, nonfarm workers, they made up 24 percent, while of all nonfarm workers, they were only 10 percent (line 12 versus line 8). The breakdown of the blue-collar occupations (lines 11 and 12) shows the foreign-born equally represented between skilled and unskilled, while for the native white the skilled outnumbered the unskilled about 4 to 3. Interestingly, those of foreign parentage were the smallest percentage of this number. Of the four groupings, only foreign-born were overrepresented significantly among the blue-collar workers.

LIVING STANDARDS FOR THE WORKING MAN

We have discussed the employment patterns of the groups comprising the new racial ethnic mix of American cities. Another dimension, which reflects the upgrading function, the effect of cities on the life chances of their inhabitants, is the standard of living.

For the working man and his family during these decades, the weight of the evidence is mixed. In some areas there was decided progress, in others things got worse. Real wages improved and hours declined. The data on earnings and hours worked look like this:

Year	Average Annual Earnings*	Average Hours per Week
1870	$380	72
1890	520	60
1910	610	55
1920	770	50

*Real nonfarm earnings in 1914 dollars.
SOURCES: Stanley Lebergott, *Manpower and Economic Growth* (New York: McGraw-Hill, 1964), pp. 526–28, and Ross M. Robertson, *History of the American Economy* (New York: Harcourt, Brace & World, 1955).

The data show that workers enjoyed steady absolute gains. However, an equally important measure is the relative gains, that is, changes in living standards compared to other groups in the society. The living standards of workers improved because the economic pie grew larger. However, it is not completely clear what happened to their slice of the pie, that is, what occurred in relation to the portions gobbled up by the upper and middle classes. What is clear is that another component of living standards is the relative social and economic dislocation generated by the shift from farm to city. Among the costs that should be taken into consideration are unemployment, exploitation of children and women, working conditions, industrial accidents, hazards, and illness. The unemployment picture looked something like this:

Years	Percent of Average Unemployment	High Year and Percent	
1870–79	10	1876	12–14
1880–89	4	1885	6–8
1890–99	10	1894	15+
1900–09	4	1908	6–8
1910–19	5	1915	9–11

SOURCE: Stanley Lebergott, *Manpower and Economic Growth* (New York: McGraw-Hill, 1964), pp. 187, 189.

We see that in two decades, the 1870s and 1890s, there were high average rates of unemployment. In the prosperous decades the normal rate was about 4 or 5 percent. In the worst of these times (second column) the rates exceeded the average by about one-half. In many years these were catastrophic proportions, for there was no unemployment compensation or systematic relief. We note that these are national rates. Urban rates, from the scattered evidence that is available, were always considerably higher. This follows when we recall that the agricultural or farm sector rarely suffered unemployment but rather, in hard times, resorted to subsistence farming.

Child labor increased sharply. In 1880 one million boys and girls, aged ten to fifteen, were "gainfully" occupied, and by 1910 the number had doubled. In 1880 women represented about 15 percent of the work force; by 1920, over 20 percent. In larger cities the percentages of women in the labor force were about 20 and 33 percent respectively. Although today women are accepted side by side with men, in most jobs as late as 1920 their position in industry was almost strictly in the lowest-paid fields, such as domestic service and cotton textile manufacturing. Furthermore, no laws protected either women or children from working hours above the normal or from wages below a level needed to survive decently.

Concrete data on working conditions, industrial accidents, hazards, and illness are not available for this period of our history. One authority (Ross Robertson) suggests that "estimates of insurance companies showed that after 1900 there were annually from 25,000 to 30,000 deaths and more than 2,000,000 serious injuries from accidents on the job." And for all practical purposes, there was no compensation for the family—there was no workmen's compensation insurance or Social Security! Certainly this was a horrible situation, one that cried out for social remedies. However, as we know, these were slow in coming. It took the Great Depression to rearrange views of economic justice, to pass the needed laws, and to bring about the organization of labor on a large scale.

These costs (which accompanied the benefits of shorter hours and higher real earnings) are examples of *spillover costs.* Usually things such as pollution or traffic congestion are thought of as examples of spillovers. However, dangerous working conditions and industrial accidents imposed great unpaid-for burdens on all society. On the one hand were the lost labor power, decreased productivity, and poorer products; on the other were the increased worker dissatisfaction and the increased costs of crime, welfare, and caring for the disabled.

The individual experienced in many cases great hardships and difficulties during this rapid growth period. As migrant, worker, family head, ethnic, or poor person, he saw many obstacles to a good life. But he also was hopeful, for the best chances were in the cities. There was some freedom to choose; and hard work, savings, and education meant better lives for his children. There was also some privacy, not in the personal sense of having a separate room but in the social sense of not having an entire village whispering about you or some member of your family, causing you to be blacklisted in the local job market. There were chances to experiment with life and be on one's own at an early age. One did not have to be a farmer like his father or grandfather if one didn't want to!

ECOLOGICAL DEVELOPMENT OF THE CITY

During this period, then, urban areas processed large numbers of foreign immigrants and internal migrants. Their movement to the city produced basic changes in their experiences, opportunities, and mobility. This large influx of immigrants and migrants, and the changing population mix, also helped to reshape the physical and social patterns of urban living.

The residents in the cities of America before World War I were not distributed as a result of chance. Nor was their distribution planned by local government or other public agencies. Rather it was the product of a number of factors that had risen to prominence in the nineteenth century. These included: intensity of land use by economic function; income level of family; family composition (stage in life cycle, age, size); ethnic clustering; transport routes and natural features; economic growth patterns; and attitudes toward mobility.

The end result was a city ecology that resembled Figure 5–1. This general view of the ecology of the city reflects the class structure of American society that emerged in the period of rapid industrialization. In turn this ecology produced severe problems in managing the city and laid the structural foundations for the problems that continue to plague many urban areas today.

The six factors mentioned above interacted in many ways. As the economic functions distributed themselves over the land area, they tended to produce a concentric ring pattern. The central area is the business district where specialized business services, banks, office buildings, large department stores, and government offices are located. It is the core for trade and commerce and cultural events, for all activities requiring constant face-to-face contact. Information, ideas, and people must move freely there, and goods and services must be made available to them. Access to this area demands a higher price; hence, improvements in mass transit, advances in information processing and exchange, as well as construction techniques, provide higher-density land use. All have given the central business district a powerful and influential role in the development of the modern metropolitan ecology.

In the area around the central business district we usually find light manufacturing and wholesaling activity as well as some of the most run-down and dilapidated housing. It is here that we frequently see the urban slum created. The next concentric area usually contains mainly residences and the economic and service facilities to provide

FIGURE 5–1   The Effects of Transportation Changes on the Ecology of the City: From Colonial Times to the Present

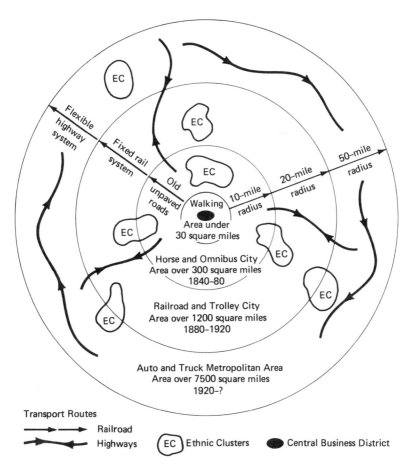

for the daily shopping, education, health, and cultural needs of the populace. Finally, we find a ring of suburbs at the edge of the city with a mixed series of land uses, light and heavy manufactures, shopping centers, and residences. The major difference there is that land is cheaper and less intensively used.

Superimposed on this concentric ring pattern, and in the case of some cities almost obliterating it, are the transportation radii of railroads and highways around whose stations and interchanges business and industry cluster. Sometimes these follow the natural features and sometimes they carve their way through the landscape.

Where do people live in this economic maze? They normally weigh alternative locations and come to some sort of choice based on a variety of factors; these include the information available about neighborhoods and residences, their income levels, the strength of their ethnic feelings, the location of their jobs, the available transport routes, and the time they want to spend in travel.

Family composition, stage in life cycle, and ethnic heritage tend to lead to people's clustering in neighborhoods. Overall economic growth and employment patterns, combined with rising family incomes, operate to expand choices and lead to value changes directed toward mobility.

In summary, during the decades 1860 to 1920 the six factors we have noted interacted to produce a more segregated, clustered city. It was a city in which the well-to-do sought to combine easy access to jobs with more space. It was one in which the poor were concentrated in the older areas at the edges of the city core where they were crowded into high-density tenements or lost in the run-down areas in the factory districts. Finally, the masses of the working class, while affected by public transit routes, continued to group for solidarity in neighborhood ethnic settlements where possible.

We have seen that in response to the waves of migrants and innovations, the residences and business firms radically redistributed themselves within the cities, leading to major internal changes in city organization. In the multiplication of varied ethnic neighborhoods and in the rapid changes of institutions, whether financial or fraternal, a group of new problems emerged. Conflicts between neighborhoods flared, especially when city service areas crossed over many such ethnic enclaves; examples are higher educational facilities, transportation lines, extensions of public utilities, sanitation, and street maintenance. The burden for adjustment fell upon politicians—to find a method of supplying such services in proportion to variations in public demand. The answer was the "political machine" system run by the "boss."

THE POLITICAL MACHINE AND THE BOSS

In the 1850s and 1860s most of the pre-Civil War city problems in public safety (fire and police) and public health (sanitation, water, and sewerage) were beginning to yield to local governmental attempts to organize a bureaucracy of city employees. Cities made use of available technics and tax dollars to build the needed facilities and maintain the system of public services. However, at the same time no coordinating agency emerged to handle the allocation of job contracts and franchises. State governments dominated by rural interests wanted only to control taxing powers and restrain local authorities—no help was forthcoming from this area. Into the vacuum of power stepped the political party—patronage and graft became the allocating tools in most city governments.

As needs grew to crisis proportions, government seemed to deteriorate. The lot of public services was marked by inefficiency, waste, and corruption. Most public utilities outside of water supply, being highly profitable, were privately run at the end of the nineteenth century. Gas, electricity, and street railways represented over $3 billion in private investment by 1900.

While the attention of most business leaders was sharply focused on the highly profitable private sector, there was a growing need for government. The increased diversity within the city in religion, race, language, and cultural origins made the exchange of information on which the provision of adequate services depends most difficult. Men who understood these situations and who were supported at local elections by faithful groups of voters were called bosses. They dominated American city politics with their machines until the mid-twentieth century.

Naturally they generated opponents in the form of reformers who frequently were tied to other causes—the ending of prostitution or gambling or the control of liquor. One wing of reform that pursued these strongly was the social gospel movement—but it failed to obtain mass support. More successful in gaining full public backing were attempts to provide better housing laws to attack the environment of poverty more directly—rather than through its apparent (to the upper-class reformers) social causes.

Both of these groups, bosses and reformers, should be seen as organic responses of the body politic to real needs. Individuals did not invent the boss system; it developed in response to basic needs. It grew as cities grew, providing jobs, services, and political influence to immigrant groups that had previously experienced few of these benefits. Patronage in public jobs, machine-run government, political corruption, and graft in construction and franchise contracts were characteristics of the system regardless of the city.

The political machines created by and for immigrant groups also changed existing structures of power and evoked a strong response from the native middle class. They tried to gain popular support by campaigning on the issue of municipal reform. Where successful, they created independent audits, the shorter ballot, nonpartisan elections, and home rule. Many of these reforms culminated in the commission and city manager forms of government. In terms of our model, the boss system created a method for reducing the costs of information, the costs of making contracts, and the costs of policing in the public service sector. Buildings and facilities were constructed, transit lines extended, streets lighted and paved, sewers laid—and the price was paid.

What did city officials control that was of value? Access to valuable urban land, improvements to given areas, control over the kinds of uses to which land could be put were potent weapons. City officials "sold" landowners and industrialists the "rights" as to when and where and how a specific area would be developed. And it did not have to be illegal. Inside information as to location decisions, control over transit rates, and granting of monopoly franchises were widely used methods for dispensing these values in return for party contributions and support.

By 1900 the worst possible outcomes were realized. Monopoly power was seized by entrenched political machines. Exploitation and corruption siphoned needed revenues out of cities, and public services fell into disarray. The story in public utilities is well documented. There, a nationwide holding company tried to build a billion-dollar monopoly over much of the urban service sector—and it almost succeeded. In the end, however, its empire turned out to be more paper than real assets. Corporation after corporation dissolved into bankruptcy—destroying investors and city organizations alike in the Great Crash of 1929–33. Other stories of attempts at reform in the World

War I era would illustrate vividly just how bad the situation was—
certainly equal to anything we have today.

THE MACHINE: A SOCIOLOGICAL VIEW

In our view the urban political machine is also an example of how
changes in economic, transportation, and other systems affect the
roles people play and the institutions within which they act.

As we have shown, the machine was an adaptive response to a
whole array of changes in urban life. The increasing density of urban
populations dramatically expanded the number of voters, and this
growing population was divided along both class and ethnic lines.
Clear and massive divisions along such lines were characteristic of
late-nineteenth-century urban America. A large working class
emerged, attracted by the new jobs created by industrialization.
Crowded into tenements and other substandard housing, they were
highly visible and easily identified, sharing common needs and desires
to which existing political systems did not respond.

This growing working class was not a homogeneous group, but
rather its members were quite conscious of their ethnicity, being Irish
or Italians, Poles or Germans. Their economic interests might be
similar, but they preferred living apart in their own little enclaves.
Moreover, they knew that railroads, utilities, and other business interests received government assistance denied to them. Yet, they lacked
the political power and skills needed to make themselves heard or to
reshape the system by the normal political processes.

In sum, the machine was an outgrowth of nineteenth-century industrialization which created an urban working class and stimulated
immigration. The political machine and the role of the boss were
understandable responses to these developments. The boss drew his
support from the ethnic working class through his knowledge of its
social organization and his understanding of its basic unit, the neighborhood. Many ethnic working-class neighborhoods followed ward
boundaries and were natural social areas to draw on for political
support. Below the neighborhood level were a variety of organizations
and groups to which the politician had to relate; these included the

parish church, the club or fraternal organization, the saloon, and the gang. Most ethnic groups had strong religious traditions, with much activity revolving around the church and parish school. The saloons and private clubs were also important centers of social life for workingmen. Young men in these poor neighborhoods informally banded together in gangs. They held social events in their clubhouses and often turned to petty crime. The boss and ward politician often called on ethnic gang members to act as "workers" at the polls and to vote early and often during elections.

In *Social Theory and Social Structure* sociologist Robert Merton presents a classic analysis of the functions of the political machine. One was to provide social services in a form acceptable to people. The local politician, who was also a neighbor, personally provided help. Recipients did not have to feel they were "on the dole," nor did they have to face the complexities of downtown bureaucracies. Second, in Merton's words, the political machine provided "alternative channels of social mobility for those otherwise excluded from the more conventional avenues for personal advancement." A working-class youth might not be able to advance in his job or learn a middle-class profession; however, power, prestige, and income were available if he successfully moved up through the party organization. Finally, it also benefited business interests such as public utilities and transportation companies by dispensing political favors. Thus, the machine and boss accommodated themselves to the economic and political inequalities worsened by industrialization. The boss did not challenge the system; he tried to wrest all the benefits he could from it while minimizing the costs to his supporters.

CITY GROWTH AND THE LARGER SOCIETY

By the 1910 American economic life was thoroughly dominated by business ways and had become urbanized in outlook. The share of workers engaged in farming had reached a peak of just under 12 million in 1920—or double the 1860 level. However, the fivefold growth of the nonagricultural sector from just over 5 million to over 25 million indicates that more than two-thirds of the American work force were no longer pursuing a living in the countryside.

There were a number of important ways in which the farm sector affected urban growth and development between the Civil War and World War I. The gradual mechanization of agriculture made it possible for a smaller and smaller proportion of the work force to cultivate the food and associated products for the entire population. Thus, while it took one farm family to feed each nonfarm family in 1870, by 1910 productivity had doubled and two urban families could be supported by each farmer.

Since the rural areas maintained relatively high rates of fertility, they produced an excess population, thus providing a significant reservoir from which the urban areas drew many workers for industry. Various figures suggest that about 30 percent of the total population growth in the urban centers came from this source during this period.

To some extent the decline in the farm sector was due to the shift to city manufactures from farm products. Notable was the substitution of coal, oil, and gas for firewood, and kerosene and oil for tallow and lard. In later decades this process continued in the shift from natural to synthetic fibers. Another related fact is the decline in the percentage of income spent on perishables as income rises: in 1860 about 50 percent of all income was spent on perishables; by 1920 it was below 40 percent and dropping. These declines in demand were offset somewhat by increased foreign demand, especially after 1900.

Though farming was declining relative to industry, this period nonetheless witnessed the full flowering of American agriculture. This may be attributed to a number of factors. First, the enormous growth in the number of farms and the improving technology of farm output and transport led to the opening up of vast new territories. Second, the pattern of increasing labor productivity through the application of science to agriculture was first established in these decades. In the light of declining relative demand for farm goods, prices fell in terms of the prices of industrial goods. Farmers had to sell and buy, therefore, in markets where they had less and less economic power and impact.

Yet the ways of farming and rural ideals seemed to dominate many aspects of social and political thought. This is a puzzle that requires explanation. Part of the answer lies in the fact that the abundance of natural resources and the wide-open spaces of the westward frontier had for over 250 years tended to shape the American character. As a people we had accepted the viewpoint of *agricultural fundamentalism,* that is, farming and living in small rural communities as the best way of life. It was close to nature, close to God, and inherently better than crowding together into cities. This was reinforced by Thomas Jefferson, Ralph Waldo Emerson, Henry David Thoreau, and other distinguished men of letters. In so doing, they directly or indirectly romanticized the rural way of life and condemned the industrial urban order (or, as they would say, "disorder") that was emerging in nineteenth-century America.

Other parts of the answer lie in the nature of the American political structure at the national level that gave great "swing" power to the farm states through the Senate (two votes per state) and political alliances. The very active role played by farm organizations is evident in the political patronage, government appropriations, and investment decisions that they shaped—a trend that continues to the present day.

In the years 1870 to 1900, the residue of the South's planter class formed a wing of the Democratic party and united its interests with the small-town businessmen of the North, who formed the core of the conservative wing of the Republican party. These groups combined with large western farm organizations such as the Grange, Greenbacks, and Populists against urban industrial interests. Examples of achievements occurred in internal improvements, transportation, tariffs, the creation of a Department of Agriculture, and land and conservation policy. These groups tried to preserve what they saw as the best apsects of rural life and to obtain a "fair shake" for the rural individual in a growing industrial-urban dominated world.

DEVELOPMENT IN CITY FUNCTIONS

Between the Civil War and World War I, the thrust toward an urban-industrial nation continued. Under the spur of increased mechanization and capital investment, the rate of economic expansion accelerated. This focused the urbanization process on the generative function of cities. Innovations and the expansion of trade through further specialization followed. The completion of the vast railroad network not only facilitated this movement but also redirected the location of many new cities away from rivers toward new resource sites. While there were many important discoveries in natural resources such as iron, oil, and precious metals, the distinctive aspect of this input expansion was the flood of immigrants from Europe. Following the pulsations of the national and regional economies, millions of new workers and consumers swarmed into our cities. Under the twin impacts of rising industrialization and mass migration, the structure of urban areas—social, political, and physical—changed dramatically.

Much of the healthy interaction function was lost in a growing segregation by income and class and a collapse of public order. Cities of larger size and increasing age made further demands on the traditional voluntary, administrative, municipal institutions and broke down their abilities to deliver services. The city was plagued by political corruption. Its upgrading abilities suffered both from declines of the interaction function and the overwhelming cycles of the generative function. New societal institutions and social order were needed. Before they could be developed, the cities were plunged into the era of full metropolitanization.

CHAPTER SIX

The Era of Full Metropolitanization: The Shaping of Urban Life since 1920

Modern American life is metropolitan. The metropolis does not merely dominate or control the surrounding hinterland: it has become the symbol and essence of this quarter of the twentieth century.

Most books on American urbanization do not fully discuss the contemporary metropolitan experience. The narrative is usually carried up to World War II, with only a few pages devoted to the past few decades. In this chapter we discuss how historical trends continue into the present as we examine the relationship between cities and the larger society.

Since 1900 metropolitan growth rates have exceeded national averages and, as a result, metropolises have increased their share of total population from less than one-third to over two-thirds. Geographers, such as Berry, estimate that over 95 percent of all Americans in the labor force work within daily commuting distance of some metropolitan market area. We are a metropolitan country.

Older trends in expansion matured and new ones appeared. Metropolitan regions grew dramatically in size and number and generated different patterns of living and working. Traditional urban institutions and forms, born in the industrial surges of the Civil War to World War I period, declined while new ones emerged. And other groups of people became involved in the benefits and costs of all this ferment and growth. One commentator, in trying to describe the forces producing this change, writes:

The functions of the metropolitan area are changing rapidly. As the functions change, the form and structure of the metropolitan area must also change. A new technology, a new affluence, new forms of corporate and governmental organization, and changing public values—all of these acting in combination are creating metropolitan areas whose size, geographic extent, and variety exceed anything previously envisaged by man. (Wheaton in Loewenstein 1971:76)

Urban areas have increased in size, number, complexity, and inter-relationships throughout the period since World War I. However, the pace of this change was not even, having been marked by fluctuations tied to wider economic system developments. Related changes in rates of industrial growth, changes in population, technology, and institutions, at different times, have contributed to the changes in metropolitanization patterns.

Throughout this book we have tried to show the relationship between economic growth an urbanization and the impact of both on the lives of urban residents. Therefore, we have organized this chapter around longer swings in economic activity, with the timing of these swings roughly as follows:

1920s	expansion
1930s	contraction
World War II	war-induced expansion
World War II– mid-1950s	expansion
Mid-1950s–1960	contraction
1960s	expansion
1970s to date	contraction

The national network of interdependent, multicentered metropolitan areas grew in power and influence as the population concentration from rural to urban residences continued. However, there were major shifts in the geographic regions where new growth focused. Within these sprawling urbanized areas, specialized subregions could be marked off. Very high rates of mobility for people, information, and goods accelerated the deconcentration of both industry and population.

OLD AND NEW FORCES LEADING TO METROPOLITANIZATION

A variety of forces were propelling American society into the era of full metropolitanization. A combination of old patterns from the nineteenth century remained active in the twentieth.

The economic growth and development ethic continued to dominate. Means, ends, goals, programs—all were blended together in an ideology of freedom, abundance, and innovation as normal to the American experience. Private property rights, individualism, free enterprise, and profits all directed societal and urban change through a competitive market. Both economic growth and urbanization were largely directed by private economic interests, motivated by profit. Thus, the shape of the new patterns of urbanization was determined by the location of industry and the activity of private land speculators and developers. The principle of private property rights remained stronger than the pressure for public control by citizens.

Certain problems, tensions, and conflicts continued to be seen as necessary evils associated with the natural progress of society. Poverty, unemployment, and the urban public service sector thus were accorded a laissez-faire approach.

By the 1920s new paths were being trod. These unfolding twentieth-century characteristics of urban development acted to increase the size and number of urban settlements, to change their regional distribution, to modify their functions and internal ecology, and to turn the entire society toward an era of full metropolitanization. These twentieth-century characteristics were the following:

Demographic Changes in the Society.   Fluctuations in fertility and declines in mortality yielded population surpluses and shortages. These were partly offset by migration and changes in social mobility. Class, race, and ethnic conflicts resulted from the tensions between this and the following characteristics.

The Increasing Impact of Science and Technology.   Scientific and technical innovations became central to the economy and produced new leading industries, such as electronics and computers. These also affected the occupational structure, with most of the jobs requiring some type of scientific or technical knowledge. These industrial and occupational changes led to job and residence shifts on a massive scale which, in turn, interacted with changes in political and social institutions. "Foot-loose" industries and services flourished with the emergence of a business culture keyed to rising living standards.

Expanding Discretionary Income.   Increases in labor productivity and labor organization resulted in the average family rising above the poverty line by midcentury. The family could now spend its increased leisure and extra income in a wide variety of new ways. Greater discretionary income also expanded the range of choices available to the average family, influencing where people lived, the kind of home they lived in, and the range of services they expected.

The Changing Role of Government.   The emerging system was efficient, but it was also highly inequitable. Despite some redistribution of income, large numbers of Americans were being left behind in poverty and squalor. The average family also faced economic uncertainty since its job and income opportunities fluctuated with the ups and downs of the national economy. A significant public debate slowly emerged over whether equal opportunity in a democracy required a framework of security and minimum economic decency. This was seen by many as a new government purpose.

Growing Sectoral Interdependence, Specialization, and Diversity. Decisions made by the government and private sectors (by rural and urban legislators, by vested interests and reformers, by corporations and unions) led to the emergence of regional markets and the tying together of all areas into national economic trends. Internally, regional sectors were more specialized. Dispersion of jobs and population followed. The role of the neighborhood was redefined and metropolitan planning emerged as a formative factor.

THE TWENTIES: A TIME OF PROSPEROUS STAGNATION

This decade is seen by some as the birth period of consumer capitalism. The dominant actors on the nineteenth-century stage—merchant, industrialist, financier—were joined by a new social type, the consumer. The problems of consumption or lack of consumption began to move to the center of the economic stage in this period. These problems were to crystallize into fundamental flaws in the American economy by the next decade, and they have continued to plague us in differing ways ever since. It was also in the twenties that another actor began to be recognized as an important member of the cast— the American worker. While the consumer's vital role was clear to the leading decision makers of the thirties, the workers had to wait until a later day.

The twin aspects of modern prosperity—mechanization and mass production—manifested themselves in terms of the typical urban householder's living style. On the average, living standards improved as wages rose, unemployment stayed low, working hours dropped, and prices remained very stable. It was the age of the consumer. Auto sales went from about 600,000 to 6 million, and total car registrations from 2 million to 26 million. The creation of the advertising industry and consumer credit fueled the sales of department, chain, and mail order stores. The American was getting his first taste of large amounts of discretionary spending power and he was learning (or being trained) to use it.

Inexpensive electric machinery and appliances, the telephone, the automobile, the radio, and new urban construction were the growth industries that pushed the prosperity of the twenties. At the same time there were depressed sectors, including agriculture, textiles, coal, shipbuilding, and leather products. In terms of urban prosperity, this meant that while some large and small centers such as Detroit and Dayton, New York and Akron expanded rapidly, some older centers such as St. Louis, Louisville, and the mill towns of New England suffered declines.

Underlying this picture were a slowdown in the rate of population growth and a shutdown of international migration, as well as increases in the mechanization of industry, in government's role in economic affairs, and in the power of the corporate and banking communities.

FLAWS IN THE SYSTEM: CAUSES OF THE GREAT DEPRESSION

These factors interacted to produce the appearance of good times, while simultaneously aggravating the flaws in the system. Closer examination shows not only that there were sick industries but also that there were growing inequities in the rewards from the economic system. While real wages grew about 40 percent, profits grew 105 percent between 1919 and 1929. If these profits had been fruitfully reinvested in new industries, more income might have been generated. Unfortunately, this was not done. Perhaps because of a slowdown in new product creation, or perhaps for reasons of personal greed, much of the excess profits went into conspicuous consumption and land and stock market speculations. The former wasted resources, while the latter bid up the value of already existing assets and created only paper gains.

The core of the problem was that the productivity of the current capital stock had consistently grown faster than wages throughout the twenties (about 1 percent per year). This productivity advance was due largely to mechanization of industry; the installation of scientific methods of plant layout, assembly, and analysis; and the development of stronger incentives for the work force. Concentrated corporate power had no major unions to bargain with, and adequate nonunionist recruits could be found as needed to keep wages low. There accumulated an excess capital capacity by the late twenties as the worker-consumer's buying power could no longer be inflated by new credit. As markets shrank, there was no longer a profit to be made in plant modernization.

Compounding this was the end of the construction boom in the late twenties. In addition to central business districts overbuilding, there was a decline in the number, size, and rate of new household formation due to the fall-off in migration from Europe and the continual slowdown in urban fertility. Unfortunately, government, which might have stepped in to improve the situation, made all the wrong moves. In addition to starting the quota system that cut back on migration, it neither prevented the growing speculation in banking, land, and financial circles nor supported workers' attempts to organize into unions.

Rather, by raising foreign trade and tariff barriers, Americans isolated themselves from the European market and further depressed agricultural export industries, forcing consumers to pay higher prices for imports. By late 1928 the handwriting was on the wall. The urban building boom had ended. The auto industry was in grave difficulty. Banks and financial institutions were beginning to restrict credit and becoming more conservative in their investments. By the summer of 1929, unemployment was rising and output was declining. Then came the stock market crash and with it the worst economic collapse of modern times.

THE THIRTIES: CRASH AND RESPONSE

The Great Depression that began in the summer of 1929 lasted twice as long and went twice as deep as any previous business cycle in America's history. Ten years later, in 1939, Americans had barely revived the average standard of living to the 1929 levels. That decade wrought major changes in the economic and socio-political life of every American. It made a special impression on urban dwellers who could not fall back on the land for subsistence and thus were particularly vulnerable to the economic aspects of this disaster.

From the urban householders' view, the depression was particularly harsh in its impact. Table 6–1 shows some varied indices of how bad conditions got during the downward spiral.

TABLE 6–1   Measures of the Great Depression

	1929	1933
Index of payrolls	100	44
Index of employment	98	64
Numbers unemployed (millions)	1.5	15
Index of industrial production	103	54
Dollar-value of exports and imports (millions)	9,640	2,934
Dow-Jones Index	365	63
GNP (current prices in billions)	104	56
Index of durable goods	40	8
Index of nondurable goods	40	28
Index of construction of residences	100	8
Dollars spent on housing repairs (millions)	50	0.5

SOURCES: Derived from Robert A. Russel, *A History of the American Economic System* (New York: Appleton–Century–Crofts, 1964), Ross M. Robertson, *History of the American Economy* (New York: Harcourt, Brace & World, 1955), and George Soule, *Prosperity Decade* (New York: Harper & Row, 1968).

In some cities unemployment rates grew to over one-third of the work force. Los Angeles was reduced to selling the animals in its zoo. Cleveland had to issue script (imitation money) to pay its schoolteachers. City welfare systems broke down. The man selling apples on the street corner was a common sight in downtown areas. Birth rates fell to an all-time low, while robberies reached an all-time high. Millions of Americans became "bums," people who rode railways from place to place trying to exist on the edge of society.

Two of the trends of the twenties continued to grow in the thirties, while two others diminished. The two that were negative in their impact were demographic forces and declining incomes. Along with the cutback in immigration, the downturn in fertility meant a reduction of the number of new consumers and eventually a decrease in the number of workers. Internal migration, which had been picking up in the twenties, tapered off, leading to slow overall growth in cities. People tended to stay on the farms where relative economic opportunity did not decline as rapidly. The picture on income decline has been painted clearly enough, but it requires one added note. While income declined, the total pie was distributed more equitably in 1939 than it had been in 1929. Profits and investments actually went negative for some years in the thirties, and top income holders received a smaller share of total income at the beginning of World War II than they had at the time of the crash. However, this was of scant importance to the one-third of the nation in deepest poverty. In 1939 there still were over 6 million unemployed Americans who had no earned income. In a society dedicated to work, savings, and upward mobility, the social and psychological damage of that decade has yet to be fully calculated, if it ever can be.

The two trends that increased their impact in the thirties were the role of science and technology and growing sectoral interdependence, specialization, and diversity. In the 1920s large American corporations had moved toward wedding science with technology and joining both to new product development and, ultimately, sales and profits. Laboratories and engineering facilities were built; corporations developed five-year plans and aimed for investment returns. Compared to the present day's massive research and development expenditures, these efforts at rationalizing the total production process seem primitive indeed. Yet mechanization, Ford's assembly lines, and Taylor's scientific-management techniques began to take hold. A specific example of the fruition of this technology can be seen in the way the internal combustion engine was beginning to fit into the picture. It illustrates well the potential that new technology holds for conflict or expanded horizons of choice.

THE IMPACT OF THE AUTOMOBILE

The automobile was adopted initially in Europe for the use of the wealthy elite. It was brought to America before World War I and attached to the high-riding carriage by Henry Ford and his peers. They visualized it as an all-weather vehicle for getting the farmer to market through mud and snow—as a rural transportation device. The twenties changed all that as the automobile became the new means of mobility for the urban middle class. Ultimately, it had an impact on all aspects of society.

In examining the impact of the automobile, the economic consequences are among the more obvious. The auto industry, in building a new mode of transportation, expands all industries supplying it, including especially rubber, oil, steel, glass and, more recently, plastics and aluminum fabrication. It also shows the need for better roads, bridges, and tunnels, expanding construction and associated suppliers to these industries. It further creates large numbers of jobs in spare parts, auto supplies, auto repairs, and servicing. These industrial patterns make an imprint upon the lives of people through shifting occupational and skill needs and upon the capital goods sector through demands for new and specialized machines, machine tools, and business services. The additional income generated by these interacting processes is located in particular older cities or leads to the growth of new urban centers (an example would be new growth at major highway intersections). National resource patterns also change. Within given metropolitan regions, residential and business choices are affected by changing transport costs, and a further reallocation of resources occurs. Nor did the spiral stop there. Tourism, insurance, recreation, and other such service industries became auto-oriented and then auto-dominated. Well might it be called the "internal combustion revolution."

Most people recognize the ways in which the automobile and truck have destroyed old industries, such as horses and wagons, in the process of creating new ones of much wider scope. And many realize that the costs and patterns of shopping and trade have changed due to this mode of transport. Yet more and more focus has recently been placed on the social costs of the automobile. Ultimately, the entire nature of our community and social life has been changed in thousands of subtle ways. We view urban life in different ways, and our values change in accordance with these new perceptions. Let us look more closely at the history of one of the above sets of interactions.

In the twenties and the thirties, the automobile and truck revolutionized our industrial and residential decision-making processes. After World War II, with funds to build adequate roads available and with a government commitment to do so, a national network of highways was completed. These changes can be viewed in two perspectives. Advances in long-distance transport complemented improvements in pipelines and water transport. Improved roads filled out the national rail network and were in turn supplemented after World War II by air freight. They have created three great belts of urban areas 450 to 500 miles long on the Eastern Seaboard, along the Great Lakes, and on the West Coast in California. Overnight short-haul trucking was extended from 100- to 300-mile trips. Business firms could purchase from or sell to other firms in a radius of 50 to 400 miles from their metropolitan location. Within urban regions, employees found their job market extended from 20 to 50 miles. Both employer and worker were free to locate in many more places than formerly. Vast parcels of land could be opened up on the urban fringe. All kinds of population densities and industrial clustering became possible as highway interchanges determined growth points and highway radials directed strip development.

However, such mobility had its costs. The metropolitan region already felt the impact in the twenties and thirties of some of the future problems of the internal combustion engine. Mass transit systems, both interurban and intraurban, were hastily overextended in the twenties and some peaked in ridership as early as the thirties. In many older eastern cities and even some newer cities, such as Los Angeles, with its extensive rapid transit system, evidence suggests that leading auto producers bought up mass transit systems to destroy competition. This was done directly through dummy corporations which dismantled existing lines and also through the passage of laws giving automobiles the right of way at intersections with rapid transit.

The car, a relatively expensive durable good, quickly became a middle-class symbol, one that poor persons could not afford. This meant that the downwardly mobile, the minorities, the new migrants, the aged, and the disabled were in danger of being without the key to mobility in the post-World War II era of plenty.

The costs to the environment have also been many. Each decade has seen more accidents, pollution, and traffic congestion. The expansion of metropolises has meant the spread of slums marked by decaying urban structures along older transportation routes. In addition our new mobility has also led to the sacrifice of valuable center city land to the automobile. This varies from city to city, although typically over one-third and up to two-thirds of a C.B.D. is used for streets, parking garages, interchanges, and service facilities. Finally, it changed the meaning of political boundaries, the scope of political patronage, perceptions of community, and our very image of the city. Everything from family life to courtship to privacy has to be understood in the framework of our new mobility. Devoting 15 percent of our resources to the automobile meant we had the potential to reshape urban living in the last two generations. That is what we did, although some would say the costs have exceeded the benefits.

THE ROLE OF GOVERNMENT

Yet another societal trend shaping urban life in the 1920s and 1930s was the increasingly active role of the government. In response to the challenges posed by the Great Depression, the government assumed new positions that directly and indirectly affected the urban dweller. The Home Loan Bank Act, Home Owners Loan Corporation, and Federal Housing Authority established the concept of the long-term mortgage. Previously, mortgages had to be renegotiated every three to five years, a policy that had allowed interest rates to be raised and made it profitable for banks to foreclose when possible. It also meant that an unemployed person could not refinance a mortgage when it was up for renegotiation. This new system, when combined with other reforms (unemployment compensation, minimum wages, Social Security, and the right to organize unions) tied home ownership to the long-term chances of the working class. Security for the working person was a possibility in 1940; it had not been so in 1920.

The Public Works Administration, the Resettlement Administration, and the U.S. Housing Authority, while making little quantitative impact on the problems of substandard urban housing conditions, did point in the right direction. It was from these beginnings that concepts such as new towns, urban renewal, regional planning, and modern zoning practices developed. Increasing federal government activity thus began to reshape urban America.

Besides attempting to revive the economy, governments at all levels played an important planning role that influenced the shape of urban areas. By the beginning of the 1920s, planning and zoning were generally defined as municipal responsibilities. Local governments responded with the incorporation of quasi-independent city planning and zoning commissions usually composed of business and civic leaders. Planning became more formalized and every planning commission began developing comprehensive "master plans"—assessments of the present functioning and problems in the city and proposals for future capital construction and land use. However, these were rarely implemented. Later critics argued that the American planning tradition showed a "physical bias," that is, an overemphasis on the physical dimensions of the city with little appreciation for the social dimension, such as cultural and life-style differences in various communities. In Herbert Gans's view, "the master planners assumed the people's lives are shaped by their physical surrounding and that the ideal city could be realized by . . . an ideal physical environment." (Gans 1968:61)

Zoning laws were adopted to control the physical dimensions of the city. At first this appeared to be a rational response to the increasing velocity of urban change. The freeing of commercial enterprise from dependence on trolley and rail lines presented a potential threat to urban and suburban neighborhoods, and it was thought zoning would protect the public from detrimental changes in land use. By the end of the 1920s, many city planners and other critics charged that zoning was a tool of the rich to realize the greatest profit from their land, rather than a protection for the average city dweller. More frequently middle-class families were moving to the suburbs that were springing up outside the city. Many officials began arguing that planning should not stop at the city limits. This led to repeated calls for regional planning for both central cities and the surrounding metropolitan areas. These new suburban communities began fighting for political autonomy and consistently opposed any regional planning. Many state legislatures formulated laws making it very easy to incorporate as an independent "home rule" political entity and very difficult for the larger central cities to absorb peripheral growth through annexation or consolidation.

The strains placed on local government led to changes in city, state, and federal governmental relations. City residents became unhappy with their limited power in state legislatures and tried to obtain greater representation in those bodies. The rural-dominated legislatures consistently opposed all reapportionment proposals, a practice that produced permanent patterns of conflict between cities and state governments. The pattern was nationwide and forged a new working alliance between cities and the federal government, partly bypassing city-state linkages. The federal government, through Franklin D. Roosevelt's leadership, assumed increased responsibility in the areas of employment, welfare, and housing. This, in turn, led to new governmental divisions in responsibility for various social problems. The National Resource Planning Board was established to coordinate national and regional resource planning. The Public Housing Administration was established to reduce slum areas and construct new housing. The new partnership between cities and the federal government in relief and housing was the most obvious and dramatic development. However, as historian Blake McKelvey notes, by 1936 "some 500 different types of services and relationships were developed in . . . planning, zoning, education, health and internal improvement." (McKelvey 1968:98)

However, there was one area of urban life where the federal government did not play an active role—ethnic and race relations.

ETHNIC AND RACE RELATIONS

As was discussed in the previous chapter, the patterns of immigration and changing population mix deeply influenced the internal structure of urban areas, as well as the social, economic, and political life of cities. In the 1920s foreign immigration, which was curtailed by World War I, began again. It increased from a low of 31,063 in 1918 to 403,000 in 1920 and to 805,000 the following year. The bulk of these new immigrants crowded into ethnic communities in the central cities, where many had friends and relatives to help with housing and jobs. Soon after the end of the war, various interest groups began lobbying for new legislation to restrict foreign immigration. A variety of nativist groups, including the Ku Klux Klan, tried to end immigration on racial grounds, arguing that the native stock must be preserved. These groups also reflected an antiurban bias, since most foreign immigrants settled in large cities. A number of labor unions whose membership included "older" immigrant groups also supported restrictive legislation, a position that partly reflected prior conflicts with immigrant groups and future fear of unemployment if the labor force grew too large.

This development increased divisions within the urban working class, separating skilled and unskilled, men and women, blacks and whites. It also produced differences between the "old" and "new" immigrants. Immigrants, denied union membership, were often used as strikebreakers, leading to a general union policy of support for restrictive legislation. Business leaders, finding sufficient manpower in domestic sources, also supported the limitation of future immigrants. Marc Fried is particularly concerned with how urban ethnic groups were affected by existing patterns of inequality.

> The ethnic character of low status populations in the United States has often helped to obscure the underlying structure of social class in this country . . . ethnic discrimination has been superimposed on the inequalities stemming from social class differences. The structure of social inequality in our society antedated the arrival of each successive population and served to incorporate the migrant into the most menial and unrewarding positions. (Fried 1973:28)

Thus, in the 1920s and 1930s there were identifiable areas of ethnic conflict. The policies of this period cast longstanding divisions in economic terms among the urban working class with ethnic groups now competing for union protection and access to preferred jobs. Migration of blacks from rural areas to southern and northern cities led to racial conflicts. Like the foreign immigrants, rural blacks looked to the cities as sources of jobs and greater freedom. However, like the foreign immigrants, they encountered resistance from already settled urban workers who feared the loss of jobs. Many factory owners consciously exploited these tensions by using blacks as strikebreakers and as a pool of cheap labor to undercut union demands.

WORLD WAR II, MOBILIZATION, AND THE LOCATION OF NEW CITIES

Government policies had changed the directions of society, but they had not pulled the country out of its economic difficulties. It was only during the war years that the American economy bounced back from the depression era. Millions of workers were employed in war production, wages rose rapidly and, as persons on the edge of the labor market became full-fledged workers, they learned new skills. Factories and industries sprouted at urban fringes or spawned entire towns. In the interest of national security, this growth was spread all over the countryside, with the result that less developed areas of the South were favored since they were considered safer and away from possible attacks on population concentrations. The West was also favored as being closer to the war in the Pacific. The government assumed vast new powers in controlling and regulating the economy which, in turn, influenced the future shape of regional urban growth.

Perhaps the most important effects of World War II on urbanization were the seeding of new industries, the initial change in attitudes toward women working, and the rising purchasing power of millions of Americans. The industries that were born in this period included aluminum, modern aircraft and associated airline travel, synthetics, antibiotic drugs, fibers, plastics and other petrochemicals. Other industries included electronics, television and computers, nuclear energy and its spin-offs. These became the great growth industries of the 1950s and 1960s.

Since World War II the number of women added to the work force has been 21 million, while the number of men has been 14 million. This shift has been fed by many sources. It began when women had to replace the millions of men in the armed forces. After the war they either stayed on or rejoined the work force after spending ten to fifteen years starting families.

During the war many people worked overtime, goods were scarce, and much money income had to be saved. This took the form of taxes, government bonds, or voluntary savings accounts. Accumulated demand prevented the expected postwar depression, and it led to fairly smooth conversion of many war industries to consumer products such as homes, automobiles, and appliances. When the soldiers returned, many had useful skills and all were entitled to veterans' loans and educational benefits. They formed new families and continued to move into urban areas in great numbers as productive workers.

These forces—expanding role of the government, creation of new industries and technology, influx of women into the labor force, and rapidly rising expectations and family incomes—ushered in the development patterns of the last thirty years.

GOVERNMENT AND PLANNING AFTER THE WAR

Relations between city and state remained poor as many state legislatures denied cities the power to levy local taxes. State governments generally maintained a hostile, passive position with regard to urban problems. Reapportionment struggles grew more complex with suburban growth, as both cities and suburbs argued that they were underrepresented at the state level.

There was a surge of concern for metropolitan planning and regional government. A wide variety of study groups issued reports, and many proposals were developed for political consolidation, but metropolitan planning was blocked by the suburban areas. The only significant agreement was in the establishment of special-function metropolitan governments to deal with matters such as water supply and sewage. Metropolitan political fragmentation was reinforced by the growing social and economic distinctions between city and suburb. The cities were increasingly black, white working class, ethnic, and Democratic, while the suburbs were white, middle and upper middle class, Protestant, and Republican. These differences were clearly reflected in voting patterns and other expressions of economic interests.

Federal government-city relations continued to develop as funds were directed toward city planning, urban renewal for slum housing, and highway transportation, moving the federal government into the area of urban development. The Housing Act of 1949 was the first major piece of legislation aimed at the total eradication of slums and the creation of "a decent home and a suitable living environment for every American family." The act gave local redevelopment agencies the legal power of eminent domain to buy up and demolish slum areas and to offer the cleared land to private developers at a subsidized bargain price. After intense political opposition to public housing, the federal government withdrew from direct involvement and instead combined a policy of federal funding with private enterprise initiatives. The general theory behind urban renewal again showed the physical bias of planners. If slum dwellers were relocated in decent housing then, supposedly, they would start moving out of poverty and patterns of personal and social disorganization. This policy was a failure, and estimates indicate that more families were forced out of their original homes and had to resettle in other slums than were adequately housed.

Because residential redevelopment was in the hands of private businessmen oriented to making a profit, the housing constructed on cleared land was often beyond the reach of the dislocated residents. Caught between the federal bulldozer and the trickle of new low-income housing, evicted families were forced into other neighborhoods, where willing landlords cut up standard housing units into instant new slums.

Many small business people also suffered. A detailed study in Providence, Rhode Island, in the late 1950s found that one-third of all businesses displaced by urban renewal or highway construction never reopened. The 1960s became the period of what some analysts called "the community revolution" as neighborhoods of both poor blacks and whites organized to block renewal schemes and prevent the demolition of their homes.

Marc Fried's study of the grief reaction of many residents of Boston's West End raised the issue of the social and psychological costs of urban renewal. The government policy was to buy up and then demolish large sites to attract investment by private developers. A consequence was the frequent destruction of entire neighborhoods and the uprooting of people who had lived there for decades.

The political response of city dwellers to centralized planning schemes led to revised thinking among many planners. One change was the attempt to integrate physical and social planning, that is, land use and physical structures, with jobs and community development. A second change was a cycle of various types of citizen participation in the development of plans. Combined with the various programs of the "War on Poverty," planners payed greater attention to low-income residents who showed they would take to the streets if ignored. The concentration of blacks and Spanish-speaking residents in the older decaying core of major cities, matched by immigrant ethnic clusters along the edge of the core, gave urban renewal planning a permanent racial and ethnic dimension. It also permanently changed the nature of the customers of social service agencies. As Glazer and Moynihan argue:

> We must be aware that all policies in the city are inevitably policies for ethnic and race relations. This is inevitable, because the ethnic and racial groups of the city are also interest groups, based on jobs and occupations and possessions. (Glazer and Moynihan 1970:xxxiii)

Relationships among housing, employment, education, and poverty became the focus of public discussions, reflecting the post-World War II population shifts. By the 1960s blacks were more urbanized than whites in the United States. The basic trends of urban growth, plus a variety of conscious policies, maintained residential segregations. As a result new other minorities were becoming the majority population in many central cities in the 1970s. Programs in housing, education, and job training took on a racial character because of the visible concentration of poor black and Spanish-speaking residents in the urban core. This in turn triggered a resurgence of ethnic identification and ethnic-based political action as poor and moderate-income white residents fought for federal assistance to counter neighborhood blight and to promote greater job opportunities.

THE EFFECT OF ECONOMIC ORGANIZATION ON SOCIAL LIFE SINCE WORLD WAR II

During the post-World War II period, the American economy assumed its modern form. The overriding factor was the organization of businesses into stabilized giant bureaucracies. Each major sector of industry became dominated by corporations that controlled their markets and integrated their functions from the refinement of raw materials to the distribution of their products. In John Kenneth Galbraith's term, this period saw the rise of the "new industrial state."

Massive growth in the size of economic units and the importance of science and technology in the production process led to a tremendous growth in productivity. Such productivity gains were reflected in rising incomes for millions of workers, in the growing power of the corporate giants, and in changes in the occupational structure. The number of workers directly involved in production jobs began a permanent decline. New jobs were primarily in white-collar occupations such as secretary, clerk, engineer, technician, and accountant. The industrial composition shifted toward the service sector, with openings in health, education, business and personal services, and trade dominant. In sum, post-war economic trends produced a new middle class, employed in white-collar and service jobs, increasingly college educated, and concerned with upward mobility and the enjoyment of the fruits of abundance.

Economic growth and the rise of giant corporate bureaucracies also had tremendous social psychological effects on people's attitudes, personalities, and beliefs. One effect was the return of economic optimism that the depression had so undermined. Most Americans saw the benefits of economic growth reflected in their lives, and came to expect them as a permanent feature. There were other social psychological changes that more particularly affected urban life. The dominance of corporate bureaucracies as a major source of employment profoundly changed the nature of many people's loyalties and commitments, especially in the new middle class. One's job and "the company" became the organizing focus of one's energies and interests. Since career mobility often required relocating from one branch to another, dedication to one's family and neighborhood began to assume a second place. Corporations responded to the erosion of prior commitments both by providing economic rewards to those who gave them up and by providing some replacements. David Riesman noted in the 1950s the pattern of "conspicuous corporate consumption" by which a corporation sought prestige and loyalty by providing new employee benefits and services and luxurious buildings.

The mobile manager was replacing the small business entrepreneur. His career hopes clearly required close identification with the company, and a willingness to follow its dictates. Since the economic interests of the corporation extended far beyond the particular city or locale where its branches were located, its executives withdrew from formal political office and decreased their active political involvement. Political activity was reduced to a public relations and lobbying function, unless a particular issue of concern, such as a new transportation system or tax increase, developed. This is not to say that major corporations did not exercise power on the local level; however, the pattern and nature of involvement changed.

Changes in economic organization and occupational structure also caused changes in suburban social and political life. As Bensman and Vidich note, the concentration of the new middle class in suburban communities caused those communities to take on many characteristics of university towns. College-educated suburban residents maintained a strong interest in educational facilities, especially local school systems, in the arts, and in local civic affairs.

The contemporary period witnessed a further restructuring of the American economy. A key change was the rise of multinational corporations, business enterprises that have production and distribution facilities in two or more countries. The sizes of corporations and the spatial patterns of industry had long been changing. However, in the last several decades one can say that industry has transcended geography, by which is meant that more and more of the world's goods and services are being financed, produced, and distributed in more and more countries, with the production process increasingly ignoring national boundaries. This is directly significant for American urban areas for several reasons. As production and distribution facilities become "internationalized," corporations become less tied to a particular metropolitan area or even a particular country. They are more able to "shop around" both the nation and the world, looking for the most favorable mix of cheap and available labor, raw materials, tax structures, and amenities. Thus, urban areas must compete more vigorously to keep and attract industry, and local government officials act like hotel managers trying to attract the best-paying clients. In complementary fashion corporations increased their power over local governments because of the implicit threat of relocation.

INCREASING URBAN SIZE AND COMPLEXITY

Since World War II the most important changes have been continuation of the trend toward increasing urban size and complexity; shift in the main focus of growth from the older urban areas of the Northeast and Upper Midwest to the newer southern and western SMSAs; redistribution of jobs and residences within the SMSAs away from the central core areas; and upsurge of socioeconomic "urban problems" associated with the above changes.

Empirical data indicate that movement cityward is slowing down and that the density of population within urbanized areas is diminishing. However, for many of us, living in urban areas seems more crowded, more rapid, and more hectic than ever. Can we explain this puzzle? Part of the answer lies in the fact that people's impressions of changing conditions are based mainly on the observance of absolute amounts of change rather than relatives or rates. Let us consider, for example, an urban area that had a history of population growth (in thousands) such as this:

1900	4	1940	64
1910	8	1950	120
1920	16	1960	200
1930	32	1970	300

The figures show a constant growth rate (doubling each decade) from 1900 to 1940. The area then experienced a slackening in the rate in each succeeding decade. Yet from the viewpoint of the average inhabitant the addition of over 230,000 persons since 1940 would seem to have had a far greater impact on his or her life style than the earlier growth. Indeed, such urban areas usually grow in size by expanding their boundaries to accommodate rapid growth. If boundaries were not changed, the area's economic, social, and political functioning would have had to undergo truly immense changes. Redistribution of jobs and residences to higher densities would have been necessary to absorb such population surges. The rest of the answer probably lies in two other facts. First, there have been increasing speed and complexity of human interaction made possible by space age technology. Second, the specialized characteristic of the service economy era, toward which we are moving, cuts up the ways in which we experience urban life. Together, these two reinforce our perceptions of much larger, more crowded, not clearly understood urban networks.

Since 1940 about two-fifths of the states have shown continuous population concentration at high rates. Another two-fifths also show increasing concentration into urban areas, but at slowed rates, and the last fifth shows constant or declining rates of metropolitanization. The first group are mainly in the South, the Southwest, and part of the North Central region. Most of the second group are on the West Coast, in the Midwest, and in the Northeast. The last group is in New England and scattered throughout the mountain, midwestern, and southern areas.

The major sources of this growth have been natural increase and a growing intrametropolitan migration. Still, in some areas a moderate reservoir of rural sources has continued to supply a significant number of new migrants. The emerging post-World War II network has been classified in the following manner by Duncan:

1. National centers performing the function of integrating the whole network are New York, Chicago, Los Angeles, Detroit, and Philadelphia.
2. Regional metropolitan communities aiding the above centers in the coordination of the system are San Francisco, Kansas City, Minneapolis-St. Paul, Seattle, Atlanta, Dallas, and Denver.
3. Major manufacturing centers are St. Louis and Pittsburgh.

Cities become linked in complex webs of interdependencies with each providing some services and goods for the others and each, in turn, served by the others. Different metropolitan communities now perform in new regional and national ways.

SHIFTS TO THE SUNBELT CITIES

Most of us recognize the competition that exists among cities. However, until recently, few realized how important to the overall picture was the shift toward the "sunbelt" urban centers of the South and West. There, suburban age, political power, and economic strength are much greater. If, for example, boundaries of SMSAs are held constant at the 1950 locations, Ann Miller has shown that only two of the leading forty-five urban areas of the nation had a positive migration to their central cities in the fifties. These were Los Angeles and San Diego. All the other sunbelt cities expanded their cores by annexation.

In addition to annexation, the sunbelt urban regions grew very rapidly. A number of factors can be identified in explaining their growth. One is the abundance of natural resources and/or favorable climate (oil, chemicals, lower land prices). A second is access by manufacturers to a relatively low-paid, less-organized work force and a very attractive tax and business atmosphere. A third is the development of new industries (for example, aircraft and space) that were mainly spurred by highly cooperative (and one might suspect, politically motivated) congressional decisions. (Key committees for national defense and public works spending were under the control of sunbelt legislators.) Perhaps underestimated were technological advances such as reliable, effective air conditioning to make the year-round living environment more comfortable. Reinforcing the above was the increase in services associated with the climate, amenities, growing population, and manufacturing industries.

The older northern tier has suffered in two ways. The slowdown in growth has seemed abrupt as capital investment and industrial expansion have not provided the private push toward renewing their aging urban centers. Public enterprise at the state and local levels tried to fill the gap, but, largely due to antiquated structures, inefficient functioning, and no way to improve productivity, it has failed. Finally, federal disinterest, ineptitude, and other priorities have prevailed. In this period, as throughout our history, urbanization has been unplanned and undirected. However, since World War II the effect of federal action has been to spur population and economic growth in the sunbelt region, which has deeply affected relationships among regions and their future course of development.

> The fact that the North continues to send money into the Sunbelt states through the Federal Government—a "prime-the-pump" philosophy that has redistributed wealth under the Federal system from the richer states to the poorer ones—may contain the seeds of a regionally divisive issue. In 1974 alone, the Sunbelt states collected from Washington in excess of $13 billion more than they contributed in Federal taxes. . . . There's going to be a terrific political issue when the Northeast wakes up to the fact that it's being milked to death for tax money going outside the region at a time when it's having a tough time paying for its own needs. (*New York Times,* February 8, 1975:42)

Table 6–2 shows the marked differences between the population growth rates of the six leading SMSAs in both areas for the last two decades and their respective sizes in 1970.

Several national patterns are quite apparent. One is the emptying of the Great Plains region, the industrialization of the Old South, and the emergence of several new major metropolitan concentrations. These new population centers are all in the sunbelt or southern crescent extending from Florida through Arizona and up the West Coast. In quantitative terms the southern and western centers increased their

TABLE 6–2   Regional Growth Patterns

	North and East SMSAs[*]	South and West SMSAs[**]
Population, 1970 (thousands)	33,184	16,525
Inside Central Cities	16,120	7,358
Outside Central Cities	17,064	9,167
Percentage Change, 1950–60	17.2	43.8
Inside Central Cities	-3.4	29.4
Outside Central Cities	59.3	61.3
Percentage Change, 1960–70	11.8	26.8
Inside Central Cities	-2.1	14.3
Outside Central Cities	29.0	38.9

[*]New York, Chicago, Philadelphia, Detroit, Washington, D.C., Boston.
[**] Los Angeles-Long Beach, San Francisco-Oakland, Houston, Dallas, Seattle-Everett, Anaheim-Santa Ana-Garden Grove.
SOURCE: U.S. Bureau of the Census, *Census of the United States, 1970* (Washington, D.C.: Government Printing Office).

size more than twice as rapidly as the northern and eastern ones in both the 1950–60 and 1960–70 decades. In the fifties almost all the growth differential was in the central city areas, but in the sixties the differences spread to the surrounding metropolitan areas. Two cautions in interpretation must be added. If the New York area (which is in a unique national position) is subtracted from the North and East, the remaining five just about equalled in size the six largest of the South and West. Second, much of the central city growth of the South and West of the fifties and sixties has been by annexation. This option was not really open to the older centers.

Yet, there will be a growing balance in the urban network among regions of the country that may bring good results in the long run. As the South and North and East and West exchange people and ideas in larger volume, a greater appreciation of the common urban experience may emerge. The hectic, growth-oriented era of the last generation may evolve into one where a more equitable national distribution of resources and people will prevail. This may help all regions in the continuing quest for a better quality for urban life.

EXPLANATIONS OF THE REDISTRIBUTION OF JOBS AND RESIDENCES WITHIN THE SMSAs

The nature of the American metropolis in the 1970s reflects the consumer choices of the past generation: single-family homes, open spaces, and private automobiles all express American individualism and freedom. This, however, has also led to problems in every area, from pollution to residential segregation. The metropolis of the seventies also reflects government policies. Subsidized middle-class housing; interstate highway systems; real estate tax systems that reward landlords for letting properties turn into slums; subsidized trucking industries and large-scale farming; tax loopholes and incentives for industrial and banking firms; rapid expansion of public higher education—the list is long. At times these have increased mobility, and at other times they have created barriers to a better-quality urban life.

The present metropolis also reflects past decisions of the business sector. Here the recent tendency has been for more and more industrial firms to become foot-loose within the metropolis in comparison with earlier eras. No longer must decisions be based mainly on access to materials, rail transportation, sources of power, or even supplies of labor. More frequently, other factors dominate. Land costs are lower in the suburbs for firms needing space to expand or shift technology. Higher levels of income among suburban buyers or higher occupational skill levels among suburban workers attract firms that find market factors dominant in location decisions. Center city locations are needed mainly for businesses requiring maximum managerial and other firm interactions.

Linked to the changes in business are changes in the household sector. Since World War II family income has doubled (after taking inflation into consideration). Expanded discretionary spending has led to more demands for living space, mobility, and services (such as education, medical care, and entertainment), which, in turn, have produced a considerable shift in the demand and consumption patterns of urban households. Technological gadgetry for the home, women working, government subsidies, and tax incentives released supply constraints. This provided further stimulus to certain kinds of output, and redistribution of residences and jobs followed. Each reinforced the other through the service sector expansion.

These changes have had different impacts on the various levels in society. The classes (lower, middle, and upper) view the urban scene from differing perspectives, and their experiences have been quite varied. We see the classes as mainly distinguished by income, education, and occupation. Upper-class families make up the smallest group in numbers, but they represent more of the leaders and decision makers than the other classes. The upper class led the flight to the suburbs, and from their viewpoint it was a rational decision; commuting time was down (thanks largely to federal highways), income was up. New houses and lots were more desirable for growing families and cheaper than rebuilding older housing. Therefore, those in the upper class used their incomes to buy the most desirable suburban land. But members of the group wanted to continue to use the resources of the city for work, play, and absorbing culture; thus, they became advocates of a "cleaner, nicer" central city.

Middle-class families represent the largest portion of the metropolitan population. Since World War II they have improved dramatically their private standards of living. This made them largely indifferent to the decline in their public lives as urban dwellers. Their homes became more spacious and beautiful, and inside, there were more consumer durables. However, their streets became dirty and damaged, their air polluted, their educational and crime-fighting systems began to break down. Today, the urban amenities are of highly irregular and haphazard quality.

Lower-class families are fewer in numbers than the middle class, but because of the income-segregating forces of the modern metropolis, they are more apparent than ever before. The poor and the near poor have uncertain incomes, bleak futures, and few skills. They have been helped little by upper-class reforms, and renewals and social welfare programs have fostered a defeatist attitude. Job ladders have broken down and educational systems are swamped with difficulties. Exploiting interests, intentional and unintentional, have multiplied, with the riots of the sixties bringing only inaction in the seventies.

URBAN PROBLEMS IN THE METROPOLITAN SETTING

Such has been the diversity of the American metropolitan experience since World War II. It is difficult to generalize about it. However, a half dozen key changes have emerged that cut across traditional problem areas. Traditional kinds of problems would be in the areas of crime, housing, pollution, transportation, jobs, health care, race and ethnicity, ghettos, taxes, and education. All of these may be encountered in numerous readers on urban studies or urban issues.

Some common analytical themes running through many of these problem areas can illuminate the common nature of some of the causes of metropolitan problems. These themes are:

Special American Traits. Each problem area is marked by several "American" traits, unique among modernized countries. These include ethnically mixed cities with a high potential for private mobility; cities that are more spread out in space; and a legal atmosphere that in its devotion to property rights makes social change difficult.

Conflicts between Social and Economic Goals.   Urban living requires expressed public goals and a sense of ownership of the whole city by its people. Many urban issues arise because of conflicts between such social goals and economic interests. Such tensions are expressed concretely in terms of job choice and residential choice. The city has in recent decades segregated itself more and more by economic criteria as its traditional social-neighborhood-oriented criteria have broken down. Some no longer see an affirmative role in their neighborhood, nor do they see many chances of upward movement in the economic sphere.

Lack of Public Choice Mechanism.   The modern metropolis has no institutional mechanism that successfully reflects public choices in the way that the marketplace reflects private choices. For example, it is difficult for citizens to exercise control over the quality and cost of public services.

Low Productivity of Urban Services.   Once the benefits of economies of scale are fully realized by our large cities, an increasing proportion of their budgets are devoted to human services. Such urban services are not as subject to productivity increases as are manufacturing or farming. We do not know how to develop the human equivalent of mechanization that would increase the output per worker of a high school teacher, social worker, or police officer unless we make substitutes for the output mix or change the method of delivering the services.

Spillover Costs.   In the private marketplace, where the dollar votes, a larger and larger number of exchanges are affecting not only the consumer and producer, but third parties as well. For example, unrestricted use of automobiles within urban regions, where they rarely pay their full social costs, has produced many spillover costs. It has led to the end of good public transit, the waste of vast amounts of resources, and the denial of jobs to the nonauto-owning poor.

Political Fragmentation.   A final reason that much of the city does not work is because the roles played by the government at the three levels (local, state, and federal) are ill-defined and confused. They overlap, conflict, compete, and leave major gaps through which the less fortunate tend to fall into desperate ways.

The themes enumerated above can be thought of as the modern expression of the imbalance among the three classic functions of the city. Urban problems are deep-seated and reflect the negative consequences of unbalanced growth, the age and size of urban areas, and lack of coordination among functions. It is to these topics that we now turn.

CHAPTER SEVEN

Sources of Urban Growth and the Evolving Network of Cities

There is a sense of crisis within many metropolitan areas. Some of this may be due to the gap between people's expectations and perceptions of their immediate urban condition. But we believe that the sources go deeper.

The quality of urban life is rooted in the fundamental functioning of cities. Cities must be able to raise the level of living of their residents above what they would experience in a nonurban setting. Ideally, this should be done with both style and grace. Unfortunately, this rarely occurs. To our knowledge a well-styled and graceful quality in urban living has been simultaneously available only for the upper classes at certain points in our history.

Today there are many indications that the older American urban areas are not successfully fulfilling their functions. We have labeled these functions interactive, generative, and upgrading. Let us briefly review them and see if we can identify the causes of our urban problems.

Cities provide meeting and exchange places. They offer economies of scale in the processes of settling, living, working, and learning. They generate, through this interactive function, externalities for the firm and the household, making a wide range of choices possible. In addition, they generate in themselves public and private services of great variety and with great efficiency. Cities give the individual the opportunity for privacy, a maximum occupational pool to choose from, and a large number of alternative life styles to develop. New ways of doing things, new inventions, ideologies, and cultural changes grow in an urban environment. Cities have been true centers for our civilizations.

Probably the most important function of the city in recent decades has been the upgrading function. Cities have taken the relatively poor from rural parts of the world and helped train, educate, and make them into more productive human beings. As nonagricultural jobs have expanded, large urban-industrial complexes have upgraded millions of workers. Sometimes it took decades, sometimes even lifetimes, but more people improved their conditions and helped one another in the urban environment than ever would have been possible in the countryside. Today this last function does not seem to be working as well as it did for previous generations. Public policy and private goals are not meeting in a coordinated fashion. Generative, interactive, and upgrading activities are seemingly in conflict or, at least, they are not complementing each other as they should.

Life in almost any city in the United States has become a battle for survival. For the poor, aged, handicapped, and children in broken families, the battle is continuous. It has turned into a war with the physical, social, and economic environment that is as real as any foreign entanglement. And we are all experiencing the results of this continuing struggle. The costs created by our urban problems are outstripping the benefits we should receive from the proper functioning of our cities.

It is here, in the ability of society to once again make the city successful in integrating its three classic functions, and especially to promote its upgrading function, that the roots of the urban crisis lie. Furthermore, we believe that an analysis of the recent process of metropolitanization is needed to understand why the city in general (and some cities in particular) do not perform as well as they could.

This chapter focuses on the three sources of growth in the modern period; these are immigration, internal migration, and changing fertility rates. It then describes and analyzes how this growth redistributed itself among the parts of the evolving urban network, suggesting some explanations for these trends within the framework of changing relative economic opportunities.

PERSPECTIVES ON IMMIGRATION AND MIGRATION

Since the 1920s the most important new source of urban growth has been the internal migration of blacks. There also has been a continued strong role for immigration from foreign lands. This foreign immigration is frequently overlooked in explanations of recent changes in American urban areas, and we will examine it in some detail. These movements are important because the upgrading function has meant, in the case of the United States, the attempted *acculturation* of peoples of diverse ethnic backgrounds into the American mainstream.

At the heart of many urban tensions today is the upward mobility of black and Spanish-speaking Americans. Many have an overriding wish to join the economic middle class, without necessarily adopting the accompanying *melting pot* value system. They do not want their cultural traditions "melted down." However, *cultural pluralism* requires a degree of economic security and the satisfaction of basic human needs as necessary prerequisites to a group's searching out meaningful spheres of activity through which it can develop a collective identity. Therefore, black and Spanish-speaking Americans, like other ethnic groups before them, look to the cities for needed job, educational, and housing opportunities. In turn, the health of our cities is tied to their abilities to respond to this demand while continuing to provide the jobs and services required by other groups.

Experts differ on the amount of openness in our social structure today as compared to yesteryear. They also differ on the question of whether or not there is a legitimate historical comparison between earlier immigrants and present-day minorities. Some point out that blacks have been here since the country began, and have a heritage of oppression. Others note that most urban, industrialized black families are only one generation away from rural poverty and lack of skills. Thus, they say, no immigrant ethnic group has done any better in upgrading in our urban history.

We will deal with this question in two ways. One is to examine the relation between patterns of growth and the performance of urban functions. The other is to put into historical perspective the black internal migration from southern rural areas to northern and western cities and compare that movement with the experience of foreign immigrants.

THE URBAN IMPACT OF CHANGING IMMIGRATION PATTERNS

From 1820 to 1970 immigrants totaled about 46 million, or 3 million per decade. From 1950 to 1970 the trend continued (there were almost 6 million new immigrants). Most of these immigrants settled into metropolitan areas in patterns similar to their forefathers'. This recent influx had significant impact on both population distribution and the labor supply in various cities and regions. Let us examine these changes in historical perspective. Around the turn of the century, four states received 65 percent of all migrants. Today the top four states receive 58 percent. The leading state, New York, earlier gained 31 percent of the migrants and now gets 24 percent. The biggest changes have been the increase of migrants in California from 3 percent to 22 percent and the irrelative decline of Pennsylvania from 18 to 3 percent. This last shift is traceable to changing long-run economic opportunities associated with the redistribution of industry westward.

Foreign migration has also had a great impact on the labor force because immigrant workers represent over 70 percent of all adult immigrants. Among natives the figure is about 40 percent. Therefore the immigrant has contributed a disproportionately large share of the total increase in the work force in recent years. Further, this was distributed so that it had a significantly greater effect on certain specific occupational categories, as well as certain local labor markets. Cities such as Chicago, San Francisco, and especially New York found such workers to be a significant proportion of net new jobholders in the late 1960s and early 1970s. The occupational distribution for a recent sample follows in Table 7-1.

These data indicate that the vast majority of the new immigrants were skilled. Of those who declared themselves workers, a full three-fourths were from white-collar or skilled blue-collar backgrounds. This is to be expected since the main requirement for admission is either to have an employment guarantee or to be in an occupation with a shortage declared by the U.S. Department of Labor. What each immigrant does represent is a net gain in human investment since some other land raised and educated him or her, thus saving us those

TABLE 7–1   Percentage Distribution of Adult Immigrants, 1969

	Entry	*1972 Registration*
White collar	25	28
Skilled blue collar	21	27
Unskilled blue collar	8	11
Service	7	12
Nonworkers	39	22
Total	100	100

SOURCE: Derived from D. North and W. Weissert, *Immigrants and the American Labor Market* (Washington, D.C.: Trans-Century Corp., 1973), pp. 100–1.

resources. Comparison of the two columns shows that between entry and later registration, recent newcomers secure jobs at least equal to their prior training. It also suggests that many declared nonworking adults (housewives and students) find work attractive or necessary soon after arriving.

A rise in occupational level and convergence toward the work force profile of the general population were the most significant changes in long-run immigration patterns. Table 7–2 lists occupational groupings of all immigrants and the general population in contrasting time periods.

The first period is 1910–30, when there were no significant restrictions. The modern period is one of highly selective in-movement, when changes in areas of origin and labor force skills act as legal as well as "natural" filters to the ebb and flow. The differences are striking between a typical immigrant in the early period and in the later one. This is especially so in categories such as professional and technical, household service, nonfarm laborer, and farm work. So sharp was the rise of the skill levels in the later period that they exceeded the white-collar share of the general population (45 percent versus 40 percent), though in the earlier decades they were less than one-half (12 percent versus 26 percent).

The current movement tends to be more family-oriented than that of the pre-World War II era (there are more housewives, students, and children), so it has been claimed that proportionately fewer immi-

TABLE 7-2   Occupational Comparisons (in percent)

| | 1910–30 | | 1940–70 | |
	Immigrants	General Population	Immigrants	General Population
White collar	12	26	45	40
Skilled blue collar	21	27	27	31
Unskilled and service	45	21	19	19
Farm	22	26	9	10

SOURCE: Derived from D. North and W. Weissert, *Immigrants and the American Labor Market* (Washington, D.C.: Trans-Century Corp., 1973), pp. 92–93.

grants would work today than around 1900. However, on arriving, women increase their labor force role and the net result in labor force participation is about the same.

These migrants came for the same kinds of reasons that their forebears did—economic opportunity and potential for a better life. Sometimes spurred by persecution or economic disaster at home, they were pulled by job openings in our major metropolises.

When we consider that current immigration is continuing at over 3 million per decade, while fertility is declining, the future impact of this source of labor may be even greater. If current natural increase and immigration trends continue, estimates are that about one-fourth of all population growth and up to one-third of all labor force growth could come from foreign lands in the next generation. Since World War II important new streams have been added to the traditional flows. Most significant has been the increase in Spanish-speaking persons from Latin America. Not contained by a quota system, these newcomers from all the islands in the Caribbean and Mexico have made up a rising share of the totals.

Another factor indicating the pressures generating such flows was the substantial increase in illegal aliens. This figure can only be approximated, but recent analysis suggests it may be as great as the legal immigrants in size. If this is so, the next decade may see the real effects of foreign sources of labor reaching higher levels than we have experienced since before World War I.

THE PATHS AND PATTERNS OF INTERNAL MIGRATION

Until the mid-1950s the internal migration patterns of Americans were fairly straightforward and easily understood. The South was the main origin area, and many tended to move from rural to urban areas in a series of steps: first was farm to village to small town within the native region, then came a longer journey to a northeastern or midwestern city. Most of these migrants were black. If they lived in Mississippi, Alabama, or Louisiana, they would usually end up in the cities of the Great Lakes crescent, such as Chicago, Detroit, or Cleveland. If they were born in Georgia, the Carolinas, or Virginia, they tended to flock to the megalopolis, the northeastern seaboard complex, to cities such as New York, Philadelphia, Washington, and Baltimore.

In the past twenty years the migration map has changed dramatically. First, most moves have become urban to urban, with many leaps across regional boundaries in all different directions. Second, there has been a consistent hollowing out of the interior of the nation, with the cities of the Gulf Coast and western rim states replacing the northern and eastern borders as the main destinations. Third, there has been a substantial reverse flow from the Northeast and North Central regions to the South. This flow has been made up mainly of white migrants who have found good job opportunities in the rapidly expanding centers of the new South. Since 1970 the outstanding upward shifts in metropolitan ranks among the top 100 have been located in a handful of states. Ten are in Florida, Texas, and Arizona, with one each in South Carolina, California, and New Mexico. The only other rapid growth metropolitan areas are two much smaller ones in Colorado. These have become the migration destinations of the 1970s.

What do we know about the typical resident's mobility? From *Public Health Monograph* No. 77, "Migration in the United States: An Analysis of Residence Histories," we conclude that average residents live in two or three different households over their life spans, and that typically such people are more mobile the further west their current residences are located. We also know that people from different geographic backgrounds have different mobility patterns.

The highly mobile group varies by region (16 percent in the East, 44 percent in the West). Another part tends to stay put in one residence. Again this varies by region (34 percent in the Northeast, 9 percent in the West). Of all size categories, persons in metropolitan areas in communities of 2,500 to 50,000 had the highest number of residences, while people in the largest cities of 500,000 and over had the lowest. Small-town folk move more frequently than large metropolitan area dwellers.

Another way of looking at residential mobility patterns is to examine the farm to town to metropolis urbanization data over a family's life cycle. Analysis of the data in "Lifetime Migration Histories of the American People" (*C.P.R. Technical Studies* Series P-23, No. 25) reveals a comprehensive picture of the nature of internal migration patterns. There are three kinds of people: those who do not move (28 percent), those who move within their own type of area, be it farm, town, or SMSA (29 percent), and the largest number, who move out of their area of origin (43 percent). This last group is of most interest to us. They had as destinations the following patterns: moved back to farms, 2 percent; moved to towns, 14 percent; moved to SMSAs, 21 percent; moved in a circle (for example, town to SMSA to town, ending where they started), 6 percent.

CHARACTERISTICS OF THE MIGRANTS

At the base of the Statue of Liberty in New York harbor are the famous words of Emma Lazarus:

> Give me your tired, your poor,
> Your huddled masses yearning to breathe free . . .
> The wretched refuse of your teeming shore

Perhaps we instinctively have extended this picture of the immigrant (and it is only partially correct) to the internal migrant of the last fifty years. Perhaps we are always ready to blame our deep-rooted urban problems on newcomers. In any event, many Americans seem to feel that migrants are relatively low-skilled poor people who generate difficulties for a city—especially if they are easily discernible by color or language. Facts about the skills, education, and demographic characteristics of the typical internal migrants of the post-World War II era are worthy of our attention.

Skills

The proportions of laborers, unskilled, and unemployed are above the average levels of the areas from which they originated and of those where they are going. There are an above average number of professional and technical workers with high educational backgrounds attracted to the largest metropolitan areas. Craftsmen and machine operators are also well represented, especially among blacks. There appear to be shortages of salespersons, managers, officials, and proprietors among most migrant groupings.

Education

Whether white or black, the migrant is more educated than the population left behind. In fact, they are frequently above the level of average schooling in the receiving areas. This characteristic is perhaps to be expected because migrants are highly concentrated (about one-half) in the prime working ages; hence, they have benefited from the most recent and highest levels of educational opportunity.

Demographic Characteristics

Resulting from the age distribution is the fact that, with the exception of special cases such as the Cuban and Puerto Rican movements, there is a relatively small family component. These three factors—education, skills, and demographic characteristics—hold for whites and blacks. However, whites have distinct advantages over blacks, as they do in the population as a whole. We conclude that the myth of the low-skilled, uneducated migrant can be dangerous, particularly when placing blame on a specific group carries with it the idea that solutions are easy to come by. So also modern attempts to stop migration and blame problems in the city on newcomers will not make cities function any better.

The most mobile can be identified more carefully within the metropolitan community by their stage in the family life cycle and by their
socioeconomic status. Clearly, three points in the life cycle tend to
dominate moves: marriage (household formation), maturing of children (family size dwindles), and retirement are the most important
decision-making stages. In addition, the two extremes of the socioeconomic ladder tend to be most highly mobile. Well-educated corporate
and professional types and blue-collar workers of moderate skill levels
and lesser education stand out. They may well reflect the two extremes
of the labor market situation: excess demand in the destinations and
excess supply in the origin areas. This last analysis shifts us from the
characteristics of the migrants to the reasons why they move.

CAUSES OF RECENT MOBILITY

People move because migration works for them. It improves the lot
of most people who decide in favor of it. Yes, there are problems with
migration, for the migrant, for the areas they leave, and for the areas
they arrive at. However, within about five years the migrants are no
longer newcomers. They are usually settled members of a community,
are earning more money, and are fairly well assimilated.

Most migrants move for economic reasons. Most have jobs waiting
for them or obtain new ones quickly. As we have seen, the new
migrant, contrary to some popular myths, is not as likely as the
long-term resident to be poor, unemployed, or on welfare. Careful
studies of a comparative nature show this to be true in almost all cases.
Available data, as in R. Wertheimer, *The Monetary Rewards of Migration Within the United States* (1971), show more clearly than words
the nature of the economic differentials that typical interstate migrants experienced by the 1960s. Gains rose with city size and education, and they were about as high for black males as for white. For
white males typical wage gains were from $1,500 to $3,700, for black
males from $1,550 to $3,000.

In the longer run a comprehensive analysis of net migration trends
and long swings since the Civil War (three volumes by Lee et al.,
Population Redistribution and Economic Growth) showed clearly that
the net migration movements responded to changes in income levels

and new job creation between regions. And blacks respond more to such changes than whites.

Of course some people choose climate, others to be with friends, and yet others may choose a particular city for its amenities. However, the evidence suggests that living conditions, such as housing and public services, play only a small part in determining the number of migrants to a particular SMSA. In the words of an outstanding researcher:

> Job opportunities produce the main flows of migrants in most parts of the world; they certainly do so in the United States. Whatever else may influence their decisions to move, the overwhelming majority of families migrate when the breadwinner is taking a new job or looking for work. When pollsters ask newcomers to a city why they came, the newcomers usually answer in terms of jobs. Long-distance migration normally speeds up in times of economic expansion and slows down in times of economic contraction. (Tilly 1976:350)

The above conclusions seem to hold whether one interviews the migrants themselves in depth or whether one investigates the objective conditions surrounding large numbers of migratory moves. Overall growth of the economy in a metropolitan area tightens the labor market quite rapidly. Given today's means of information exchange, the word gets out through formal and informal communication linkages. The sharp turnaround in the economy of certain SMSAs between the 1960s and early 1970s, as illustrated in Table 7–3, suggests this sensitivity.

TABLE 7–3 Changing Migration Patterns of SMSAs

	Average Annual Net Migration (thousands)	
SMSA	1960–70	1970–73
Sharp reversals	+10	-35
Continued expansion	+21	+34
Slowdowns	+39	+18

SOURCE: Derived from U.S. Department of Commerce, *Statistical Abstract of the United States, 1975* (Washington, D.C.: Government Printing Office, 1975).

Such net migration figures are among the best available indicators of the social and economic health of a given metropolitan area. This table shows that the early seventies produced three different patterns among these SMSAs: Los Angeles, Philadelphia, Seattle, Chicago, and St. Louis were the sharp reversals; Dallas-Fort Worth, Anaheim, Baltimore, Houston, San Jose, and Washington, D.C., were the slow-downs; and Tampa, Denver, San Diego, Atlanta, and Miami were those of continued expansion. No national policy informs potential migrants of such changes, and in the sharp economic reversal of 1974–75 many of these areas suffered severe problems with too many new arrivals. With unemployment over 10 percent, the lags in information feeding back did not sufficiently discourage in-migrants.

MIGRANTS IN THE METROPOLITAN ENVIRONMENT

The city has had a varied and generally positive impact on most migrants and they have adjusted fairly well to metropolitan ways. Yet we can see clearly that a great ethnic diversity is still strong in our urban areas. Although Americans today live in a pluralistic culture, they have not been "melted down" by the urbanization process. They still retain and are renewing many of the traditions and customs of their origins. In many ways the migrants and their children have advanced their standards of living. Better health and education, more skilled occupations, and higher incomes have been the lot of most. Some, however, have fallen behind.

One classic myth should be put to rest, and that is the idea that newcomers suffer all kinds of social and mental disturbances as a result of relocating. Careful analysis of unemployment, family stability, delinquency, crime, and other such indicators fails to show any significant differences between recent arrivals (under five years) and long-term residents. In fact, in each of these areas the data show that there is less social disorganization for those who move long distances than for nonmovers in destination areas. While there is greater social disorder in areas of high turnover, the mobile group is not the cause. One conclusion, then, might be that it is primarily the poor quality of the social environment into which the migrant comes that eventually fosters the urban problems said to be dominant in ethnic clusters.

Migrants have had significant effects upon the shaping of metropolitan America, both quantitatively and qualitatively. They provided key elements in the growth of the metropolitan labor force, and contributed to the rapidly growing household sector, leading to the expansion of construction, home furnishings, and consumer goods. This in turn stimulated urban trade and commercial services, as well as education, health, and public services such as transport, fire, and police protection.

Naturally, all this was not accomplished without costs. Crowding; segregation; the flight of the middle class to the suburbs; the blending of slums, ghettos, poor areas, and old industrial belts into giant, decaying bands between CBDs and higher-income, exclusively zoned suburbs—the list is long and requires analysis of the internal changes in metropolitan areas (see Chapter Eight).

Most of the post-World War II migrants adjusted well to the new environment. The city made good use of their talents and provided potential paths for upward social mobility. Those coming from the countryside to the city are frequently assimilated into the urban social structure through working-class communities since these provide the places of entry to the industrial world of work. They are centered on close-knit neighborhood social relationships, usually based on extended families, church, and local organizations. In the words of Marc Fried, they are based on "the ready availability of members, the binding set of expectations for mutual assistance and dependability in emergencies" (Fried 1973:18).

However, other kinds of adjustment mechanisms of a more impersonal nature are possible: skills in handling urban institutions, finding jobs through newspapers and agencies, and such can take the place of a friendly community. What appears is that the paths, both economic and social, to upward social mobility frequently lead out of traditional neighborhoods. Therefore, the very nature of assimilation into the wider urban society tends to break down certain ethnic values through the pursuit of the new occupational roles of metropolitan life.

Another aspect of the interaction of the newcomer and the city arises when we view this upward mobility question at close range. The migrants traditionally have filled the bottom rungs of the ladder when they first entered the metropolitan environment. Knowing less about the city, frequently being without the skills to find their way among urban institutions, feeling left out and discriminated against, they have had to fill in wherever openings appeared in the job market. This we know. However, we are less sure of their upward mobility patterns. This is especially so for the black migrants since World War II. Until 1960, census data enabled us to distinguish occupational upgrading between generations for the foreign-born and foreign stock, but no such categories separate blacks into recent and earlier migrant groupings.

It is possible, however, to make this distinction for one new minority: the Puerto Ricans who have moved to the mainland are broken down into those born in Puerto Rico and those born here. (By definition, anyone with one parent born in Puerto Rico is declared Puerto Rican.) A careful analysis of census data of the occupational profiles of those born on the island (comparable to foreign-born) and those born on the mainland (comparable to foreign stock) suggests that this group made progress between 1950 and 1970 comparable to almost any made by earlier immigrant groups during the first generation after arrival.

In the few studies done of black mobility that take into consideration the timing of migration, the picture is more mixed, with some substantial progress and some retrogression. In New York, for example, black females made significant penetration (greater percentage gains than whites) into white-collar clerical, sales, and professional categories in this period. To a great extent they were moving out of the household service category of their rural and small-town mothers. However, black males, while moving out of laborers' jobs, tended to concentrate in operative (semiskilled, blue-collar) categories. They did not make as much headway into the white-collar fields as their sisters or as their white urban counterparts.

These are important considerations around which the resolution of many policies revolves. The openness of our socioeconomic system, the long-term needs for quotas and special hiring practices, and the whole strategy for reinforcing the upgrading and generative functions of cities are all at stake. At present we need more research to help guide our policy and our politics on these matters.

THE GROWING IMPORTANCE OF NATURAL INCREASE IN METROPOLITAN GROWTH

Before leaving the sources of city growth, it is necessary to describe and analyze the role played by natural increase in recent decades. Traditionally cities only grew by migration, with death rates about matching birth rates. Since the 1930s natural increase has played an increasing role.

By the 1960s natural increase accounted for 75 percent of all metropolitan area population increases. (Changes in the fertility rates that were part of this are discussed below.) Migration from abroad accounted for 14 percent, and internal movement about 11 percent. However, this statement overlooks differences between whites and blacks and among different sections of the country. Migration accounted for 21 percent of the white increase and for 42 percent of the nonwhite, and almost all of the latter was internal.

By the 1960s natural increase and migration accounted for the following proportions of net metropolitan growth in each of the major regions:

	Migration	Natural Increase
Northeast	3	97
Midwest	2	98
West	50	50
South	30	70

The West and South had high rates of immigration to metropolitan areas for whites and blacks. The picture was:

	West	South
Whites	48	38
Blacks	58	10

Thus natural increase became the main source (52 percent) of population increase for urban areas (for whites, 58 percent; for blacks, only 25 percent). Examining these factors in more detail, one finds that from the 1930s to the 1950s, the roles of migration and natural increase varied greatly as elements in metropolitan growth. Ann Miller in her monograph (Miller 1964) makes a number of important contributions to the analysis of the role of the sources of urban growth. First, she adjusts for annexations, keeping SMSA size constant. Second, by analyzing age groupings, she adds the important insight that the age group twenty to thirty-four, when most people enter the labor force, shows positive migration even when the overall figures are negative. The rates of these age groups are always two or three times as high as the average and sometimes much higher. Of the total net flow, persons aged twenty to thirty-four made up over 70 percent for whites and over 56 percent for blacks. She suggests the interplay of migration and natural increase as follows:

> To summarize, population gains for whites ten years of age and over in
> the forty-five areas came primarily from natural increase during the
> 1930s and 1950s and primarily from migration during the 1940s but the
> factors underlying the differences among the decades varied. (Miller
> 1964:5)

Most of the natural increase in the population since World War II that has fostered metropolitan growth originated in changing fertility rates. The sharp upsurge in the birth rate between the end of World War II and the late fifties has been called the "American baby boom." It was followed by a sharp decrease in the sixties, which continued into the seventies. In the mid-seventies the fertility rate was down to the very lowest levels in our history, comparable to those of the Great Depression. Needless to say, such a fluctuation had profound effects on metropolitan regions.

The echoes of such a fertility swing work their way through the age groups in a population. Thus, between 1965 and 1970 there was an increase in the eighteen- to twenty-five-year-olds of almost 22 percent. Between 1970 and 1975 the impact was in the twenty-five to thirty age group, and since 1975 the age groups after age thirty are beginning to swell. Eventually there will be a dramatic increase in the numbers eligible for Social Security (probably in the first decade of the next century).

Between 1955 and 1970 the problems and opportunities connected with the younger age groups came into their own: the need to find more room in which to live—movement to more open spaces and bigger houses; the need to increase educational and recreational capacities; the problems of juvenile delinquency and vandalism; the challenge of integrating large groups of young workers into employment markets; the creation of a baby, then child, then youth, then young adult market. And no sooner were these adjustments made in urban living when the needs started to diminish and the challenge became one of reallocating shrinking resources to new needs while still effectively using old facilities. Since 1970 the work force has felt a major impact of this ripple effect. As young marrieds have faced relatively poor economic growth, they have slowed down family formation, with the result that urban construction has slid sharply downward. The work force has increased rapidly, but so has unemployment as trained and skilled workers force less trained and unskilled workers out of jobs. Other, older workers have stopped seeking work, and still others have been shut out of jobs. Educational expansion has halted and all urban schools suffer as low enrollment forces consolidation and sometimes leads to conflict. Much of the explanation for these changes lies in the directions taken by Richard Easterlin.

He suggests that the interaction of young peoples' aspirations for goods (tastes for material things) with their actual affluence is a key relation. Their actual affluence can be seen largely as the interaction of their numbers and skills in the labor market relative to older groups (their competitors in a sense) and the general level of economic growth creating labor demand.

A pattern of interaction can be drawn thus:

	1920s	1930s	World War II to Mid-1950s	Mid-1950s to Mid-1970s
Tastes for goods	High	High	Low	High
Income growth	Normal	Low	High	Normal
Fertility	Normal	Low	High	Low
Number of young workers and skills relative to older workers	Normal	Normal	Low	High

In summation, prior fertility determines current age structure and thus the ratio of younger to older workers. This ratio operates through the labor market to raise or lower the relative income levels of these two groups. Current income is measured against what one hoped to receive. This latter is determined largely by the individual's historical experience when growing up (the father's or older worker's prior income). The interaction of current income and aspirations for material goods determines fertility. As Easterlin has suggested, the evidence of the American case since 1920 seems to support such a causal chain. This implies that swings in fertility have replaced migration swings as the dynamic segment in the demographic forces in urban areas. It also implies that judgments about the early cessations in urban population growth may be premature.

Such changes in the components and rates of urban population change have great impact on the social and economic institutions in our society. The resulting changes in age distribution may lead to declines in educational priorities and increases in health care needs. Residential and housing patterns also change as the proportion of two-career and one-or-two-children families increases. The nature of the urban market also shifts, as do labor force characteristics. Industry responds in the usual manner, generating new products and services, opening some plants and closing others. These forces accumulate in rearranging the distribution of population and jobs among the varied cities in the entire national network.

A DESCRIPTION OF THE EVOLVING NETWORK OF CITIES

Patterns of specialization have been changing within the modern city network over the past fifty years as the maturing national economy generated growth in a variety of ways. The demand for steel aided expansion in centers such as Pittsburgh and Cleveland, and increased use of the automobile spurred on Detroit and Akron (the latter specializing in tire products). The regional centers of Dallas, Houston, and Tulsa benefited from the demand for oil, and drew many rural southern migrants. New commercial and service activities aided growth in a variety of regional centers such as Cincinnati, Indianapolis, Minneapolis, Portland, and Seattle. There was also rapid expansion in recreational centers such as Miami, St. Petersburg, Tampa, Phoenix, and Las Vegas. These areas attracted both an increasing number of tourists and many retired persons who settled there permanently.

What happened to the leading cities of 1970? The first forty, which represented almost all of those above 25,000 city population in 1870, developed into the leading thirty-five SMSAs of 1970. Three notable overall trends were the relative stability in the top third; the appearance of new centers to make up one-half in the next two-thirds (eleven of twenty); and the loss to the large SMSA category of almost one-half of the original group. The changes can be broken down into four categories: the largest SMSAs (dominant metropolises), the old centers, the new centers (southern and western rim), and the dropouts.

Table 7–4 shows the dominant metropolitan changes. The top group of the 1970s was similar to that of 1870 with four exceptions: Los Angeles–Long Beach, Dallas–Ft. Worth, Houston, and Nassau-

TABLE 7–4   Ranking of Cities, 1870, and SMSAs, 1974

Area	1870	1974	Type of Shift
New York–New Jersey	1	1	None
Chicago	4	3	Upward
Los Angeles–Long Beach	Under 25,000	2	New SMSA
Philadelphia	2	4	Downward
Detroit	15	5	Upward
San Francisco–Oakland	9	7	Upward
Washington	11	8	Upward
Boston (and vicinity)	6	6	None
Pittsburgh	14	12	Downward
St. Louis	3	11	Downward
Baltimore	5	14	Downward
Cleveland	13	17	Upward
Dallas–Ft. Worth	Under 25,000	10	New SMSA
Nassau–Suffolk (N.Y.)	Under 25,000	9	New SMSA
Houston	Under 25,000	13	New SMSA

SOURCES: Sam Bass Warner, Jr., *The Urban Wilderness: A History of the American City* (New York: Harper & Row, 1972), pp. 70–71; U.S. Department of Commerce, *Statistical Abstract of the United States, 1975* (Washington, D.C.: Government Printing Office, 1975).

Suffolk (counties on Long Island usually considered part of a New York-New Jersey SCSA). The upward and downward shifts are visible when one examines Table 7–4.

THE REMAINDER OF THE TOP FIFTY

Of this next group of areas, eleven were new centers: Minneapolis, Seattle, Atlanta, San Diego, Denver, Phoenix, San Antonio, Birmingham, Oklahoma City, Jacksonville, Miami.

If we include Houston and Dallas-Ft. Worth, their share of the urban population was 2.5 percent in 1890; by 1970, it was 10.6 percent. From a total population of about 560,000 in the 1890 city bounds, they grew to almost 16,000,000 in the 1970 SMSA boundaries. Average SMSA size was approximately 1,212,000. Average city size was just about one-half of that.

Milwaukee, Indianapolis, Louisville, Memphis, and Columbus (Ohio) were old stabilized centers that were the big losers from the top group in 1870, along with Cincinnati, New Orleans, and Buffalo. Of the leading forty cities of 1870, ten had dropped out by 1970 by losing rank steadily. Five others had been absorbed. The stories of their decline are the stories of the industrial decline of the old second-order manufacturing growth centers of the nineteenth century in the northern states.

Each of these new centers began to spurt in particular decades, for example, Houston in the 1940s and Dallas and Miami in the 1950s. Each tended to be associated with a particular constellation of industries, but as is evident in the following section, these were not the same industries as in the pre-World War II period. They were petrochemicals, aerospace, agribusiness, government, tourism and recreation, and communications—the leading industries of the mid-twentieth century.

ANALYZING THE EVOLVING NETWORK OF CITIES

The historic patterns of industrial location in the United States were that market-directed firms chose the Northeast; those requiring large amounts of unskilled labor picked the South; and those needing raw materials ended up near their supply sources. Since 1920 these patterns have been changing dramatically. Raw materials are less important as inputs, synthetics and energy-intensive products are more common, and energy and transportation costs have dropped sharply. The migration of millions of workers discussed earlier also affected labor costs by causing movement toward equalization between regions. As a result industry today is most likely to locate and expand in the growing metropolitan market areas where millions of consumers and workers form deep and ready pools for participation in buying and selling, consuming and producing.

World-wide developments have also affected the evolution of the national network of cities. A great decade of depression followed by a generation of "hot" and "cold" wars has reshaped the national economy. There has been an accompanying and interacting series of widespread political and social changes that have seen dozens of new policies and programs instituted by an expanding government. New approaches to land policy, zoning, transportation, and commerce have helped reshape the framework within which cities grew and evolved.

Typical urban dwellers have prospered as average living levels have gone up threefold over the past two generations. Science-based knowledge, technological changes, and the increased education and skills of the work force have been the main driving factors behind these higher living standards. Specifically, the key ideas that need comment and elaboration are the growth in the market (rising population and income), the rapid changes in technology, the focus of administration on manufacturing, and the shift of resources into service industries and occupations.

GROWTH IN URBAN MARKETS

The importance of rising incomes in the growth of the largest areas is not immediately apparent; yet we realize that these are the best-paying areas of the country, and they contain a larger share of the highest-paid occupational groupings than their size alone would lead one to expect.

As incomes rise, people spend less and less on necessities. First, food and clothing and, later, consumer durables decline as a proportion of the total dollar spent. Spending on luxuries and services rises rapidly as income advances into the middle range. Hence those urban regions that offer the richest markets and broadest-based services and best sources of labor have managed to more than hold their own as industries and population have shifted about. Beverly Duncan has noted that it is the capturing of new industries that has been the best single explanation of which cities have grown more rapidly than the average since 1920. If a city just maintains a constant mix of jobs, it inevitably declines, but when a city can develop a new function or latch onto a current trend, it moves rapidly up the ladder. Witness New Orleans (always a great port for commerce) emerging since World War II as a major tourist attraction. Such industrial changes are all ultimately linked to consumers' changing demands.

What have been the main changes in the nature of the metropolitan consumer's marketing habits since America has become a fully industrialized nation?

Before the Civil War urban areas represented only about 25 percent of the total consumption expenditures for all American households. By World War II the city share had risen to over 70 percent, with the turning point coming sometime between 1900 and World War I. It was the growth of an urban middle class, made up of both blue- and white-collar workers, that become the dominant factor in market expansion in the twentieth century. Fortunately, the legacy of the large, consuming, rural middle class of independent farmer, village merchant, and craftsman made the transition for our marketing and production techniques fairly smooth. As mass-produced, standardized, and yet high-quality goods flooded the urban sections of the nation in the first half of this century, demand expanded rapidly, making possible greater economies of scale. As more firms flocked to locations specializing in certain lines of products, there resulted a drop in labor, transport, information, and by-product costs. The circle of reduced costs and expanding markets continued. Such interactions operated especially in some fields such as food marketing, apparel, and household appliances.

How did these changes affect family life on the urban scene? In food marketing the diffusion of mechanical refrigeration from wholesale to retail to the household level made for a wider choice of foodstuffs and drove down prices. Gas and electric refrigerators replaced the icebox. Food could be kept fresh longer, thus requiring fewer deliveries. Less time and effort were now devoted to shopping and cooking. Other changes in simple kitchen utensils and techniques of home canning were equally important. Such changes expanded the alternative choices available to women in the everyday tasks of raising a family. The impact was felt first among the upper middle class, which had the income needed to purchase such devices by the 1920s. And changes outside the home interacted with those within, as Dorothy Brady notes:

> By the 1930s, many disadvantages of urban living had been overcome —largely by the extension of city water and electric power systems, and by the introduction of an array of electrical equipment. Burdensome housekeeping tasks like carrying in water and fuel and carrying out wastes were eliminated. Ways had been found to secure all the comforts found in wealthy establishments without the problems associated with servants. (Brady 1972:80)

By the post-World War II period most American urban families could hope for such conveniences, and the electric kitchen and clean heating (and sometimes cooling) of the house were taken for granted. Again Brady puts these consumption patterns (market changes) into beautiful historical perspective:

> Today, the great majority of American families live on a scale that compares well with the way wealthy families lived 200 years ago. Of the essentials, food and clothing have become less important in the aggregate, but housing and household operation, with all the array of modern facilities and equipment, have become a more important element in the total. The purchase and operation of automobiles represent a larger fraction of aggregate spending than did outlays for clothing in the past. Of the other kinds of goods and services, equipment for recreation and public entertainment has increased considerably, and direct and indirect expenditures for education have grown dramatically. (Brady 1972:84)

Such advances in material well-being have resulted from advanced levels of technology and industrial development. These same changes in techniques and industry have been responsible for much of the evolution in the urban network.

CHANGES IN TECHNOLOGY AND INDUSTRY

The appearance of new products and technologies is most clearly seen in the shifting industrial characteristics of the manufacturing labor force. Table 7–5 indicates these changes over the half century 1910 to 1960.

Examination of the two columns reveals the fact that almost all of the leading industries of 1960 were different from those of 1910. And the two that were the same, machinery and steel, maintained their respective positions. Machinery, nonelectrical and electrical, remained first in ranking. Iron and steel became simply steel and stayed fourth. These basic building blocks of manufacturing were joined by chemicals (sixth) and structural metals (ninth). These four not only took up the slack of the declining lumber firms, but also pointed toward the increasing captial intensity of all modern industry. Two other noteworthy additions to the top ten were aricraft and motor

TABLE 7–5 Leading Manufacturing Industries (ranked by value added)

1910	*1960*
Machinery	Nonelectrical machinery
Lumber	Electrical machinery
Printing and publishing	Motor vehicles
Iron and steel	Steel
Malt liquors	Aircraft
Men's clothing	Basic chemicals
Cotton goods	Beverages
Tobacco goods	Dairy products
Railroad cars	Structural metals
Boots and shoes	Newspapers

SOURCES: U.S. Bureau of the Census, *Census of the United States, 1910,* Vol. 8 (Washington, D.C.: Government Printing Office), and U.S. Bureau of the Census, *Survey of Manufactures, 1959-60* (Washington, D.C.: Government Printing Office).

vehicles. Actually they were numbers one and two in employment, but as ranked here (by the *value added* by the manufacturing process) they are fifth and third respectively. How did all these changes occur?

In established industries increases in the scale of operations caused functions to split off from the main firm to smaller outside service firms or manufacturing suppliers. This tendency multiplied economies within the locale more than in the plant, leading to more specialized training and to increases in pools of skilled labor. In turn, new firms that could make use of such labor supplies were attracted to these areas. There were many improvements in converting raw materials into finished products and in the substitution of artificial materials and synthetics. Since 1900 the raw material input has declined by about 50 percent in importance as a factor in determining the location decision of the manufacturer. Now, the focus of site selection is toward available services and markets that reduce finished product transport costs and distribute city growth among the leaders in population (major market and purchasing power areas).

Another aspect of the shift in manufactures was the spectacular increase in value-added per worker, on the order of 400 percent, or about twice the advance of the 1860–1910 period. This productivity change, combined with declining transportation costs and the shift in discretionary spending toward services, led to stabilization (and recently decline) in manufacturing workers' share of total jobs. The drop was from 33 percent in 1910 to 28 percent in 1970. Note, however, that in absolute numbers manufacturing employment tripled from 7.8 million to 21 million. Thus, there was about a twelvefold increase in real output of manufactured goods (a fourfold per worker increase times a threefold increase in employment). This growth, with a pattern that varied widely, was not evenly distributed among the cities of the nation.

Sometimes it developed originally in one or two cities; examples are automobiles in Detroit and aircraft and space in certain southern and western metropolises such as Los Angeles, Seattle, Houston, and Ft. Worth. As output levels increased, it became profitable to decentralize some of the stages in the production process. Assembly plants, parts suppliers, service industries, capital goods manufacturers, and such located in other cities shared in the phenomenal growth of these products. By 1970 it was estimated that almost one-third of the

American work force was employed in jobs directly or indirectly related to just two of these industries, aircraft and automobiles.

The most important growth industries besides those in the top ten were plastics and synthetic fibers, rubber products, office machines and computers, photographic equipment and petrochemicals, oil and coal. The newer centers (indicated in the previous section of this chapter) show little of the profiles of older centers—no railroading, printing, food-processing, or metal-working complexes. But they do show trade, finance, and service sectors supporting the twentieth-century growth industries. Thus the South and West do not compete directly in the same industries by and large as the North and East, where the growth of the older industries showed some expansion and slow evolution.

Other industries such as chemicals, machinery, and steel expanded and split into five basic groupings: chemicals, steel, structural metals, electrical and nonelectrical machinery. These were scattered all over the country although the cities in the southern region dominated chemicals and the Midwest steel and machinery.

Older centers have declined or stayed at about the same rank dependent on how they adapted to the changing industrial environment. Pittsburgh, for example, slipped sharply because it continued to remain overly dependent on steel. While steel stayed at the same rank in value-added, it lost sharply in employment potential. In addition, Pittsburgh lost a large share of the national market to other regions as the technology in steel production favored nearness to markets and skilled labor rather than proximity to coal and iron deposits. Plants opened up near Trenton, New Jersey, and on the West Coast.

Other older centers such as New York have held their own. The decline of New York since 1970 has been centered in the city. The larger SCSA still maintains about 10 percent of the nation's manufacturing employment, the share it has had since before the Civil War.

How have some older centers stayed relatively healthy? One explanation favored by Wilbur Thompson is that older, larger cities attract more innovators and generate many new firms, products, and industries that are then spun off into smaller cities further down the urban hierarchy. The recent revitalization of the Boston area around the knowledge, computer, and electronics industries is such an example.

Thompson adds the idea that in the long run it is the quality of the socioeconomic resource base (human and physical) that determines the trend in the health of the city rather than a series of short-run changes in national demand patterns.

Since World War II the more rapid diffusion of technical knowledge has required a very firm base in human and business services. How did this development take place? By World War I most of the larger cities had laid the groundwork for diversified and profitable service bases. With their large trading areas, they captured new growth like magnets.

Business services growth provided one of the major reasons for new manufacturing to develop near these major centers. The internal changes in manufacturing mentioned above essentially made factors such as the business executive's liking for golf, fine weather, or good schools deciding factors in site location. The centers and fringes of the largest metropolitan areas have provided for these amenities in a complementary manner. What has happened is that manufactures have tended to locate in the suburban areas and services have split between the suburbs and the center city. The long-term trend is shown in the date in Table 7–6.

This growth has led to population dispersal described in Chapter Eight. In turn, this population growth requires human services from shopping to education to health care. These again tend to split between center city (for large-scale hospitals, higher education, cultural,

TABLE 7–6   Wage Jobs in Manufacturing

Year	Percent Inside Central Cities	Percent Outside Central Cities
1919	80[*]	20
1939	63	37
1958	51	49
1967	47	53
1972	44	56

[*] Estimated from Census of Manufactures and Census of Population.
SOURCE: National Research Council, Toward an Understanding of Metropolitan America (San Francisco: Canfield Press, 1974), p. 22.

and special shopping services) and suburbs or local neighborhoods for all general residential needs, including retail trade, local schools, firefighting, police, and recreation.

Our analysis of the evolution of the urban network shows the importance of economies of scale, agglomeration, and growth. We think of the resulting urban complexes as big places; yet, we know they can be too big. If an urban area becomes so large that it generates inefficiencies, we say it has reached the point of diseconomies of scale. An example is the sprawling size associated with managing the New York SCSA. We also know that if urban areas grow too slowly or too quickly, they can create all sorts of serious problems.

These processes of multiplication and division and duplication and growth have been viewed by social scientists such as Constantine Doxiadis (*Ekistics*) as not only revealing an analogy with organic life but also as a true mirror of such processes as cell division, nervous (communication) systems, and other living functions. Doxiadis is convinced that the system of cities is evolving on a planetary scale and that world-wide development is inevitable. He has suggested that the origins of most urban difficulties lie in too rapid or too slow growth rates, too large a scale or *dysfunction*. His general solution has been to try to develop a new multidiscipline science called "ekistics," which looks at the basic components of living at a number of levels. Perhaps the most important question that he raised was the one of controlling the future course of the evolution of the urbanizing world. He held up as the ideal a modular series of large regions made up of vast numbers of small neighborhood communities with occasional vital civilizing centers. To us, in light of recent growth patterns, the question shifts slightly as to how to revitalize our present centers and keep our smaller cities livable and economically attractive.

As Joseph Spengler has pointed out, "the greatest promise may lie in the development of an adequate number of additional cities of size one hundred to two hundred thousand." He ties this to "Key Decision Makers" who can launch a city from an economic base of ten to twenty thousand persons in one plant. This attracts forty to eighty thousand others gainfully employed and supports this size city. Since about one-third of all Americans work for fewer than one thousand corporations, such decisions could be made with motivation and incentive.

The above analysis has shown how the changing functioning of the network of cities reflected the patterns of twentieth-century industrial change. The form of this system of cities evolved in new ways. Different locational factors became important to key decision makers in large corporations and government. As a result many new cities joined the dominant metropolitan chain; most older, larger centers of the early nineteenth-century held their own; and many of the smaller original manufacturing areas were overshadowed when they did not adapt to the new order or innovate. Just as the relationships within the family of urbanized areas grew and shifted, so also their internal structures changed under the impact of wide societal and national forces in the twentieth century. The next chapter will detail how these forces reshaped the ecology of the modern metropolis.

CHAPTER EIGHT

Internal Change and Metropolitan Ecology, 1920-70

The symbol of the twentieth-century metropolitan region is the skyscraper, whose architectural father was Louis Sullivan. He believed that buildings should have an organic unity; that once you knew the functions of a building, its form naturally followed. He held that form follows function.

The changing industrial-occupational mix of the city has led to changing functions and to changes in physical and social forms. It was these new forms that in turn shaped both the equity and efficiency with which the city functioned or, perhaps more precisely, dysfunctioned or did not function in a positive manner. Changing functions and new innovations have also led to new patterns of population redistribution throughout the metropolis. This produced new settlements, changing both the types of communities that urban residents live in and the range of problems they face.

AN OVERVIEW OF HISTORICAL FORCES SHAPING THE MODERN METROPOLIS

As anyone who has been to another city can recognize, no American metropolis exactly resembles any other. Diversity of social shape and physical layout depends on when the city was built, local geography, industrial mix, and a number of other factors. Nonetheless, there were similarities in all the historical development patterns of the great cities of the nineteenth century. Likewise there are great similarities among the new metropolises that have become prominent in the urban network since 1920.

The older areas are plagued by obsolescence in their land usage patterns; they are more densely settled, cover less land, and have more dominant central business districts. They show more serious signs of economic and fiscal decay and face almost insurmountable barriers to socioeconomic health. In many of their neighborhoods and subareas, the future seems bleak indeed unless there is massive outside aid. The newer areas are less locked into old land usage patterns. Having lower densities, more land in which to expand, fewer signs of neighborhood decay, and less dominant CBDs, they are more flexible and open to future population needs and development patterns. Since their economies are healthier, they do not face serious imbalance of revenues versus expenditures.

The older centers found themselves at World War I largely congealed in a nineteenth-century form dictated geographically by political boundaries, economically by the growth of manufactures and commerce, and socially by the vast immigration from Europe. These limits proved more and more difficult to extend with every passing decade.

Superimposed on the river- and horse-dominated cities of the pre-Civil War era came the railroad-trolley car era. Dirt roads, ditches, and springs became paved streets with lights and curbs, sewer pipes and water mains. Gas, electricity, and telephone lines further froze the layout of the city. Large industrial plants, noisy, polluting, using huge amounts of coal and raw materials, which were in 1870 at the city fringe, now found themselves in the middle ring. The shanty towns of the poor were bypassed by new residential building booms and the incorporation of early "suburbs" under the city's jurisdiction. So also the rich and growing middle class found their residential neighborhoods lost in a patchwork of mixed usages. Old did not blend with new, and redirecting major segments of the old city to new uses was terribly expensive, time-consuming, and open to all kinds of political corruption.

Some older urban centers continued to grow and prosper as the CBDs assumed new functions. Office buildings, containing insurance, real estate, finance, and business services, joined specialized light manufacturers and subcontractors in apparel, machinery, and printing. Mass transit and skyscrapers made it possible to concentrate 10,000 workers on a single acre of land. By World War I, despite difficulties, much of the city area around the expanding CBDs was still occupied by tax-paying family residences. Expansion outward was promoted vigorously as swarms of new migrants bolstered the work force and quickly formed consuming households.

It was the movement of people and jobs to new locations that fundamentally changed the shape and nature of urban areas. How do social scientists analyze the factors determining movements of people and business? One way is to build an abstract model of the process and, after quantifying the variables, attempt to simulate the decision process through interactions on a computer. Frequently the core of the analysis can be reduced to a housing market and a labor market wherein *supply* and *demand* for houses and workers become the determinants of both the quantity of each exchanged at any given time and the price of these exchanges.

Typical of the variables determining the shape, position, and shifts of these relationships would be the following three kinds. Some are shared in common, such as value placed on travel time, funding and investment decisions, available sites for expansion, and in-moving and out-moving workers. Each market would also have variables unique to itself: in residential decisions, neighborhood amenities and desires to maintain ethnic ties; in job market decisions, national and regional economic growth and the historical industrial mix. Finally some variables can be thought of as links between the two decision-making processes: leading to job choices—the skills and education of workers, the value placed on travel time, and the kinds of jobs available in given locations; leading to residential decisions—available housing and income levels of the workers.

Such "modeling" of how the real world allocates urban land is sometimes misleading. In reality, rather than a series of choices that leave all parties more or less satisfied, the result is often conflict among different interest groups. This is particularly so in land use patterns in the reconversion of many central city downtowns. High-income housing and institutional users such as large hospitals and universities have become deeply enmeshed in political struggles. Low-income residents, some middle-income residents, and even retail trade and small businesses are frequently aligned on the other side. Although city fathers dislike taking political sides, problems in assembling large parcels of land frequently force choices upon them with the result that planning is replaced by warfare. Government pressures are brought to bear as the simple free-choice pattern of the picture depicted above breaks into fragments under political tension.

AGGREGATION VERSUS DISPERSAL AS FORCES IN METROPOLITAN ECOLOGY

As we have argued, the redistribution of people and jobs to new locations is the basic force changing the ecology of urban areas in the modern period. However, choices made by households and institutional land users, and the political conflicts among them, occur in the context of national socioeconomic patterns. Chief among these are *aggregation* and *dispersal.* The ecology of metropolitan areas also reflects the cross-currents of these conflicting trends.

Having discussed how form follows function, how the internal shape of urban areas is influenced by social, economic, and political activities, we will now focus this discussion further by analyzing how aggregation and dispersal shaped metropolitan ecology, especially the location of jobs, residences, and the central business districts.

Until the early twentieth century there were powerful factors that kept people and industry concentrated in central cities. The consequence was the emergence of densely populated, heterogeneous cities. With many industries competing for limited space, the cost of land was being continually bid upward, making city land more expensive for purchasers and renters, and more valuable for owners. The dominant use of sections of the city for industry and commerce then affected overall patterns of land use. Residential areas were pushed further from the center of the city, and since transportation was slow and limited, housing increased in cost the closer to the center it was located.

In an urban property market, the value of any particular site is affected by changes in the use of other sites. Through the 1920s property markets were dominated by the need for industries to locate near each other and near rail and shipping lines. Since jobs were concentrated in specific sections of the city and people wanted to live close to their work to reduce commuting time, the value of residential land was determined by proximity to the business district. This, in turn, affected land use and land value for service professionals such as doctors, lawyers, and bankers, who depend on population concentrations.

The skyscraper is the classic example of the culmination of these trends. In the 1920s and 1930s the demand for prime locations, coupled with falling construction costs and technological advances in structural and electrical engineering, led builders to erect taller and taller structures. Cleveland's fifty-two story Terminal Tower, Chicago's thirty-six story Tribune Tower, and New York's eighty-six story Empire State Building symbolized the need for the efficient use of space in dense cities, as well as new prosperity and growth.

However, along with the dynamic of aggregation there has been a second overlapping trend of dispersal. As people continued to move toward urban centers, these centers have increased in territorial scope, with population scattered over large metropolitan areas. As the small town served for many years as a staging area and filter for population migration from rural to urban areas, so the past fifty years have seen urban populations spilling over the boundaries of central cities, the new staging areas for the growth of suburbs and satellite towns along the urban fringe.

Density dropped in the last generation from over 5,400 per square mile to less than 3,400. In central cities it dropped from over 7,700 to less than 4,500. This process began in cities such as New York as early as 1850. After World War II it entered a new phase as the central cities started to lose jobs very rapidly to the suburbs. Indications are that the population shift led the industrial shift until about 1960, and since then jobs have shifted out slightly more rapidly than people. The cities are today spreading out faster than ever. In the 1960s metropolitan areas grew by 26 million; one-third was by annexation at the edges and two-thirds by growth within the boundaries. This trend has had profound impact on the people remaining in central cities and the type of services performed in these areas. An example is the failure of numerous attempts to revitalize older CBDs.

Since World War II the decaying central business districts have had billions of dollars of private and public funds pumped into them in a massive effort to bring about their "renewal." To a large extent this has been a failure when measured by net new jobs created, net population gains, retail sales, or any other standard economic indicator. It is a case study of how misdirected resources can produce results of questionable long-term value when counter trends are not recognized.

We believe that the thrust of modern metropolitan development is away from one central business district, as regions may be developing many smaller, specialized business districts. The largest urban areas will probably always have one dominant center; however, it may not be business-controlled in the present sense of the term. New central city forms are appearing. In the older cities the core has always evolved and expanded; until 1920 the sequence was from commerce to manufacturing to trade and office centers. Since then personal and business services, cultural functions, educational and health services have joined the older mix and shifted it around.

Of the newer cities, many never had a core. Los Angeles, Houston, Phoenix, and other sunbelt cities are so spread out that no one center yet seems dominant. And, because of the automobile, none may appear.

As indicated previously, modern transport and communication have released the bonds of space and the costs of decentralization. Thus, newer cities tend to be less dense from their beginnings, and the older ones are spreading out rapidly. Mills suggests that the *density gradients* of population and assorted economic activities (manufacturing, services, wholesale and retail trade) have dropped on the average over 50 percent since 1910.

FORCES BEHIND DISPERSAL

A particularly important factor accelerating this metropolitan trend was the widespread use of the automobile. Just as the skyscraper symbolized the trend of aggregation, the automobile symbolized dispersal. As architect Frank Lloyd Wright put it, "The future will involve a race between the elevator and the automobile, and the wise man should bet on the auto." (Wright in Segel 1965:4)

As the automobile allowed for the dispersal of population over wider areas, so the truck, and improved highways and communication systems permitted the decentralization of jobs. With mechanized, assembly-line production becoming more prevalent, firms now needed one-floor operations, rather than multistory lofts. With cheap suburban land now increasingly accessible, central city locations became less desirable, and factories began moving from urban cores to suburbs. At the same time, a separation of production from management was occurring. Thanks to transportation by means of streetcars or highways and telephone communication, firms could separate functions and locate their offices in central cities and their factories in suburbs. As the urban economy was transformed into a metropolitan economy, there grew a variety of metropolitan communities, including the old central cities, new suburbs, satellite towns, and a growing urban fringe. All were increasingly interdependent and linked by common social and economic institutions.

Industrial relocation and outward-moving population interacted and produced a new locational pattern with the suburbs becoming the generative industrial basis for the metropolitan areas. In a recent study, Dorothy K. Newman found that from 1954 to 1965 half of the new, private, nonresidential building in metropolitan areas took place in the suburban rings. She also discovered that the figure was even greater for industrial building—63 percent. John Kain's well-known study of decentralization population and four industry groups in forty large urban areas shows dramatic changes after World War II. His data are given in Table 8–1.

TABLE 8–1 Suburban Share of SMSA Manufacturing Employment and Population, 1948–63

Percent	1948	1963
Population	36	54
Employment in manufactures	33	52

SOURCE: John F. Kain,"The Distribution and Movement of Jobs and Industry," in *The Metropolitan Enigma,* ed. James Q. Wilson (Cambridge, Mass.: Harvard University Press, 1968), p. 30.

Our discussion of the growth of metropolitan areas and the movement of industry and households from the central city to fringe areas follows most analyses by stressing the role of new transportation and communication systems and the relocation of jobs to the outer fringes.

But an exclusive focus on these factors can be misleading. An additional factor, the life cycle of cities must also be included.

If an historical examination is made of patterns of land use and the movement of people and jobs from central cities to fringe areas by the size of American cities, a clear pattern emerges. The trend we have discussed, where land use densities in the oldest part of a city decline and are displaced by the rapid growth rates of fringe areas, occurs within fifty years after a city reaches a population size of 50,000.

It is clear that the truck and automobile were very important in the modern period, but in terms of general growth trends of American cities they were just another transportation innovation, like the electric streetcar before them, in facilitating the growth of suburban residential areas around older central cities.

The concept of a *life cycle of cities* helps explain not only the timing of metropolitan dispersal, but also which industries tend to move and which remain. The *economic base* of an urban area, as well as its overall pattern of land use, is deeply affected by both its size and age. If the dispersal of jobs and people is seen as part of the life cycle of cities, then we can recognize that it occurs at different times for different cities. The younger metropolitan areas tend to develop around highway networks and have ample land for construction. Such cities capitalize on their advantage of roads and open spaces to become manufacturing specialists. However, as the city ages and becomes more densely populated, land values change, causing changes in economic activity. The older a city, the more its manufacturing and wholesale and retail trade decline.

THE EFFECTS OF CHANGING ECOLOGY
ON THE INDIVIDUAL

There are at least two major effects of the increasing scale and mobility and declining density of the modern metropolis. There is the increasing social isolation that accompanies the greater physical isolation of social and economic groups. There is the high level of sensory stimulation that accompanies life in the modern metropolis, with the accompanying danger that overload will lead to high stress, strain, and tension.

As a result of the first factor (and perhaps others), there has been an upsurge in attempts to rebuild some of the sense of ethnic communities of the industrial city. This move toward social organization is intended to help control the impact of the city on the individual.

People need a social place in which to locate their lives and aspirations. The social organization is the local neighborhood system. As Dorfman notes:

> The most superficial glance at an American city will disclose that it includes a wide variety of people who sort themselves out into neighborhoods largely on the basis of ethnic affinity and socioeconomic similarity. These neighborhoods have neither economic nor administrative nor legal significance. They are social entities purely, and they discharge most of the social functions of the city insofar as they are discharged at all. (Dorfman in Hochman 1976:34)

Although weakened by increasing scale and mobility and the dramatic changes in economic activity, neighborhoods continue as important social units. They are the physical and social expressions of generations of creative activities by residents trying to carve out a satisfying environment.

We view this creativity in defensive and offensive ways. That is, it protects and assures a social position and simultaneously provides the base from which the ethnic can (if he or she wishes and has the opportunity) move into the American mainstream. Within such locales, styles of life different from the American way of life can be maintained—and they are. Indeed, indications are that such localism is being adopted by suburbanites as well. As the central city declines, new "urbs" throughout the metropolitan region are becoming focal points for new specialized functions and interactions. All are interconnected by the new technics, and the interconnections are growing.

We suggest that the movement to the "suburbs" and also the attempted revival of the urban neighborhood concept represent similar kinds of responses to the same underlying metropolitan shaping forces. These act upon individuals who respond in various ways, depending upon the resources they can bring to bear. There is an absence of effective regional planning and public policy. There is the presence of political fragmentation and private interests that do not pay their full social costs. Therefore, many of these social places that groups try to build have no firm economic or political base. They cannot function well within an inefficient city or an inequitable metropolitan framework.

SUBURBANIZATION: CHANGES IN COMMUNITY

Historically, suburbs have been a major mechanism of urban growth. In the era of full metropolitanization, they become particularly important. Today a full understanding of urbanization requires an examination of suburban areas, their composition and patterns of growth. In a sense such areas are as old as cities since they designate residential locations resulting from the redistribution of population outward from the urban core. In America the preconditions for suburbs have existed since before the turn of the century, when trolley and commuter railroad lines were extended beyond the city limits. However, patterns of urban growth are uneven, wavelike, with the result that the rapid growth and redistribution of population following World War II captured the attention of many people. The outpouring of articles and books on this "suburban boom" was accompanied by the development of a specific picture of suburban life that some analysts eventually called "the suburban myth."

The essence of this myth is that suburbs are fundamentally different from cities, that they foster quite different forms of social organization, patterns of child-rearing, political participation, life styles, and even "cultures." In this view, popular through the late 1940s and 1950s, suburban residents were viewed as more mobile, willing to move from one development to another if it would further their careers, as well as more upwardly striving (very concerned with success and status symbols). For this reason education is a prime concern, and they give great attention to the local school system. Finally, they were seen as more sociable and child-centered than urbanites, spending more time together and participating more in local civic, political, and social activities.

Several sociological studies of the period tended to reinforce this view. William H. Whyte's *The Organization Man* discussed the suburban communities of the aggressively mobile corporate executives whose life style revolved around job success and the affluence it provided. Seeley and his associates studied an upper-middle-class suburb near Toronto and in *Crestwood Heights* painted a similar picture. Seeley especially emphasized the importance given the local school and the socialization for achievement so prominent in their child-rearing practices.

Many other analysts also drew a negative picture of suburban life. They did not just discuss its differences from city living, but rather tried to show how it symbolized many negative trends in the society. Peter Hall summarizes the negative view in the following way:

> . . . the possibilities for fruitful human interaction are much reduced . . . there is a premium on conformity . . . social relationships are shallow . . . the growth of a really popular, democratic culture is stultified. (Hall 1975:85)

However, enough time has passed to evaluate these views so that we can now consider what suburban growth tells us about the urbanization process. We argue, along with many other social scientists, that the distinctive features of suburbs are transitional. They are indistinguishable in operation (rather than location) from portions of central cities. Put another way, the same urbanization process that creates cities also creates suburbs; both types of settlements can be comprehended in a single model. The factors discussed throughout this book—economic growth, demographic change, technological innovation, rising incomes, and changing social and political institutions—can be used to explain the pattern of American suburbanization.

The major problem with earlier analyses is that they were too close to the phenomena, focusing on only one stage of suburban growth. We would argue, along with Herbert Gans and Bennett Berger, that most of the city-suburban differences in behavior and life styles pointed out in the 1950s are really due to race and class factors. Thus, researchers were identifying characteristics of the specific groups that settled in the suburbs, not features of suburban life itself.

A classification of suburbs suggested by Alvin Boskoff helps make this point, and identifies the variety of American suburbs. (Boskoff in Halebsky 1973:220–36)

1. The Traditional Upper-Class Suburb. These are small in number and primarily located around older northeastern cities such as Boston and Philadelphia. Their social composition is of older, upper-class families. Their development is due to the social differentiation and specialization basic to urban life: wealthy families desired distinctive residential areas and could afford the higher transportation costs.

2. The Identity-conscious Suburb. This is the type most focused on by commentators who developed the suburban myth. Its social composition is of upper-middle-class families, primarily employed in the middle levels of various corporations. These settlements are constructed to appeal to upwardly mobile families who want the feeling of space, security, and freedom from urban problems. Complete with a "tasteful" name and including a swim club and other recreational facilities, they form a total community environment. Since such suburbs can be found outside every major urban area, a family can relocate any number of times whenever job movement may require and continue to live in similar environments.

This type of suburb reflects social class variation, demonstrates urban status systems of classification, and delineates the process by which status symbols are diffused; that is, first upper-class styles are copied by the upper middle class, and then by large segments of the lower classes of the population.

3. The Mass-produced Suburb. This kind contains a more varied population, encompassing middle-class professionals, small businessmen, and skilled blue-collar workers and, compared to previous suburbs, these are stable. Most residents identify with the community and have occupations permitting them to reside there permanently. They commute to work in nearby cities, but prefer living in a suburban setting.

Gans's study, *The Levittowners,* was of a typical mass-produced suburb. He found that the residents were not unlike their urban counterparts, having a good degree of similarity in age and income. Most were in the earlier phases of family formation with several children; however, there was considerable difference in ethnic composition, regional backgrounds, and sources of income. One family might be headed by a skilled worker at the peak of his earning power, another by a professional at the start of his career.

These suburbs are the result of a more advanced phase of the urbanization process. Improved transportation and communication, rising incomes, and government policies facilitating home mortgages have extended freedom of residential choice to greater numbers of urban residents. Highway systems make larger sections of metropolitan areas accessible, while rising incomes and diversity of community types permit more choice in terms of a family's life style and values.

4. The Industrial and Variegated Suburb.   This reflects the full trend of metropolitan growth. As businesses and industries, as well as families, relocate throughout the metropolitan region, suburbs become more variegated or mixed. In the earlier phase suburbs are of the "bedroom" or "dormitory" type, with residents commuting to work in nearby cities. However, the decentralization of jobs and relocation of industries mean that many residents can both live and work in the suburbs. By the 1970s the majority of people living in such areas worked in them, not in central cities, and many central city areas had become bedroom communities.

This type best shows that the distinctive features of suburbs are transitional. As they fill in with population growth and develop mixed land use with industrial relocation, other changes occur. Commercial concerns increase and many of the service and recreational facilities found in cities also spring up. Suburbs cannot develop the full range of specialized goods and services available in central cities, but they can provide for most of the needs and desires of their residents. With the growth of suburban shopping centers, recreational facilities, and various commercial establishments, many residents need rarely travel to central cities.

A POLITICAL UNDERSTANDING OF SUBURBS

Our attempt to locate suburbs within the general process of urbanization raises an important question of how to distinguish the nature of suburbs. Since they differ significantly among themselves, result from typical mechanisms of urban growth, and do not fundamentally differ in life style or social organization from sections of cities, they raise difficult problems of definition.

Our view is that they should be understood in political terms. Suburbs result from the redistribution and growth of population through metropolitan regions. They begin as spatial additions to the urban core and, as they grow, become distinct subcenters of urban population and activity. However, this population redistribution occurs across political boundaries. Suburbanization refers to the process of population migration outside the legal jurisdiction of central cities. Because political boundaries so affect revenues, services, and political institutions, suburbanization can also be viewed as ecological changes in metropolitan stratification systems, in the changes of income, wealth, and power.

As distinct racial, ethnic, and income groups in the population become localized and socially patterned throughout the metropolitan region, political boundaries create significant differences and divisive conflicts become clearer. Residential location becomes an important factor determining access to resources, such as good-quality schools and recreational facilities, and it also influences the ability of families to insulate themselves from various social problems, such as crime.

NEIGHBORHOODS IN THE INTERNAL STRUCTURE OF THE METROPOLIS

The study of suburbanization reveals important information about the dynamics of urban growth and the social and political consequences of metropolitanization. The study of how city neighborhoods have changed over time discloses other forces altering the metropolitan ecology. Particularly important are increased scale and mobility.

In the period 1860–1920, neighborhoods were shaped by rapid industrialization that was expressed in the physical shape, the use of space, the growth of industry, and changes in occupational and social structure. Thanks to many dedicated researchers, there is a great deal of data available about urban neighborhoods as they underwent change. In the 1920s sociologists Robert Park, Ernest Burgess, and others, commonly called the Chicago School of sociology, began detailed studies of urban social life. Their starting point was that the city resembled a mosaic of social worlds; in other words, there are clear physical and social distinctions among urban populations. In their view cities are distinguished by distinct neighborhoods (what they also called natural areas) where neighbors share common cultural traditions, life styles, and occupations.

These distinctive areas tend to develop for two reasons. One is economic competition and the ability of powerful groups to control the use of choice land. Thus, the distribution of population and industry is not planned but results from the conflict, struggle, and efforts of urban residents. However, urban neighborhoods are not only the result of competition. They also persist because they express the institutional patterns, life styles, and values of the ethnic and racial groups that live in them. Thus, distinctive immigrant communities, the Chinatowns, Little Italys, and the Polish and Irish neighborhoods endured both because of the poverty of their residents and because of their desire to maintain distinct cultural values and ways of life.

Differing institutional patterns, life styles, and values are expressed in measurable statistical differences. Chicago School researchers mapped the occurrence of various phenomena in terms of their distribution throughout neighborhoods. As Robert Park notes:

> The differences in sex and age groups, perhaps the most significant indexes of social life, are strikingly divergent for different natural areas. (Park 1952:172)

Park's studies found areas of the city with high proportions of single people, while other areas had concentrations of large families. There were areas with many gangs and high rates of delinquency, while others had few youth problems.

The statistical differences noted by Park were seen as a reflection of the social reality of neighborhoods. The neighborhood was a significant community for its residents, maintaining and imposing what Park called "a moral order." Neighborhoods, being relatively homogeneous, that is, composed of similar types of people, contained institutions and groups expressing common norms and values.

In the Chicago School's studies of urban social life, one of the key terms was *disorganization,* or the weakening of social bonds. The strength and vitality of cultural traditions lessened; parents lost control over children; the community generally had less influence over the behavior of its members—all of which were expressed in rising rates of divorce, crime, and delinquency. We now recognize that Park and his associates were writing as these neighborhoods were undergoing changes, as traditional patterns were breaking down.

Maurice Stein has suggested that for this reason the view of the Chicago School is a useful but limited one. Park and others studied cities at one historical period in their development. The descriptions are invaluable, but they must be placed in a broader historical context. They studied one type of community formed by city residents at a particular stage of urbanization. Such settlement patterns, therefore, need to be compared with other types of urban communities to obtain a comprehensive view of urban social life. Let us try to place the Chicago School's picture of neighborhoods in the 1920s in perspective and examine some of the changes that took place in the era of full metropolitanization.

When these researchers began their investigations, they found urban neighborhoods undergoing profound changes—changes that have continued into the present, deeply altering the nature of residential areas. They focused on the pressures that urbanization exerts on communities and the problems these raise for planning and control in the city.

Two such pressures can be identified and their effects charted over time. One is population increase and the growth in size of urban areas, what we have called increasing scale. This is important because increases in the size of urban units lead to the dispersal of families, friends, functions, jobs, and facilities over a widening area. Through the turn of the century, the neighborhood was the area where people found the greatest opportunities for friendship, voluntary action, leisure, and political participation. In the era of full metropolitanization, the primacy of the neighborhood is broken. The use of the automobile and better communication permitted people to develop friendships and engage in social and leisure activities over larger areas and to live further from their jobs. Put simply, the destinations of neighborhood residents increasingly shifted outward, and the significance of the immediate neighborhood diminished.

A second pressure is the increase in secondary groups in the city. Sociologists make a basic distinction between primary and secondary groups. Primary groups are relatively intimate groups whose members interact on a face-to-face basis and are involved with one another in a variety of ways. Secondary groups are more functional and impersonal; they are established to perform specific functions, interrelationships are restricted, and members tend to know only single facets of one another (for example, a student and teacher, worker and foreman). One consequence of the urbanization process is the development of secondary groups. People continue to interact in a variety of primary groups, such as family and social club, but the number and variety of secondary groups increase. An example of this in terms of neighborhoods is the transfer of many functions they previously performed to more formal secondary groups, such as the range of city service agencies.

To summarize, at the beginning of the metropolitan era, the neighborhood was a working part of urban social structure. Cities were socially and physically divided into distinct residential areas where diverse immigrant cultures were maintained and modified. Neighborhoods were also communities in two senses. One was that they were spatially bounded areas where people carried on a collective life through a common set of institutions. In a deeper sense of community, neighbors lived close together and were united by common interests and values and concern for mutual aid. Facing a new and bewildering urban environment, often not speaking English, and lacking public services, residents of even the poorest immigrant neighborhoods organized themselves for mutual aid and support. They were able to do this through common institutions, such as church, political club, school, and settlement house, because they shared common values and a common culture. The contemporary geographer Brian Berry expresses the picture of the immigrant resident in the following manner:

In the search for self-identity in a mass society, he seeks to minimize disorder by living in a neighborhood in which life is comprehensible and social relations predictable. He seeks an enclave of relative homogeneity: a predictable life style, a safe area, free from status-challenging ethnic or racial minorities; a haven from complexity, to be protected and safeguarded. (Berry 1973:53)

SLUMS AND THE INTERACTION OF URBAN PROBLEMS AND POVERTY

It has been argued that each type of residential area comprising the internal structure of urban areas reflects particular forces that change the metropolitan ecology. Suburbs reflect long-term patterns of growth and the political fragmentation of modern urban areas. City neighborhoods are shaped by the increased scale and mobility found in the modern era.

Yet another type of area in which urban dwellers all too frequently live is called a slum. These areas significantly affect the social, economic, and political life of their residents, and reflect other trends in urbanization. Slums are the physical and social expression of inequalities in the distribution of the benefits of economic growth, as well as the structure, performance, and spatial patterning of the urban economy.

The term "slum" is often used loosely, and its meaning is sometimes unclear. As Charles Abrams notes, the term usually refers to two types of conditions. On the one hand it designates physical conditions of a neighborhood, especially substandard housing and physical deterioration. On the other hand it highlights certain social conditions of life, such as overcrowding. Slums, understood in these terms, have always been a part of urban life, reflecting the fact that jobs and income have always been unequally distributed throughout urban populations. These trends gave high-income groups the resources to monopolize the choicest residential areas and pushed the poor to the least desirable areas. Put another way, income and housing, poverty and slums, and other urban factors must always be considered together. For example improved transportation systems, such as the introduction of the trolley car and then the automobile, produced quite uneven benefits. For the middle- and upper-income groups, improved transport provided greater range of choice. As distance shrinks, the range of possible residences and jobs expands; however, for low-income groups it often leads to greater social and economic isolation.

The course of American economic growth and urbanization has produced some significant changes in city slums. Through the turn of the century, since cities were compact, slums were densely populated, but covered rather small areas of cities. When slum dwellers went to work or shopping, they usually walked. Slums were also close to the industrial areas where the residents searched for work. Since there were few public social services, such places were much worse than anything we find today.

Raymond Vernon points out another trend in the nature of urban slums. As the compact cities of the nineteenth century became the nuclei of large, sprawling metropolitan regions, slums also expanded in area. Densities declined in slum areas as they did through other sectors of cities as populations dispersed throughout the region. This expanded the stock of older housing available to low-income groups and caused a massive increase in the size of slums. Thus, although slum conditions are not as severe as in previous decades, they are much more noticeable and have greater impact on the environment of poor people. Wilbur Thompson notes that as these locales increase in size to equal the area of a high school district, they become self-renewing.

Slums are the by-product of many urban problems. An examination of these interactions shows that they reflect the course of urban economic growth and its impact on jobs, income, and public services. They also reflect the characteristics of residents, such as degree of power, motivation, and social problems. What follows is a discussion in more detail of the interrelation of these factors in producing urban problems.

The starting point is a downturn in the national economy that produces a more severe than usual loss of jobs in a specific city because its industrial mix is particularly vulnerable to those kinds of spending that are hampered by a depression (for example, construction, machine tools, consumer durables). The long-term unemployment rates go up and local inventories rise as spending declines in a geometric fashion. This leads to more layoffs and a reduction in business plans to expand. Local government tax revenues will fall or expand only very slowly while the costs of and the demands for government services will increase. Public investment frequently suffers as, for example, cutbacks in transportation or health programs. The results of this downward spiral are many: among the unemployed, a loss of hope and motivation and a cynical acceptance of the welfare way of life; disregard for family requirements leading to increases in crime rates and the need to devote more of shrinking public resources to public safety; young people turning to a street way of life, making neighborhoods into battle zones. Working people may try to leave the city to flee the rising tax and crime rates. Those who stay frequently face deteriorating school systems that leave their children lacking in skills and with few good educational chances. This lack of training for young people reduces their productivity potential to employers, leading to bleak futures in low-wage jobs. The life of "hustling" and petty crime beckons strongly. With low incomes, at least two people must work in each household and even then poor nutrition, housing, and health are common in such areas.

The increased spatial, economic, and social isolation of the poor can create a fiscal crisis for the central city that feeds on itself. Separated from the growth sections of the region by political boundaries of past generations, the tax base of the city grows much less rapidly than do the demands of its citizens for local services. The city, forced to assume new duties such as welfare and health care and trying to increase productivity of services that are very difficult to manage efficiently (public education and recreation, for example), is driven to raise tax rates. Businesses and residents seeking mainly short-term benefits can move to the less problem-beset suburbs and still use the city as work place and service center. The city may in turn trim services in an effort to slow tax increases—and the trimming hurts the neediest the most. Recently the activity of strong public service unions has further complicated cities' attempts to keep costs low.

While we realize that any of these problems can be overcome, the key issue is where are the best places to put resources to get maximum benefits for least costs. There have been so many counterproductive and frustratingly inadequate programs over the past generation that this question must be answered in a new and more successful way.

Most social scientists see the societal question of poverty as pivotal in the cycle of urban problems. Many argue that poverty should not be measured only in dollar terms. Poverty, of course, involves a lack of money, but it also can be viewed as an inability to fully participate in modern society, an inability to benefit from and to command the goods and services available to most other people. Christopher Jencks gives a good example of this.

He discusses how the goods and services that made it possible to live on $15 a week during the Great Depression were no longer available to a family with the same "real" income (that is, $40 a week) in the 1960s. This is because many societal and urban trends have altered the meaning of poverty. Eating habits have changed, and many cheap foods are no longer available to families. The location of industry shifted with decentralization, and many jobs required ownership of a car. A telephone is also often needed to find out about new employment openings. In Jencks's view, the cost of living is really the "cost of participating in a social system" (Jencks 1972:5). Changes in consumption patterns, transportation systems, and labor markets all increasingly isolate the urban poor in slums and continually raise the cost of participation in urban society.

Since poverty is the inability to participate, to command the goods and services available to others, let us examine the experience of poverty for those trying to cope in an urban setting. We focus on three important aspects of life: health care, crime, and employment.

Many studies show that the nature, availability, and quality of health care are unequally apportioned among urban residents. One study in Chicago found that there were about twice as many doctors per one hundred thousand persons in nonpoor as in poor areas. The same study also examined indexes of health in poor as compared to other neighborhoods.

> It was found that the poverty area had a 60 percent higher infant mortality; 200 percent higher incidence of premature births; . . . 200 percent more new cases of tuberculosis; 550 percent more new cases of venereal disease; and 100 percent higher death rate from carcinoma of the cervix. (Gordon 1971:316)

Many studies have found that poor people are unlikely to have a private physician, instead using the emergency rooms of city hospitals and visiting doctors much less often. They have less nutritional diets and suffer some diseases unique to their environment. In 1969 one researcher estimated that at least 400,000 poor children had lead poisoning, contracted from eating chipped, lead-based paint in deteriorating housing.

Another important aspect of life is the sense of personal security. The quality of life in a community is partially determined by the amount of crime that occurs, and the perception of crime by residents. People fear violence, theft, and fraud, and want to control the factors causing them. Crime data clearly indicate that ecological patterns are significant: crime is unevenly distributed throughout urban areas; a family's security is greatly affected by the type of community in which it lives.

A third important area of life is employment. The poor today face a very different labor market from the one entered several generations ago. The contemporary urban labor market differs in two significant ways, one of which is its spatial dimension. With the decentralization of jobs and population, the labor market extends throughout the entire metropolitan region. Today a worker's price of participation includes his or her residence and type of transportation. The second difference involves changes in the labor market. The job experiences of various racial and ethnic groups have been quite different, leading some economists to develop the concept of a segmented or dual labor market. An example is the phenomenon of the working poor: millions of urban residents work full time, year round, yet remain poor. Thus, the urban labor market must be viewed as unable to generate enough adequate-paying jobs for all those able and willing to work.

In the mid-1970s a widely discussed policy to alleviate this condition is guaranteed public employment, all the more necessary now because the generative function of the city has been weakened with businessmen refusing to invest in areas with high tax rates. This brings to the center of the urban problems cycle the fiscal crisis: not enough revenues to cover expenditures and demands for services rising annually. Raising taxes tends to be self-defeating since it drives middle-class income earners away to the suburbs that want no part of the city's fiscal problems. At some point the cycle must be broken. Many programs have been proposed, but none have looked adequately to the question of the underlying imbalance among the functions of the city.

THE METROPOLIS AND THE LARGER SOCIETY

A final issue to be discussed is the relationship between the modern metropolis and the larger society, the interrelation of urban and societal trends, important aspects of which are the transformation of agriculture and the alteration of the rural sector of American society.

After stabilizing in the decades 1920–40, the number of rural residents, farmers, and farms has declined steadily since World War II. Farm acreage has increased slightly, productivity and net farm output have soared, and farm size has grown sharply. These changes have been called a "second agricultural revolution" by agricultural experts. Data supporting these generalizations are shown below.

	1920	1970
Farm population (mills)	32.0	9.7
Number of farms (mills)	6.5	2.7
Farm acreage (mills)	95.6	1,103
Average farm size (acres)	147	383

SOURCE: U.S. Department of Commerce, *Statistical Abstract of the United States, 1975* (Washington, D.C.: Government Printing Office, 1975).

To account for these dramatic changes and their rapid acceleration after World War II, one must understand the long-term transformation of agriculture. In the words of economist William Parker:

The developments since 1940 are the payoff on a continental scale of the whole U.S. agricultural history: the expansion of a commercially minded farm population over the soil, the development of the institutions and attitudes from which scientific agriculture could grow, and the raising of productivity and national wealth to levels at which capital formation—in the soil, in equipment, in ideas, and in the training of human beings—could proceed. (Parker in Davis, Easterlin, and Parker 1972:373)

Clearly, advances in scientific agriculture were fundamental in the post-World War II increases in farm productivity. This was the crystallization of the historical tendencies referred to above. We must also look to such changes to explain the altered relations between farm and metropolis. A useful overall measure of the huge increases in farm productivity is farm output per man-hour. The data below reveal why the last generation's fivefold increase in efficiency can properly be called a "second agricultural revolution."

(1967 = 100)	Farm Output per Man-Hour
1950	33
1960	64
1973	133

SOURCE: U.S. Department of Commerce, *Statistical Abstract of the United States, 1975* (Washington, D.C.: Government Printing Office, 1975).

In analyzing the nature of the changes measured, three categories can be distinguished:

Mechanization: The development of the internal combustion engine and its adaptation to many farm tasks stands out as the major breakthrough in this area. In the 1940s there were only one tractor and less than one truck per three farms. By the 1970s the figures were about two tractors and one truck for each farm. Between 1950 and 1974, the value of all farm machinery and equipment per farm grew fourfold in constant dollars.

Biochemical invention: More than matching these increases were changes in seed, feed, livestock breeds, and the use of chemicals. Fertilizer, lime, and pesticide expenditures rose fivefold since World War II. These innovations increased output per acre as well as per man-hour. Hybrid seeds improved yields and fertilizing techniques added to productivity advances. The land released from feeding work animals was put to good use as the earnings from exports purchased the gasoline to drive the machines.

Programed scientific research with government financing: The long history of land grant colleges and experimental stations has paid off handsomely in the last generation. Between 1965 and 1975 alone, the federal expenditures for the Department of Agriculture's research and development program grew from $200 to $428 million. It should be noted that the Department of Housing and Urban Development typically received a research and development budget on the order of $1 million per year! As one urban commentator remarks:

Although only a small fraction of the economy is now involved with agriculture, a separate Department of Agriculture exists but though 70 percent of the population is now urban, there is no Department of Cities.

If there were a Department of Cities, the same needs of the urban dweller and the same interests of the government in the city would be generated as are presently generated by the Department of Agriculture for the nation's farmers. (Abrams 1967:3447)

The most important change in the organization of the farm sector was the appearance of the very large farm and the direct linking of large producers to the world of business, which can be termed the birth of agribusiness. These larger farm units meant specialization and integration of functions. Food from raw product to retail outlet could be handled more efficiently and could be processed to suit changing consumer tastes. These changes also meant the decline of the family farm because it could not compete; it could not invest, mechanize, and perform operations on the scale necessary for modern commercial agriculture. By the mid-1970s we find that, of all the farmers, 44 percent were over fifty-five years of age, with the average age about fifty-two years. The youth are still seeking out the metropolises and the remaining few family farms are dying off rapidly. Another factor contributing to the decline of the family farm is the fact that though prices received by farmers grew, the prices they paid grew more rapidly.

Did the government, through its price subsidy programs to farmers, attempt to stop this decline? From the viewpoint of many, unfortunately, the answer is no. The data indicate that the majority of government support has been shifting rapidly to the largest agricultural businesses—those with sales over $20,000. Their share has risen from 31 percent to 76 percent over the past fifteen years.

Since the benefits from government subsidies and price supports were realized by farmers in the best economic position, marginally successful ones were given no inducement to stay. Government policy also aggravated rural poverty because little assistance was given the low-income farmer who stayed on the land.

As the last pages of Chapter Five indicated, the farm sector was economically interwoven with the urban by World War I. By the 1970s the rural farm sector was, for all intents and purposes, fully urbanized and industrialized. It still played a most important role in American life, but the role was now fully integrated. A final figure suggests the scope of this integration: by the 1970s, per capita personal income of the farm population from nonfarm sources equaled that from farm sources. And of all the rural population, farm population fell from 53 percent in 1940 to 18 percent in 1970.

Ultimately, these changes provided a reserve of labor power for our expanding urban centers. They also provided food and its by-products to our population at higher and higher levels of choice. It was these higher levels of choice, along with shifts in the international markets for grain, that have been principally responsible for the recent sharp rises in food prices.

Since 1970 food prices have exploded. Poor government planning, the sharp rise in fertilizer costs (due to the oil crisis), drought and other natural disasters were mainly responsible. In addition, the expanding demand in modernized countries for high-grain-consuming meats (12 lbs. of grain = 1 lb. of beef) was added on to growing world population. Simply reducing beef consumption for urban Americans back to the 1950 levels (assuming no other changes) could reduce corn grain demand by about 500 million bushels annually. Such a change would make it possible to increase our food grain exports considerably (other crops could be planted instead of corn), thus providing added earnings for farmers or the needed reserves for a world food bank. This could also mean lower food prices for urban dwellers and the ability to pay for more imports (such as needed oil) with the foreign exchange earned by farm products.

This chapter illustrated how job and residential choices reshaped the modern metropolis. It showed how the size, age, and rate of growth of an urban area interacted with such decisions to affect the nature of the urbanization process and the internal structure of the city. In turn, these changes in form reflect back on the functions the city performs. The balance or imbalance among these functions generates new social patterns and ways of life. Such social innovation requires adaptation and flexibility in urban society and leadership from its members.

When these qualities are lacking, deeply rooted individual and social problems become more evident and require strong policy measures. Whether or not we as a metropolitan nation are willing to make the decisions on priorities and long-run strategies to carry through such measures is still an open question, as we enter the last quarter of the twentieth century.

CHAPTER NINE

Conclusions and New Perspectives

Social scientists hold at least three views on cities and urbanization. One group, in which we could place Mumford and Doxiadis, stresses universal similarities among cities and sees world-wide modernization leading to a coming together of urban form and structure. In their view cities merge into a world network of urban areas closely resembling one another and closely linked in ways of life. A second group, led by Sjoberg, sees the same kind of similarities in the common city form and the tightly knit urban network, but believes that urbanization is not universal but rather is culturally specific (Indian culture helps to create cities that are in some way Indian). Thus, for this group, cultural differences play a stronger role in the urbanizing and modernizing processes. The third group, of which Berry is a leading exponent, sees urbanization operating in different ways that vary with the times and the cultures. It believes, with the second group, that cultural factors dominate over technology and that both vary greatly as to their timing and rates of change. However, unlike the other two groups, members of this third group believe that the results are a growing divergence of urban forms in different regions of the world. Thus, the cities of Europe, the United States, and those of less developed countries are different as are the urbanizing influences at work.

Our views draw from each of these, while adding a new emphasis. We suggest that all the cities of modern history performed three similar, fundamental functions in shaping their societies.

Thus, urbanization has an underlying set of purposes—to create population settlements that perform certain functions for society.

However, we believe further that the forces (demographic, technological, institutional) shaping the urban thrust, while similar in nature, are complex in action. In different resource and cultural settings, they interact with the balance or imbalance among the city functions to produce different forms of cities—of varied physical, socioeconomic, and political structure. Then this urban ecology reacts back upon the balance points of urban functioning to change neighborhood activities and customs, family manners and life styles. These further influence the values, expectations, and beliefs of the entire societal change process in subtle and far-reaching ways. The result is the continuing, complex story that we have studied over the preceding chapters.

THE DYNAMICS OF URBANIZATION AND THE COMPLEXITY OF CITIES

This book has described and analyzed cities and urbanization. The great problem of a short study such as this one is to recognize and do justice to the dynamic nature of the urbanization process and to view the city as an evolving organized complexity. For example, any study of urbanization must begin at the demographic level. Urbanization, in the strict sense, refers to the concentration of population through growth and redistribution. Throughout the book we showed changes in population size and distribution during different historical periods. However, changes in the distribution and size of population have many consequences, affecting people's economic and political activity, social organization, and culture. When such changes have a different distribution from the emergence of new technics and industries, tensions and conflicts accompany the mutual interaction of expanding trade and income.

There is no neat and simple way of understanding the multiple interactions among these aspects of life. We tried to illuminate them in several ways. One was to concentrate on the American experience, and to provide points of comparison with England, the ancient world, and medieval European society. We hoped that the rich texture of urbanization would be clearer through such societal and historical comparisons. A second approach was to give a detailed, historical analysis of American urbanization so that the changes within the mix of urbanization could be better appreciated. For example, we discussed the consequences for neighborhood, city, and region and focused on particular features of urban life such as the nature of community and the interaction of city living with changing class structure. A third approach was to develop the idea that the study of urbanization raises the question of what cities are as distinctive types of settlements. In one sense urban areas are constantly changing their effective boundaries—village to town to city to metropolis to urban region. Meanwhile the city limits signs are hammered down at political boundaries without reference to operating socioeconomic realities. This gap reflects and influences the patterns of jobs and incomes, wealth and resource distribution.

Our central theme was the repetition of the threefold continuity in historical functioning:

1. *The interactive function* leads to the exchange of ideas and the development of complex interrelationships. These profoundly impact on the city's culture and life styles and give support to the other functions below.

2. *The generative function,* through scale economies and agglomeration, creates goods, services, technologies, and ideas. Innovations and specialization are central to this concept. Strongly generative cities become radiating centers for new industries, technics, and social-political changes, and continuously specialize in their services for one another.

3. *The upgrading function,* in conjunction with the above two, assimilates migrants on a vast scale and raises their standards of living. Becoming urbanites, they add to the richness and diversity of the culture and develop the next generation of human resources for continuation of the generative and interactive functions.

THE CHANGING BALANCE OF CITY FUNCTIONS

It is a major thesis of this book that in order to understand our current urban environment, its future direction, and the nature of its problems, we must comprehend the origins of our present cities. This understanding cannot simply be limited to a historical description, but it must be centered on a socially valid analysis of their functions. We believe these functions to be fairly constant; however, the wider forces intertwined with urbanization, and its societal causes and effects, have changed over time. These forces shifted the relative importance or balance of city functions.

Historically, cities show a long period of change before the emergence of these three functions to their positions of current dominance. In low-technology-level agricultural societies these three were present in only primitive forms.

In retrospect, what we call civilized societies originated among the organized groups centered in city settlements. They exchanged goods, services, and ideas and generated innovations in ways of life and means of earning a living other than hunting and farming. But the network of relationships among the earliest cities was very weak and fragile. The internal structure focused on protective and priestly activities, providing little room for upgrading through investment in human resources. Large populations could only be organized in a pyramidlike social structure, with the few ruling the many. Absolute control was in the hands of religious or quasi-religious leaders. The technics did not permit communication and specialization on a level adequate to continue upgrading large numbers of immigrants. Instead, such societies had extensive slavery systems built like great living machines that made possible a high flowering of culture in many of the ancient cities of the eastern Mediterranean. When these cities combined their power of organization with great military might, they could politically control an empire. This the Persians and Romans did quite effectively for centuries. Eventually internal contradictions prevented expansion of generative and interactive functions. External forces, such as disease and barbarian invasions, contributed to the urban stagnation of subsequent centuries. Revival came slowly, but it finally led to the creation of a new urban form—the premodern city of the Middle Ages.

In medieval times, with the increase in trade, the generative function became more important. But it was controlled carefully through social structure and political institutions. Guilds, manors, and church focused life on equilibrium values and the promise of the hereafter, while the villagers and feudal nobility dealt with the problems of this world. Toward the end of the Middle Ages, the generative function rose to a stronger position. This was accomplished in two stages. There was the slow ascendancy of urban centers spurred by the growth of world commerce, and the development of new ideas in science and in politics. There were few cities and each was a center for a far-flung trade network. However, the urban influence had not penetrated the hinterlands of agriculture.

Then around the middle of the eighteenth century change accelerated as the forces of the previous two centuries (focus on world trade, advances in learning and the social organizing principles of society) met at the crossroads of England. There emerged the first industrial revolution fueled by knowledge and technical breakthroughs in a handful of industries. It was driven by the impersonal organizing principles of laissez faire and supported by capitalists, businessmen, and the remaining feudal elite who were anxious to retain some social control.

It created new kinds of urban life styles. Industrial cities appeared; producers were differentiated from consumers, and vast agglomerations of the population and residences were centered around the factory. Gradually the benefits of increasing productivity, the growth in scale, and the use of machines spread to the urban working classes.

These processes changed the form and structure of cities as well as the ways in which they performed their functions. The generative function leaped to dominance with rapid economic growth and extensive innovation in ways of life. The interactive function grew more impersonal with the separation of man from his craft as the growth of machines laid down an industrial discipline that tended to reduce values of community and social life. The upgrading function, while operative, seemed to be frequently swamped by the cycles of business growth and the accompanying dislocation of the enclosures in the countryside.

While these changes occurred in England, parallel changes took place in America. From small beachhead settlements in the seventeenth century, urban towns evolved under British colonial rule. Serving the commercial goals of mercantilism and testing the mother country's institutions and laws in the American resource mix of abundance and openness set the tone for the unifying of the nation after the Revolution. Despite a strong interactive function, the colonial city had a weak upgrading potential and a limited generative function, for it operated in a slow-growth agricultural society. In the nineteenth century the generative function came to the fore as the western expansion of the frontier, the growth of world trade, transportation innovations, and a positive government policy toward economic growth fostered new industries and ideas. Early industrialization followed a pattern similar to Great Britain's, but with the American stamp of greater interaction through sociopolitical institutions and little rural dislocation. The earliest mass migrations from Europe also signified that the upgrading function would be expanding to match the other two.

However, after the Civil War, with the full flowering of the industrial city, the generative function seemed to dominate the interactive and upgrading functions. Certainly upgrading continued, but at great private and public costs as many individuals and groups were caught in the conflicts and imbalances generated. As the community declined in importance, so did the interactive function, and internal communication became a problem.

Industrialization led to new imbalances among the functions as well as new urban problems. Varied political and social responses from political machines in cities to new national political parties to a strong social reform movement were attempted. But the flows of migrants, technology, and trade continued to test fully the upgrading function of the cities. This was similar to the earlier period in urbanization, but the American pioneer environment gave our experience the special characteristics that were carried into the present century.

A major portion of our work has examined the tensions and balance among the three functions as they evolved into the network of modern metropolitan centers that dominate American society today. We looked at the economic, social, and political factors that influenced the functioning of cities. These were the broad societal trends leading to full metropolitanization. We then analyzed the rise of the upgrading function and the contributions of migration and natural increase to the rhythm of urban growth since the 1920s. Following this, we traced the impact of changing markets and technology on the regional redistribution of economic opportunities in metropolitan areas. This evolutionary growth pattern shaped the relations between the generative and upgrading functions. Under the impact of a new industrial and technical mix, the very structure and form of cities changed. This involved simultaneously a gathering together at certain points in the network and dispersal within these aggregates.

The adaptation of urban institutions became pronounced as new blocks of voters, vested interest groups, and economically segregated areas developed rapidly. The generative function that raised the standard of living seemed to continue, but the upgrading and interactive functions were again out of balance. The community, as the center of interaction, was losing its identity, and the paths of upward mobility were, for many, harder to climb. From these imbalances a series of themes suggest themselves as to why the city could not fulfill what has become its critical societal function—that of upgrading.

If our cities are to do more than provide baby-sitting functions for the poor, we must face the root aspects of urban problems. These include: the notion of optimum or best size for manageable cities; the hard societal question of the best distribution of growing affluence; the lack of investment in human resources; the problem of city age and overgrowth; the political takeover of government policy-making apparatus by corporate economic interest groups; the multiplication in urban regions of social costs due to inefficiency, waste, and pollution; the growing questions of how many resources should be made available in what manner to the different levels of government—state, local, and federal—and how political leaders should expend these resources to provide a better-quality urban life.

TOWARD A WORLD-WIDE PERSPECTIVE

In the history of humankind, rapid and large-scale urbanization is a recent occurrence. Before 1850 no society was mainly urban, and by 1900 only one, Great Britain, could be so regarded. Today, only three-quarters of a century later, all industrial societies are highly urbanized, and throughout the rest of the world the dynamic of urbanization is gathering momentum.

As this process has spread from Western Europe throughout the world, two major trends have become clear. One is that the later a country becomes industrialized, the faster its urbanization. As Kingsley Davis notes, "The change from a population with 10 percent of its members in cities of 100,000 or larger to one in which 30 percent lived in such cities took about 79 years in England and Wales, 66 in the U.S., 48 in Germany, 36 in Japan, and 26 in Australia" (Davis 1974:94).

A second trend is the continued close connection between urbanization and economic growth. The process of change from a spread-out pattern of human settlement to one of concentration in urban centers is intimately linked to the transition from an agrarian to an industrial economy and the concentration of industry in urban locations. Therefore, as more countries proceed on the road to industrialization, the world-wide degree of urbanization also rises.

Over the last fifteen years roughly 577 million people, out of a total world population of 4 billion, either moved into or were born in settlements of 100,000 or more inhabitants. Although migration from rural areas is important, a sizable and growing proportion of this newly urbanized population is due to natural increase, that is, born to parents already living in urban areas. With high rates of natural increase, the urban explosion continues even with migration from the countryside.

The present pattern in less developed countries is fairly clear—the bigger the unit, the faster it seems to grow. As one commentator puts it, "Towns grow more rapidly than villages, cities faster than towns; cities of more than a million faster than cities with less than a million; and multi-million cities, with over 2.5 million people, fastest of all. The result is that, by the year 2000 New York and Tokyo will be joined, on present trends, by at least 25 other contenders in the super-city class. Of these, no fewer than 18 will be in the under-developed countries." (Wilsher 1975:E3)

At first glance the current urbanization process in the poorer, less developed countries of the world seems to be unlike the historical process previously described. Indeed, all of these countries are deeply enmeshed in traditional ways: farmers use primitive methods and implements; there is little or no modern manufacturing; illiteracy is prevalent; effective transportation and communication networks are lacking—in short, modernization has not arrived. Yet, their urban areas are growing at rapid rates. We will use our view of the way cities function with a changing mix of urbanizing pressures to explain this puzzle. It would seem that, fundamentally, the same forces (demographic, technological, institutional) are at work in urbanizing these nations that were at work in the past history of the West. But now they must be understood from different perspectives.

THE TECHNOLOGICAL, INSTITUTIONAL, AND DEMOGRAPHIC MIX

Rapid diffusion of modern farming technology into backward areas of the world exposes them to disruptions within their traditional landholding institutions similar to those caused by the enclosure movement in Great Britain. This has a twofold effect. The best farmers modernize their inputs (seed, fertilizer, water pumps, insecticides), commercialize their greatly increased output, and sell their product for higher profits in frequently distant markets. The rapid growth of world trade has brought all countries into a close-knit network, where world prices dominate most grains and cereals, raw materials and manufactures. This is where the well-to-do farmer sells and buys and makes a profit; however, these world prices are higher than the poor peasant can afford. (This is the other or second effect.) He cannot raise enough to feed himself and does not have the capital to increase his output. To help the poor farmer who must buy grain at higher world prices, governments in nations such as India have kept basic foodstuffs (rice and wheat) below the world price. This further stimulates local well-to-do peasants to plant larger holdings, to invest in modern ways, and to sell their farm production in world rather than local markets. The majority of poor peasants working small patches, using oxen and wooden plows, cannot raise enough to feed their families and cannot get enough cash from sales to buy the food and other essentials to live. They are reduced to a marginal existence and must begin to wander about seeking jobs and food. In order to survive, they flee the land for the cities where government distribution of food subsidies is more certain and rations are frequently more generous.

Since the early seventies, regional droughts, skyrocketing oil and fertilizer prices, and continued demand for grain-fed animals in developed countries have made the situation a crisis.

These technological and institutional forces must be seen in a special demographic perspective—in a few words, a drastically lowered death rate without a comparable reduction in the birth rate. Recall that in the American experience of the nineteenth century, immigration was the main source of urban population increases, while in this century natural increase has become more and more important. By the 1970s their relative roles have been just about reversed. The estimate is that in the earlier period less than one-third of urban growth was from natural causes, and since World War II the figure has been consistently over two-thirds. The nineteenth-century American urban birth rates were significantly lower than rural rates and the death rates were probably as high or higher. In the twentieth century the differences have narrowed greatly, and we have fairly low birth and death rates at slightly above replacement levels of natural increase. In the last third of the twentieth century, less developed areas show high rural and urban birth rates and low rural and urban death rates. This produces very high rates of natural increase in both sectors. If we impose the substantial rural to urban migration figures on top of this, the reason behind the term "urban crisis" becomes apparent. In the British and American experiences, demographic factors shifted slowly over a 150-year period. In the less developed areas the transition to low death rates took one generation, while birth rates have been slow to fall.

The consequences for the quality of life, and even survival itself, for these newly urbanizing peoples are quite serious. We know of the tremendous difficulties experienced by large urban centers in highly industrialized and technically mature countries in developing the administrative resources needed to cope with large-scale problems. The problems involved in providing jobs, housing, medical care, and necessary services to urban residents in less developed countries are even more staggering. As one United Nations report put it, there are "exploding cities in unexploding economies." The rapidly growing cities create such overwhelming problems that governments in less developed countries have tried numerous plans to create more balanced growth between rural and urban areas. These include relocation of the capital (Brazil and Tanzania), damping of wage differentials between urban and rural areas (Zambia), reorientation of education toward agricultural interests (Indonesia and Tanzania), subsidies for industrial location (Togo), rural land reclamation (Kenya), and a "citizenship tax" on living in the city (Seoul in South Korea). (Freeman and Berelson 1974:38)

TOWARD A LONG-RUN PERSPECTIVE

In the American experience the generative function is clearly tied to the long swings in economic growth and population, especially the immigration component. The interactive function has shifted with each new breakthrough in transportation, power, and communication technology. This was linked to the upgrading function through the operation of changing political and social institutions and the changing city form and structure. Imbalances among functions were normal, with such imbalances leading not only to new urban problems but also to creative opportunities for urban adaptation.

Today to keep this dynamism working seems to require a full understanding of the already completed transformation from the nineteenth to mid-twentieth-century industrial-occupational patterns and the many-sided effects of the full metropolitanization of the population. In the coming decades the service-oriented post-industrial society of America will shape a new urban order. The decentralizing metropolis will be the container, and new points of population, the product. The growth and shifts within the urban network will continue to change power relations within the society as we become completely urbanized.

In a global perspective, our analysis indicates that in much of Asia, Africa, and Latin America the commercial and industrial cities are still forming while the modern city functions are gaining momentum.

Due in good part to the patterns of western development (especially commercial, political, and technical), the generative function is usually fragile and unprotected from world-wide pressures. Further, the interactive function is not supportive of the generative and does not provide the climate for proper operation of the other two functions. The societies of these less developed areas are deeply enmeshed in differing ways of life, beliefs, and values. In closed, agricultural societies such traditional ways formed social, political, and economic divisions that were self-contained and balancing. Today, though, they act as serious barriers to the successful exchange of ideas and innovations. This is most obvious in urban centers, exhibited by the disastrous human consequences caused by the failure to promote the upgrading function.

In both advanced and developing countries, the focus of change is in urban centers. In today's world with its new viewpoints on the concepts of limited resources and human needs, we must learn to balance the costs with the benefits of living in cities. We must also learn ways to distribute the costs and benefits more justly.

We hope you have begun to understand the nature of our urban condition and its impact on behavior patterns and institutions so that you can join in considering how to bring under control the forces that will continue to shape the quality of urban life for coming generations.

Selected References

The following books and articles have been culled from the vast and rapidly growing literature of the field with the needs of the student in mind. Asterisked works are highly recommended: The single asterisk indicates introductory material; the double asterisk, material at a higher level of difficulty.

General

U.S. Bureau of the Census
1960   *Survey of Manufactures, 1959–1960.* Washington, D.C.: Government Printing Office.

U.S. Bureau of the Census
1968   "Lifetime Migration Histories of the American People." *C.P.R. Technical Studies,* Series P–23, No. 25. Washington, D.C.: Government Printing Office.

U.S. Department of HEW, Public Health Service
1968   "Migration in the United States: An Analysis of Residence Histories." Public Health Monograph, No. 77. Washington, D.C.: Government Printing Office.

U.S. Department of Commerce
1975   *Statistical Abstract of the United States, 1975.* Washington, D.C.: Government Printing Office.

U.S. Bureau of the Census
         Census of the United States 1860, 1910, 1960, 1970. Health, Education and Welfare, Washington, D.C.: Government Printing Office.

Chapter 1

*Adams, Robert M.
   1960   "The Origin of Cities." *Scientific American* 203 (September): 153–
           72.
Argan, Giulio C.
   1969   *The Renaissance City.* New York: Braziller.
Childe, V. Gordon
   1965   *What Happened in History.* Baltimore: Penguin.
*Goodman, Paul, and Percival Goodman
   1947   *Communitas, Means of Livelihood and Way of Life.* New York:
           Random House.
Gutkind, E. A.
   1964   *International History of City Development,* vol. 6. New York: Free
           Press.
Hammond, Mason
   1972   *The City in the Ancient World.* Cambridge, Mass.: Harvard Univer-
           sity Press.
**Haworth, Lawrence
   1963   *The Good City.* Bloomington, Ind.: Indiana University Press.
*Jacobs, Jane
   1969   *The Economy of Cities.* New York: Random House.
Laslett, Peter
   1966   *The World We Have Lost.* New York: Scribner.
Lewis, Oscar
   1973   "The Rural-Urban Continuum." In John Walton and Donald E.
           Carns (eds.), *Cities in Change: Studies on the Urban Condition.*
           Boston: Allyn and Bacon.
Martindale, Don
   1958   "Prefatory Remarks: The Theory of the City." In Max Weber, *The
           City,* trans. by D. Martindale and O. Neuwirth. New York: Free
           Press.
Mayer, Harold M.
   1971   "Definition of the City." In Larry S. Bourne (ed.), *The Internal
           Structure of the City: Readings on Space and Environment.* New
           York: Oxford University Press.
Meadows, Paul
   1957   "The City, Technology and History." *Social Forces* 36 (December):
           141–47.
Mumford, Lewis
   1938   *The Culture of Cities.* New York: Harcourt Brace.

**Mumford, Lewis
  1961 *The City in History: Its Origins, Transformations and Its Prospects.*
         New York: Harcourt, Brace & World.
Pirenne, Henri
  1939 *Medieval Cities.* Princeton, N.J.: Princeton University Press.
Roebuck, Janet
  1974 *The Shaping of Urban Society.* New York: Scribner.
**Schnore, Leo R. (ed.)
  1968 *Social Science and the City: A Survey of Urban Research.* New
         York: Praeger.
Scientific American Books
  1969 *Cities.* New York: Knopf.
Sennett, Richard
  1969 *Classic Essays on the Culture of Cities.* New York: Appleton-Cen-
         tury-Crofts.
Sjoberg, Gideon
  1960 *The Preindustrial City: Past and Present.* Glencoe, Ill.: Free Press.
Thomlinson, Ralph
  1969 *Urban Structure.* New York: Random House.
Tisdale, Hope (Eldridge)
  1942 "The Process of Urbanization." *Social Forces* 20 (March): 311–16.
Weber, Max
  1958 *The City.* New York: Free Press.
Williams, Raymond
  1973 *The Country and the City.* London: Oxford University Press.

Chapter 2

*Ashton, T. S.
  1948 *The Industrial Revolution, 1760–1830.* London: Oxford University
         Press.
Banks, J. A.
  1973 "The Contagion of Numbers." In H. J. Dyos and Michael Wolff
         (eds.), *The Victorian City,* vol. 1. London: Routledge & Kegan
         Paul.
Briggs, Asa
  1963 *Victorian Cities.* London: Odham Books.
Choay, Francoise
  1969 *The Modern City: Planning in the Nineteenth Century.* New York:
         Braziller.

Deane, Phyllis, and W. A. Cole
    1969   *British Economic Growth 1688–1959,* 2d ed. Cambridge at the University Press.
Dickinson, Robert E.
    1951   *The West European City.* London: Ròutledge & Kegan Paul.
Dyos, H. J., and D. A. Reeder
    1973   "Slums and Suburbs." In H. J. Dyos and Michael Wolff (eds.), *The Victorian City,* vol. 1. London: Routledge & Kegan Paul.
Engels, Frederick
    1952   *The Conditions of the Working-Class in England.* London: Allen & Unwin.
Gauldie, Enid
    1974   *Cruel Habitations: A History of Working-Class Housing 1780–1918.* New York: Harper & Row.
Hobsbaum, Eric J.
    1964   *The Age of Revolution 1789–1848.* London: Weidenfeld and Nicolson.
*Lampard, Eric E.
    1957   *Industrial Revolution: Interpretations and Perspectives.* Washington, D.C.: American Historical Association, Service Center for Teachers of History.
Landes, David S.
    1970   *The Unbound Prometheus: Technological Change and Industrial Development in Western Europe from 1750 to the Present.* Cambridge, Eng.: Cambridge University Press.
**Polanyi, Karl
    1962   *The Great Transformation. The Political and Economic Origins of Our Time.* Boston: Beacon Press.
Smith, Adam
    1937   *An Inquiry into the Nature and Causes of the Wealth of Nations.* New York: Modern Library, Random House.
*Taylor, Philip A. M.
    1958   *The Industrial Revolution in Great Britain: Triumph or Disaster.* Lexington, Mass.: Heath.
Thomis, Malcolm
    1974   *The Town Laborer and the Industrial Revolution.* London: B. T. Batsford.
Thompson, E. P.
    1964   *The Making of the English Working Class.* New York: Pantheon.

Chapter 3

Blumenfeld, Hans
  1973 "The Urban Pattern." In J. Walton and D. Carns (eds.), *Cities in Change.* Boston: Allyn and Bacon.
Borchert, John R.
  1967 "American Metropolitan Evolution." *Geographical Review* 57 (July, 1967): 301–32.
Davis, Lance, et al.
  1965 *American Economic History: The Development of a National Economy.* New York: Richard D. Irwin.
**Davis, Lance; Richard Easterlin; William Parker et al.
  1972 *American Economic Growth: An Economist's History of the United States.* New York: Harper & Row.
*Eckhardt, Wolf von
  1964 *The Challenge of Megalopolis.* New York: Macmillan.
*Glaab, Charles N., and A. Theodore Brown
  1976 *A History of Urban America,* 2d ed. New York: Macmillan.
**Gottmann, Jean
  1961 *Megalopolis, The Urbanized Northeastern Seaboard of the United States.* Cambridge, Mass.: MIT Press.
Gras, Norman S.
  1922 *An Introduction to Economic History.* New York: Harper.
Jackson, Kenneth A., and S. Schultz (eds.)
  1972 *Cities in American History.* New York: Knopf.
Lebergott, Stanley
  1964 *Manpower in Economic Growth.* New York: McGraw-Hill.
McWilliams, Wilson Carey
  1973 *The Idea of Fraternity in America.* Berkeley: University of California Press.
*Miller, Zane L.
  1973 *The Urbanization of Modern America: A Brief History.* New York: Harcourt Brace Jovanovich.
Pickard, Jerome P.
  1973 "Growth of Urbanized Population in the United States: Past, Present and Future." In David W. Rasmussen and Charles T. Haworth (eds.), *The Modern City.* New York: Harper & Row.
Robertson, Ross M.
  1955 *History of the American Economy.* New York: Harcourt, Brace & World.

Russel, Robert A.
  1964   *A History of the American Economic System.* New York: Appleton-Century-Crofts.
Schnore, Leo F. (ed.)
  1975   *The New Urban History.* Princeton, N.J.: Princeton University Press.
**Vidich, Arthur J., and Joseph Bensman
  1958   *Small Town in Mass Society.* Princeton, N.J.: Princeton University Press.
Wakstein, Allen M. (ed.)
  1970   *The Urbanization of America: An Historical Anthology.* Boston: Houghton Mifflin.
**Warner, Sam Bass, Jr.
  1970   "A Scaffolding for Urban History." In Allen W. Wakstein (ed.), *The Urbanization of America: An Historical Anthology.* Boston: Houghton Mifflin.
Warner, Sam Bass, Jr.
  1972   *The Urban Wilderness: A History of the American City.* New York: Harper & Row.

Chapter 4

Bremmer, Robert H.
  1970   "The Discovery of Poverty." In Allen M. Wakstein (ed.), *The Urbanization of America: An Historical Anthology.* Boston: Houghton Mifflin.
*Bridenbaugh, Carl
  1964   *Cities in the Wilderness, The First Century of Urban Life in America 1625–1742.* New York: Capricorn.
*Bridenbaugh, Carl
  1964   *Cities in Revolt, Urban Life in America 1743–1776.* New York: Capricorn.
**de Tocqueville, Alexis
  1961   *Democracy in America,* vol. 1. New York: Schocken.
Eaton, Clement (ed.)
  1963   *The Leaven of Democracy.* New York: Braziller.
Lane, Roger
  1970   "The Expansion of Police Functions." In Allen M. Wakstein (ed.), *The Urbanization of America: An Historical Anthology.* Boston: Houghton Mifflin.

Lockridge, Kenneth A.
    1970   *A New England Town: The First Hundred Years.* New York: Norton.
Nettels, Curtis
    1962   *The Emergence of a National Economy.* New York: Harper & Row.
Schlesinger, Arthur M., Jr.
    1945   *The Age of Jackson.* Boston: Little, Brown.
**Taylor, George R.
    1951   *The Transportation Revolution, 1815–1860.* New York: Harper & Row.
Taylor, George R.
    1970   "Building an Intra Urban Transportation System." In Allen M. Wakstein (ed.), *The Urbanization of America: An Historical Anthology.* Boston: Houghton Mifflin.
*Wade, Richard C.
    1964   *The Urban Frontier.* Chicago: University of Chicago Press.
Zevin, Robert B.
    1971   "The Growth of Cotton Textile Production After 1815." In Robert W. Fogel and S. L. Engerman (eds.), *The Reinterpretation of American Economic History.* New York: Harper & Row.

Chapter 5

Brady, Dorothy
    1972   "Consumption and the Style of Life." In Lance Davis; Richard Easterlin; William Parker et al.; *American Economic Growth: An Economist's History of the United States.* New York: Harper & Row.
Burlingame, Roger
    1938   *March of the Iron Men. A Social History of Union Through Invention.* New York: Scribner.
*Cochran, Thomas C., and William Miller
    1942   *The Age of Enterprise, A Social History of Industrial America.* New York: Macmillan.
*Handlin, Oscar
    1951   *The Uprooted, The Epic Story of the Great Migrations That Made the American People.* New York: Grosset & Dunlap.
*Hays, Samuel P.
    1957.   *The Response to Industrialism, 1885–1914.* Chicago: University of Chicago Press.

Jackson, Kenneth
    1975   "Urban Deconcentration in the Nineteenth Century: A Statistical
            Inquiry." In Leo F. Schnore (ed.), *The New Urban History*. Prince-
            ton, N.J.: Princeton University Press.
Jones, Maldwyn A.
    1960   *American Immigration*. Chicago: University of Chicago Press.
Josephson, Matthew
    1962   *The Robber Barons: The Great American Capitalists 1861–1901*.
            New York: Harcourt, Brace & World.
Merton, Robert
    1968   *Social Theory and Social Structure*. New York: Free Press.
Moore, Barrington, Jr.
    1966   *The Social Origins of Dictatorship and Democracy*. Boston: Beacon
            Press.
*Osofsky, Gilbert
    1963   *Harlem, The Making of a Ghetto*. New York: Harper & Row.
**Park, Robert, et al.
    1967   *The City*. Chicago: University of Chicago Press.
Pease, Otis (ed.)
    1962   *The Progressive Years*. New York: Braziller.
Pred, Allen R.
    1966   *The Spatial Dynamics of U.S. Urban Industrial Growth, 1800–1914*.
            Cambridge, Mass.: MIT Press.
*Riis, Jacob A.
    1957   *How the Other Half Lives: Studies Among the Tenements of New
            York*. New York: Hill and Wang.
Riordan, William L.
    1963   *Plunkitt of Tammany Hall: A Series of Plain Talk on Very Practical
            Politics*. New York: Dutton.
**Rischin, Moses
    1962   *The Promised City: New York's Jews 1870–1914*. New York:
            Harper & Row.
Schlesinger, Arthur M.
    1933   *The Rise of the City 1878–1898*. New York: Macmillan.
Schnore, Leo F.
    1970   "Metropolitan Growth and Decentralization." In Allen M. Wak-
            stein (ed.), *The Urbanization of America: An Historical Anthology*.
            Boston: Houghton Mifflin.
Segel, Arthur (ed.)
    1965   *Chicago's Famous Buildings*. Chicago: University of Chicago Press.

Thernstrom, Steven
    1964   *Poverty and Progress: Social Mobility in a Nineteenth-Century City.*
            Cambridge, Mass.: Harvard University Press.
Ward, David
    1971   *Cities and Immigrants.* New York: Oxford University Press.
**Warner, Sam Bass, Jr.
    1962   *Streetcar Suburbs.* Cambridge, Mass.: Harvard University Press.
Wirth, Louis
    1957   "Urbanism as a Way of Life." In Paul K. Hatt and A. J. Reiss, Jr.,
            (eds.), *Cities and Society.* Glencoe, Ill.: Free Press.

Chapter 6

**Banfield, Edward
    1974   *The Unheavenly City, Revisited.* Boston: Little, Brown.
Bensman, Joseph, and Arthur J. Vidich
    1971   *The New American Society.* Chicago: Quadrangle.
Bollens, John C., and Henry J. Schmandt
    1975   *The Metropolis: Its People, Politics and Economic Life,* 3d ed. New
            York: Harper & Row.
Burgess, Ernest W.
    1967   "The Growth of the City: An Introduction to a Research Project."
            In Robert E. Park et al. (eds.), *The City.* Chicago: University of
            Chicago Press.
**Chinitz, Benjamin
    1964   *City and Suburb: The Economics of Metropolitan Growth.* Engle-
            wood Cliffs, N.J.: Prentice-Hall.
Clark, Kenneth
    1967   *Dark Ghetto: Dilemmas of Social Power.* New York: Harper &
            Row.
*Cochran, Thomas C.
    1957   *The American Business System: A Historical Perspective 1900–1955.*
            New York: Harper & Row.
Fried, Marc
    1973   *The World of the Urban Working Class.* Cambridge, Mass.: Har-
            vard University Press.
Galbraith, John K.
    1967   *The New Industrial State.* Boston: Houghton Mifflin.
Gans, Herbert
    1968   *People and Plans.* New York: Basic Books.

*Glazer, Nathan, and Daniel P. Moynihan
    1970   *Beyond the Melting Pot, The Negroes, Puerto Ricans, Jews, Italians and Irish of New York City,* 2d ed. Cambridge, Mass.: MIT Press.
*Greely, Andrew M.
    1971   *Why Can't They Be Like Us? America's White Ethnic Groups.* New York: Dutton.
Greer, Scott
    1962   *The Emerging City.* Glencoe, Ill.: Free Press.
Greer, Scott
    1972   *The Urbane View.* New York: Oxford University Press.
*Jacobs, Jane
    1961   *The Death and Life of the Great American Cities.* New York: Random House.
Leuchtenberg, William
    1968   *The Perils of Prosperity 1914–1932.* Chicago: University of Chicago Press.
Leuchtenberg, William
    1963   *Franklin D. Roosevelt and the New Deal 1932–1940.* New York: Harper & Row.
**Long, Norton
    1975   *The Unwalled City.* New York: Basic Books.
**Lynd, Robert S., and Helen M. Lynd
    1956   *Middletown.* New York: Harcourt, Brace.
**McKelvey, Blake
    1968   *The Emergence of Metropolitan America 1915–1966.* New Brunswick, N.J.: Rutgers University Press.
Riesman, David
    1950   *The Lonely Crowd.* New Haven: Yale University Press.
Rose, Arnold (ed.)
    1948   *The Negro in America: The Condensed Version.* New York: Harper & Row.
Soule, George
    1968   *Prosperity Decade.* New York: Harper & Row.
*Vernon, Raymond
    1962   *The Myth and Reality of Our Urban Problems.* Cambridge, Mass.: Joint Center for Urban Studies of MIT and Harvard University.
Vernon, Raymond, and Edgar M. Hoover
    1962   *Anatomy of a Metropolis.* New York: Doubleday Anchor.
Wheaton, William L. C.
    1971   "Form and Structure of the Metropolitan Area." In Louis K. Lo-

ewenstein (ed.), *Urban Studies: An Introductory Reader.* New York: Free Press.

Chapter 7

Berry, Brian J. L.
  1973   *Growth Centers in the American Urban System,* vol. 1. Cambridge, Mass.: Ballinger.
Doxiadis, Constantine
  1968   *Ekistics.* New York: Oxford University Press.
Duncan, Beverly, and Stanley Lieberson
  1970   *Metropolis and Region in Transition.* Beverly Hills, Calif.: Russell Sage.
Easterlin, Richard
  1974   "Population." In Neil Chamberlain (ed.), *Contemporary Economic Issues,* 2d ed. Homewood, Ill.: Irwin.
Gordon, Milton
  1964   *Assimilation in American Life.* New York: Oxford University Press.
Hansen, Niles
  1975   *The Challenge of Urban Growth.* Lexington, Mass.: Heath.
Lampard, Eric E.
  1968   "The Evolving System of Cities in the United States." In Harvey S. Perloff and Lowdon Wingo (eds.), *Issues in Urban Economics.* Baltimore: Johns Hopkins Press.
Lampard, Eric E.
  1975   "Two Cheers for Quantitative History: An Agnostic Foreword." In Leo F. Schnore (ed.), *The New Urban History.* Princeton, N.J.: Princeton University Press.
Lee, E.; D. Thomas; R. Easterlin et al.
  1957–64 *Population Redistribution and Economic Growth,* 3 vols. Philadelphia: American Philosophical Society.
*Lewis, Oscar
  1966   *La Vida.* New York: Random House.
Lieberson, Stanley
  1963   *Ethnic Patterns in American Cities.* New York: Free Press.
Miller, Ann R.
  1964   *Net Intercensal Migration to Large Urban Areas of the United States, 1930–40, 1940–50, 1950–60.* Philadelphia: University of Pennsylvania.

**National Research Council, Social Science Panel on the Significance of Community in the Metropolitan Environment
   1974   *Toward an Understanding of Metropolitan America.* San Francisco: Canfield Press.
North, D., and W. Weissert
   1973   *Immigrants and the American Labor Market.* Washington, D.C.: Trans-Century Corp.
*Sale, Kirkpatrick
   1975   *Power Shift, the Rise of the Southern Rim and Its Challenge to the Eastern Establishment.* New York: Random House.
Spengler, Joseph J.
   1972   "Population Pressure, Housing and Habitat." In Joseph E. Haring (ed.), *Urban and Regional Economics.* Boston: Houghton Mifflin.
**Tilly, Charles
   1968   "Race and Migration to the American City." In James Q. Wilson (ed.), *The Metropolitan Enigma.* New York: Doubleday Anchor.
Wertheimer, Richard
   1971   *The Monetary Rewards of Migration Within the United States.* Washington, D.C.: Urban Institute.

Chapter 8

Abrams, Charles
   1965   *The City Is the Frontier.* New York: Harper & Row.
Abrams, Charles
   1967   "Federal Role in Urban Affairs." In United States, Congress, Senate, 89th Cong., 2d sess., *Hearings, Subcommittee on Executive Reorganization of the Committee on Government Operations.* Washington, D.C.: Government Printing Office.
Berger, Bennett
   1960   *Working-Class Suburb.* Berkeley: University of California Press.
*Birch, David
   1970   *The Economic Future of City and Suburb.* New York: Committee for Economic Development.
Boskoff, Alvin
   1975   "Emergence and Structure of the Urban Region: Suburb, Satellite and Fringe." In Sandor Halebsky (ed.), *The Sociology of the City.* New York: Scribner.
Bourne, Larry S. (ed.)
   1971   *The Internal Structure of the City: Readings on Space and Environment.* New York: Oxford University Press.

Edel, Matthew
  1972   "Planning, Market or Warfare?—Recent Land Use Conflicts in American Cities." In M. Edel and J. Rothenberg, (eds.), *Readings in Urban Economics.* New York: Macmillan.

*The Editors of Fortune
  1958   *The Exploding Metropolis,* 2d ed. New York: Time, Inc.

Fellner, David, et al.
  1975   "Jobs in Philadelphia: Experience and Prospects." *Business Review,* Federal Reserve Bank of Philadelphia (December).

Fried, Marc
  1963   "Grieving for a Lost Home." In Leonard J. Duhl (ed.), *The Urban Condition.* New York: Simon and Schuster.

**Gans, Herbert
  1962   *The Urban Villagers.* Glencoe, Ill.: Free Press.

Gans, Herbert
  1967   *The Levittowners.* New York: Vintage.

**Gordon, David (ed.)
  1971   *Problems in Political Economy, An Urban Perspective.* Lexington, Mass.: Heath.

Hall, Peter
  1975   *Urban and Regional Planning.* London: Halsted Press.

**Harrison, Bennett
  1974   *Urban Economic Development: Suburbanization, Minority Opportunity and the Condition of the Central City.* Washington, D.C.: Urban Institute.

Hochman, Harold (ed.)
  1976   *The Urban Economy.* New York: Norton.

Jencks, Christopher
  1972   *Inequality.* New York: Basic Books.

Kain, John F.
  1968   "The Distribution and Movement of Jobs and Industry." In James Q. Wilson (ed.), *The Metropolitan Enigma.* New York: Doubleday Anchor.

*Liebow, Elliot
  1967   *Tally's Corner.* Boston: Little, Brown.

*Lowe, Jeanne
  1967   *Cities in a Race with Time.* New York: Random House.

**Milgram, Stanley
  1970   "The Experience of Living in Cities." *Science* 167 (March): 1461–68.

Mills, Edwin S.
    1972   *Studies in the Structure of the Urban Economy.* Baltimore, Md.:
            Johns Hopkins Press.
Newman, Dorothy K.
    1974   "The Decentralization of Jobs." In Bennett Harrison, *Urban Eco-
            nomic Development.* Washington, D.C.: Urban Institute.
Park, Robert
    1952   *Human Communities.* Glencoe, Ill.: Free Press.
**Report of the Social Science Panel, Assembly of Behavioral and Social
Science, National Research Council
    1974   *Toward an Understanding of Metropolitan America.* San Francisco:
            Canfield Press.
Seeley, John, et al.
    1956   *Crestwood Heights.* New York: Basic Books.
Srole, Leo
    1970   "Mental Health in the Metropolis." In Frank L. Sweetser (ed.),
            Studies in American Urban Society. New York: Crowell.
**Stein, Maurice
    1960   *The Eclipse of Community.* New York: Harper & Row.
Sternlieb, George
    1971   "The City as Sandbox." *The Public Interest,* no. 25 (Fall): 14–21.
Suttles, Gerald
    1972   *The Social Construction of Communities.* Chicago: University of
            Chicago Press.
*Tabb, William
    1970   *The Political Economy of the Black Ghetto.* New York: Norton.
Vernon, Raymond
    1959   *The Changing Economic Function of the Central City.* New York:
            Committee on Economic Development, Supplementary Paper No.
            1.
Whyte, William H.
    1956   *The Organization Man.* New York: Simon and Schuster.

Chapter 9

**Berry, Brian J. L.
    1973   *The Human Consequences of Urbanization.* New York: St. Martin's
            Press.
*Boulding, Kenneth
    1964   *The Meaning of the Twentieth Century.* New York: Harper & Row.

Davis, Kingsley
    1959   *The World's Metropolitan Areas.* Berkeley: University of California
           Press.

Dorfman, Robert
    1976   "The Functions of the City." In Harold Hochman (ed.), *The Urban
           Economy.* New York: Norton.

Fabun, Don
    1971   *Dimensions of Change.* Beverly Hills, Calif.: Glencoe.

Fava, Sylvia F., (ed.)
    1968   *Urbanism in World Perspective.* New York: Thomas Y. Crowell
           Co.

Freedman, Ronald, and B. Berelson
    1974   "The Human Population." *Scientific American* 231 (September):
           30–39.

Hall, Peter
    1966   *The World Cities.* New York: McGraw-Hill Publishing Co.

Horowitz, Irving L.
    1966   *Three Worlds of Development.* New York: Oxford University Press.

Hoselitz, Bert, and Wilbert Moore (eds.)
    1963   *Industrialization and Society.* Paris: Mouton.

Lewis, Michael
    1973   *Urban America, Institutions and Experience.* New York: Wiley.

Loewenstein, L. K. (ed.)
    1971   *Urban Studies: An Introductory Reader.* New York: Free Press.

Meadows, Paul and Ephraim H. Mizruchi, (eds.)
    1976   *Urbanism, Urbanization and Change: Comparative Perspectives.*
           Reading, Mass.: Addison-Wesley.

Reissman, Leonard
    1964   *The Urban Process.* New York: Free Press.

Thompson, Wilbur M.
    1965   *A Preface to Urban Economics.* Baltimore: Johns Hopkins Press.

Tibbitts, C.
    1960   "Aging as a Modern Social Achievement." In C. Tibbitts and W.
           Donahue (eds.), *Aging in Today's Society.* Englewood Cliffs, N.J.:
           Prentice-Hall.

Walton, John, and Donald E. Carns (eds.)
    1973   *Cities in Change: Studies on the Urban Condition.* Boston: Allyn
           and Bacon.

*Ward, Barbara
    1976   *The Home of Man.* New York: Norton.

Index